W9-BEV-127

Glossary
of Graphic
Communications

ISBN 0-13-096410-7

90000

9 780130 964106

Glossary of Graphic Communications

Third Edition

Compiled by
Pamela J. Groff

Prentice Hall PTR, Upper Saddle River, NJ 07458
http://www.phptr.com

Prentice Hall books are widely used by corporations and government agencies for training, marketing, and resale.

The publisher offers discounts on this book when ordered in bulk quantities.
For more information phone 800-382-3419; fax 201-236-7141;
email corpsales@prenhall.com or write
    Corporate Sales Department
    Prentice Hall PTR
    One Lake Street
    Upper Saddle River, NJ 07458.

Printed in the United States of America

10 9 8 7 6 5 4 3 2 1

ISBN 0-13-096410-7

Prentice-Hall International (UK) Limited, *London*
Prentice-Hall of Australia Pty. Limited, *Sydney*
Prentice-Hall Canada Inc., *Toronto*
Prentice-Hall Hispanoamericana, S.A., *Mexico*
Prentice-Hall of India Private Limited, *New Delhi*
Prentice-Hall of Japan, Inc., *Tokyo*
Simon & Schuster Asia Pte. Ltd., *Singapore*
Editora Prentice-Hall do Brasil, Ltda., *Rio de Janeiro*

Contents

Introduction

With over 3,500 terms, lists of frequently used computer file extensions and common abbreviations and acronyms, and an extensive bibliography, this book can help you master the things you need to know to participate more fully in the electronic publishing business.

This third edition of the *Glossary of Graphic Communications* is the most extensive revision to date, combining, for the first time, Internet and computer networking terminology with technical print-publishing terms in a single volume. Prior to the explosive growth of the Internet and networked electronic publishing systems, graphic designers were among the few outside of accounting and data processing who were interested in what computers could do for them. Since the first edition of this book was released in 1991, the computer has become a ubiquitous presence in every area of business and in many households as well.

Computers excite us by giving us greater control over our communications—from simple email and printed documents to more complex creations, such as CD-ROMs or Internet World Wide Web pages. Yet the experience can turn frustrating rather quickly if we don't understand the key words and phrases that more experienced users banter about, or we are unaware of the principles developed for the traditional printing field that underlie some "desktop" publishing computer applications.

In closing, I'd like to offer special thanks to GATF's editor in chief Thomas M. Destree who, in addition to suggesting many new and revised terms, created the layout and illustrations for this edition and proofread the entire manuscript. Rich Adams, GATF research scientist/digital imaging and color reproduction; Phil Green, senior lecturer at the London (UK) College of Printing; Frank Kanonik, GATF's director of on-demand printing; and Dillon Mooney, the GATF technical consultant who manages Foundation's technical inquiry desk, all provided valuable insights into this swiftly changing field we now call graphic communications. Again, my thanks.

Pamela Groff
GATF Technical Editor
April 1997

A

abatement. Reducing the degree or intensity of, or eliminating, pollution.

aberrations. Errors in a photographic lens that prevent the lens from producing a single focus of all intensities of the light rays reflected from the subject, resulting in poor image definition at the film plane. Astigmatism, chromatic aberration, distortion, and spherical aberration are some specific optical aberrations.

ablation. Process of writing data to optical memory with a laser that burns holes into thin metal film.

abort. A computing command that instructs the system to abandon a program or ignore all data transferred after a given point.

abrasion. (1) Scratching or wearing away a sheet of paper or paperboard either through contact with another sheet of paper or paperboard or with some other object. Alternative term: *scuffing.* (2) The wear on paper manufacturing equipment, particularly machine wires, caused by filler pigments and other components of the paper furnish, which develop as the sheet is formed.

abrasion marks. Streaks or scratches that appear on a photographic print or film because of the condition of the developer. Such marks may be removed by swabbing the print or film with alcohol.

abrasion resistance. The inherent ability of a substrate to inhibit deterioration or destruction by friction. Alternative term: *rub resistance.*

abrasion test, paper. Test incorporating motion that is used to determine the dry rub, wet rub, wet bleed, and smear and rub qualities of a paper.

abrasion test, washability. A test that determines the scrub resistance, cleanability, and abrasion resistance of coating materials, such as waxes, anodized metals, and plastics.

absolute address. A permanently assigned storage location usually in a computer.

absorbance. The ability of a layer of a substance to absorb radiation expressed mathematically as the negative common logarithm of transmittance.

absorbency. A paper or other porous material's ability to soak up the liquids or vapors (e.g., moisture) with which it comes in contact.

absorption. (1) The first stage of print drying in which a portion of the ink vehicle is absorbed by the paper. (2) An optical term for selective transmission or partial suppression of light.

accelerator. (1) An alkali, or base, used to activate a developing agent to make it more effective. (2) A substance added, or a method used, to hasten the natural process or progress of an event or series of events, such as ink drying.

acceptance sampling. Inspection of a sample from a lot to decide whether or not the lot meets the criteria specified.

acceptance sampling plan. A directive that indicates sampling sizes and the criteria for acceptance.

access. To retrieve data from a hard drive or other physical storage medium or another computer connected via network or modem.

access control. In a network, a means of ensuring the system's security by requiring users to supply their names and passwords each time they log on.

access control list. In a network, a database that holds the names of the valid system users and notes the level of access that each has been granted.

access time. The interval between the instant at which a call for data is initiated and delivery of the data is completed.

accordion fold. Two or more folds parallel to each other with adjacent folds in opposite directions, resembling the bellows of an accordion. Alternative term: *fanfold.*

acetate base. A photographic film support used to prepare overlays or used as a clear base for stripping.

Accordion fold

acetic acid. (1) An organic liquid used in testing the acid resistance of a material. (2) The active ingredient in a stop bath, an acidic processing solution that neutralizes the developing solution remaining on a photographic material.

acetone. (1) A solvent used in gravure inks to accelerate drying. (2) An ingredient in many lacquer thinner compounds and adhering liquids that is used to remove lacquer-adhered knife-cut stencils and lacquer blockouts from screen-printing fabrics.

achromatic. (1) Without color or hue (black and white). (2) A lens corrected for black-and-white photography.

achromatic color removal/replacement or reproduction (ACR). See *gray component replacement* (GCR).

acid. (1) In lithography, a dampening solution ingredient that enables gum arabic to cling to the nonimage areas of the plate. (2) Perchloride of iron used to etch gravure cylinders. Alternative term: *etchant.*

acid fixer. A chemical solution containing sodium thiosulfate (hypo) and diluted acetic acid, among other additives. Immersing photographic film or paper in an acid fixer for a specific time period renders the images permanent by removing unexposed silver halides from the film or paper. Alternative terms: *fix, fixer,* or *fixing bath.* See also: *hypo.*

acid resist. An acid-proof protective coating applied to metal plates to limit areas of etching.

acid stop bath. An acetic acid photographic solution used to halt development on positives, negatives, films, or paper prints.

acid-free paper. A paper with no acidity and no residual acid-producing chemicals.

acidity. A pH measurement of lithographic fountain solution.

acid-proof. A material that resists contact with or immersion in acid. Alternative term: *acid resistant..*

Acrobat. See *Adobe Acrobat.*

acrylic ink. A screen printing ink that contains acrylic polymers and is used to print on some plastics and other substrates, especially ones that will be exposed outdoors.

actinic. The range or color of light emitted from mercury vapor lamps, arc lamps, and photo-flood bulbs that will expose sensitized photographic films, paper, or printing plates.

activated carbon. A highly adsorbent form of carbon used to remove odors and toxic substances from liquid or gaseous emissions.

activator. In photography, a high pH solution that permits the developer to diffuse into the film emulsion to develop the image.

active matrix display. A full-color liquid crystal display that offers higher resolution, contrast, and vertical refresh rate than a passive matrix display. See also: *passive matrix display.*

acutance. An objective measurement of the sharpness of the edge of a printed shape against the substrate or background color.

adaptation. Adjustment that the visual mechanism makes to its sensitivity to light after a period of exposure to a given light level.

adapter. (1) Device used to connect two different types of electrical terminals. (2) A circuit board that is inserted into an expansion slot of a computer system to extend its capability, for example by connecting a peripheral that cannot communicate directly over the host computer's bus, enhancing multimedia, or adding memory.

addition agent. In gravure, a material added in small quantities to plating solution for the purpose of modifying the character of a deposit.

additive. (1) Any compound which, when combined with another, reduces or improves flow (workability), or otherwise changes the composition of a lubricant to a predetermined state. (2) A substance added to another in relatively small amounts to impart or improve desirable properties or suppress undesirable properties. In printing, these substances may be added to ink, paper, and dampening solutions.

additive color process. Mixing red, green, and blue lights in various combinations to create a color reproduction or image. A color television system is an example of the additive color process.

additive primaries. Highly saturated red, green, and blue lights that, when mixed together in varying combinations and intensities, can produce any other color. See also: *subtractive primaries.*

additives/modifiers. Ingredients added to a printing ink to give it special characteristics or properties. Modifiers promote adhesion and film flexibility, provide abrasion resistance and slip, and serve as antiblocking and antipinholing compounds.

additivity failure. A common condition occurring when the total density of the overprinted ink films is not equal to the sum of the individual ink densities.

address. (1) A character or group of characters that identifies a particular part of computer storage or some other data source or destination. (2) In data communication, the unique code assigned to each device or workstation connected to a network.

address resolution. In a local-area network with an Internet connection, the automated process by which the LAN address of each workstation is converted to an IP address. See also: *transmission control protocol/Internet protocol.*

addressability. In a line of printed digital information the number of positions per unit length, usually per inch, at which successive pixels are placed.

adhering. In screen printing, attaching indirect film to the screen fabric.

adhesion. A mechanical or chemical reactive bond causing two surfaces to stick together.

adhesion test. Any of a variety of test methods used to determine adequate bonding of an ink or coating to a substrate.

adhesive binding. Applying a glue or another, usually hot-melt, substance along the backbone edges of assembled, printed sheets. The book or magazine cover is applied directly on top of the tacky adhesive. Alternative term: *perfect binding.*

adhesive bleed. Adhesive that seeps from pressure-sensitive stock before or after processing the finished product. This condition is caused by cold flow or clamp pressure. Alternative term: *adhesive ooze.*

adhesive-coated paper. Paper covered on one side with an adhesive that is activated by moistening (for gummed papers) or heating (for heat sealing). Adhesive-coated paper may also be permanently tacky on the coated side (for pressure-sensitive applications).

adjacency. The overlap or spacing of neighboring pixels in an array.

adjacency effect. The property of the eye that causes the same color to look different when surrounded by or adjacent to other colors. A color will appear darker when surrounded by a lighter color, or lighter when surrounded by a darker color.

adjacent color effect. The visual influence of a highly saturated color on a nearby color.

Adobe Acrobat. One popular portable document file (PDF) format. Through Acrobat or another PDF, users can read electronic versions of printed documents that maintain the attributes (bold and italic type and other formatting choices) assigned to a printed original. See also: *portable document file.*

adsorption. The adhesion in an extremely thin layer of molecules (gases, solutes, or liquids) to the surfaces of solid bodies or liquids with which they are in contact.

affinity diagram. A tool for grouping related items together following a brainstorming session.

afterburner. In incinerator technology (such as that found on web presses), a burner located so that the combustion gases are forced to pass through its flame in order to remove smoke and odors. It may be attached to or separated from the incinerator proper.

afterimage. An image that a viewer continues to see after the actual object is no longer in sight. Because of cone fatigue in the eyes, the color and shape of the afterimage may be complementary to the color and shape of the actual object.

after-tack. Tack that develops after an ink should have dried or after a heat-drying operation.

agate. (1) Body type measuring approximately 5½ points. The agate is frequently used to specify the depth of newspaper advertising. Fourteen agate lines are equivalent to one column inch. (2) A polished stone tool used in bookbinding to burnish the edges of books after applying metal leaf.

agitation. (1) The darkroom procedure used in developing to ensure an interchange of solution over the surface of the negative or positive. (2) In gravure, the use of air to stir solutions.

air bars. A device that aids in securing the press sheets to the impression cylinder. Air bars prevent the sheet from making premature contact with the blanket, which would cause a double image to print. They are also found on web sheeters.

air bells. (1) A surface defect in paper. Alternative terms: *blisters; foam marks.* (2) In photography, small bubbles of air that adhere to photographic surfaces during development, leading to visible defects on the processed film.

air eraser. A miniature, hand-held sand-blasting device used to remove unwanted images from lithographic plates. Air erasers are also used to remove art without destroying the texture of the medium.

air jets. The tiny holes in a sheet, plate, or similar configuration in a drying system through which compressed air is forced onto the freshly printed substrate to accelerate drying.

air pollutant. Any substance in air that could, in high enough concentrations, harm humans, animals, vegetation, or materials.

air pollution control device. Mechanism or equipment that cleans emissions generated by an incinerator by removing pollutants that would otherwise be released to the atmosphere.

air pull. Coating the screen with ink (during screen printing) without making an impression on the substrate. See also: *flooding.*

air shaft. A special roller in the roll stand of a web press that uses air-actuated grippers to hold the core of the roll of paper.

air shear burst. A break in a paper roll or web caused by air trapped in the roll during winding. Alternative term: *burst.*

air-blast nozzles. Devices that use forced air to separate the top sheets of the pile. Alternative terms: *rear blowers; air-blast pipes.*

Air-blast nozzle

airbrush. (1) A miniature, pencil-shaped hand sprayer used to retouch drawings, photographs, and density values on continuous-tone negatives. (2) Adding or removing process color values in a designated picture area displayed on the screen of an electronic color imaging system. The operator airbrushes the image by using a mouse or guiding a stylus on a digitizing tablet and adjusting the strength and width of the electronic "spray."

airbrushing. (1) Manually retouching an image by spraying dyes or pigments on it with air forced from a small, hand-held device. (2) Electronically retouching images on a computer or larger color prepress system. With an electronic airbrush, an artist can avoid the coarse splatter effects and brush strokes common in manual airbrushing.

air-knife coater. A device that applies excess coating to paper and then removes the surplus by striking the fluid coating with a flat jet of air, leaving a smooth, metered film on the paper.

album binding. To enclose and cover a document on the short side of a page instead of in the more common method of binding upright on the long side of the page.

albumin process. A method of sensitizing metal plates with a bichromated, natural water-soluble protein.

alcohol. (1) One of a family of organic solvents used in flexographic and gravure inks. (2) An organic substance added to the dampening solution of a lithographic printing press to reduce the surface tension of water. Alcohol makes the dampening solution more uniform, allowing for a thinner application of solution to the plate.

alcohol, percentage. The proportion of alcohol in relation to the amount of water in the dampening solution.

alcohol substitutes. Chemicals used in lithographic dampening solution in place of isopropyl alcohol.

algorithm. An ordered set of well-defined rules for the solution of a problem in a finite number of steps.

alias. An alternate or duplicate label for a data element in a computer system. For example, one email address may have several aliases representing different departments or individuals. On a Macintosh, an alias icon makes a program, such as Microsoft Word or QuarkXPress, accessible from different areas on the desktop instead of just where the actual program is stored.

aliasing. A jagged or "staircase" effect in a raster image, caused by an insufficient number of image samples. See also: *anti-aliasing*.

alignment. (1) The horizontal positioning of characters. In base alignment, characters rest on a common horizontal line, excluding descenders and irrespective of aesthetics and design proportions. (2) In typesetting, alignment denotes the exact (even) relationship at the top (or bottom) of the letters in a font. The term can also refer to setting lines of type so that the ends appear even. See also: *justification*.

alkali blue. A strong, organic blue pigment with a bronzy cast. Alkali blue is dispersed in lithographic varnish and used as a toner for carbon black inks. Alternative term: *reflex blue.*

alkali removable resists. Inks that can be wiped off with a caustic compound or alkaline solution after drying.

alley. The spaces between tabular copy. See also: *gutter.*

alpha channel. An eight-bit channel reserved by some image-processing applications for masking or retaining additional color information.

alpha test. The first pre-release evaluation of computer software usually conducted by programmers and developers. Also any initial evaluation of a product or equipment.

alphabet length. The space required for letters of a given font expressed in points, or the length of the lowercase alphabet of a particular type font.

alphabet sheets. Type in a variety of fonts and faces printed on transparent material with a pressure-sensitive adhesive backing or on a waxy sheet, which the designer burnishes to adhere the type to the new substrate. Type on alphabet sheets is used to select unusual typefaces and symbols that may not be found in a typical typesetting or computer system. Alternative terms: *rub-down type; transfer lettering.*

alphabetic character strings. Linear segments of related characters represented by letters instead of numbers.

alphanumeric. Code representations of information in machine-readable form. The data consist mainly of letters and numerals with additional symbols and punctuation marks.

alum. (1) A mineral sulfate used in manufacturing paper. (2) Any compound composed of ammonium sulfate, chromium, potassium, or sodium and aluminum that is used as a hardening agent in photography and for various other purposes in the graphic arts.

aluminum ink. (1) An ink pigment consisting principally of finely pulverized aluminum particles that leave a silver appearance on the printed substrate. (2) Small flakes of aluminum that are mixed with a varnish or lacquer vehicle and used to achieve special effects in printing.

aluminum plate. A thin sheet of specially grained aluminum used as surface and deep-etch lithographic image carriers.

American Standard Code for Information Interchange (ASCII). A standard code approved by the American National Standards Institute that uses a set of seven-bit coded characters (eight bits when the parity check is included) to facilitate information interchange without formatting codes among data processing, data communications systems, and associated equipment. The ASCII set consists of both control and graphic characters.

ammonium fixer. In photography, a fixing bath containing NH^+ (univalent ion of ammonia), which is used for removing silver halides from photosensitive emulsions.

amplitude modulation. Method of varying the strength (amplitude) of a fixed-frequency carrier signal in accordance with that of an information signal in the communications process. See also: *frequency modulation.*

analog device. A computer or other device that uses continuous signals of varying intensity rather than digital signals that can only be "on" or "off." Some color scanners use hard-wired electronic circuits to perform analog color correction and tone reproduction, while other scanners use digital data to perform similar functions. See also: *digital device.*

analog transmission A communications process in which a continuous signal is varied by amplification. See also: *digital.*

analog-to-digital converter (A/D). An adapter that permits a digital computer to interpret analog transmission signals.

anamorphic. A lens on a graphic arts camera that creates distortion negatives by reducing copy in one dimension while allowing the other dimension to remain unchanged.

anamorphic scan. Altering or manipulating an original piece of artwork electronically so that the width and height are not enlarged or diminished in proportion, but are altered to produce an image that is taller and skinnier or shorter and fatter than the original.

anastigmat. A photographic lens corrected so that the rays from different points meet in a focal point instead of dispersing. Process lenses are anastigmats, meaning that they prevent a blurred and imperfect image from forming. Alternative term: *anastigmatic.*

angle, screen. See *screen angle.*

angle, squeegee. In screen printing, the angle formed by the face of the squeegee blade in the direction of the printing stroke, and the plane of the screen fabric. The squeegee is held in printing position but without pressure applied.

angle bar. A metal bar at a 45° angle horizontal to the direction of the printing press. It is used to turn the web when feeding from the side, or to bypass turning it in ribbon printing. The angle bar is usually filled with cooled air and perforated to reduce the friction resulting from web travel. See also: *folder, ribbon.*

angle of attack. In screen printing, the position of the face of the moving squeegee blade and the plane of the screen under pressure. Because the blade is flexible, the angle of attack differs from the squeegee angle, which is measured without movement or pressure.

angle of incidence. The angle created when the incident (incoming) light ray strikes the normal line perpendicular to the surface of an object.

Normal

Angle of incidence (I) and angle of reflection (R)

angle of reflection. The angle drawn at the point of incidence (intersection) of a reflected ray and the normal line perpendicular to the reflecting surface.

angle of refraction. The angle that results when a light ray bends as it passes from one medium to another. Refraction makes an object appear to be in a different position from where it really is.

angle of view. The portion of a scene visible through a camera lens.

angle of wipe. The setting between the doctor blade and the engraved gravure cylinder.

aniline dyes. Colorings made from coal-tar derivatives.

aniline print. An insoluble glue or cold enamel image that has been stained with an aniline dye.

aniline printing. An early name for rotary letterpress printing with rubber plates and fluid, fast-drying inks that contained dyes derived from aniline oils. See also: *flexography.*

anilox rollers. A steel or ceramic ink metering roller. Its surface is engraved with tiny, uniform cells that carry and deposit a thin, controlled layer of ink film onto the plate. In flexo presswork, anilox rollers transfer a controlled ink film from the rubber plate (or rubber-covered roller) to the web to print the image. Anilox rollers are also used in remoistenable glue units and to create "scratch-and-sniff" perfume ads.

anilox system. The inking method commonly employed on flexographic presses. An elastomer-covered fountain roller supplies a controlled ink film from the ink pan to the engraved metering roller. After ink floods the metering roller, the fountain roller is squeezed or wiped usually with a doctor blade to remove the excess. The ink that remains on the metering roller is transferred to the rubber printing plate.

anti-aliasing. In computer graphics, a procedure whereby pixels at the edge of a diagonal or curved surface are averaged with those of the background in order to produce a smoother edge and minimize the effect of unwanted patterns (jaggies). Alternative term: *dithering.* See also: *aliasing.*

antifoaming agent. An additive that disperses bubbles that may form in offset dampening solution or screen printing inks during printing. Antifoaming agents are also added to plate developers and processors.

antihalation. The property of a film or paper or poly plate with an opaque backing that prevents light rays from reflecting.

antihalation backing. A coating on the back of a film base that contains a light-absorbent dye or colored pigment. See also: *halation.*

antioffset spray. See *antisetoff spray.* Alternative term: *spray powder.*

antioxidant. An agent that prevents drying oils and other substances from changing when exposed to air. See also: *antiskinning agent.*

antique finish. A natural or cream color and/or rough finish frequently used for book pages and cover stock.

antisetoff compound. An ink additive that prevents the inked image on a press sheet from rubbing off on the sheet above it in the delivery pile by forming a protective layer on the ink surface or shortening the ink's jelling time.

antisetoff spray. Ground starch particles sprayed onto sheets to keep the ink on each press sheet from direct contact with the ink on another sheet in the delivery. Alternative term: *spray powder.*

antiskinning agent. A material added to ink to prevent a rubbery layer from forming on its surface when it is exposed to air. See also: *antioxidant.*

antivirus program. The essential software that is used to detect and destroy rogue applications designed to damage a computer. See also: *virus.*

aperture. (1) A lens opening through which light passes. Alternative term: *f-stop.* (2) The open spaces between the threads in a screen printing fabric.

aperture percentage. The portion of the screen printing fabric area through which ink can pass. It is expressed as a percentage of the total fabric area.

apochromatic lens. A color separation lens that has been highly corrected for spherical and chromatic (color, astigmatism, and flatness of field) aberrations. See also: *color-corrected lens.*

AppleShare. A network operating system for Macintosh computers.

applet. A small application program that performs a simple task or, in the case of Java, can be used to add animation or multimedia to an application. See also: *Java.*

AppleTalk. A local-area network standard for Macintosh computers.

application program. The computer software designed to perform actual jobs as opposed to the system programs that manage equipment operation.

applications program interface (API). System software that allows computer programmers to create interface features or, in a network, determine how the various features will be used.

applicator roll. A cylinder used to spread coating, tints, lacquer, or varnish.

apron. A blank space at the edge of a foldout that permits the sheet to be folded and tipped in the finishing process without marring the copy.

aqueous dispersion. Pigments scattered in a water-soluble binding medium that changes to a water-insoluble form when a screen-printed cloth is steamed or heat-cured.

arc lamp. A device that produces an intensely bright light from a sustained discharge of electricity across a gap in a circuit or between two electrodes (slightly separated carbons). The carbon arc lamp was once commonly used for exposing offset plates and engraving photoresists, but, because it was a fire hazard and its light emissions fluctuated greatly, it has largely been replaced by quartz-halogen and pulsed-xenon light sources in the graphic arts.

archival paper. A long-lasting, nonacidic paper used increasingly to print books and other important records and documents.

archival printing. Techniques for printing books, documents, and records intended to last 150 years or more.

archival storage. The long-term storage of image information on photographic, magnetic, or other media.

archive. A group of compressed computer files.

area composition. Preparing data for typesetting in such form that all or as many elements of the final page as possible are typeset in place. This reduces or eliminates pasteup. Area composition output falls somewhere between galley output (requiring extensive pasteup) and full page makeup with all elements in place.

argon-ion laser. A laser light source in which argon-ion gas is stimulated to produce a monochromatic blue-green beam of light that is used to expose images onto orthochromatic or blue-sensitive photographic film, paper, or electrostatic printing plates.

arithmetic-logic unit (ALU). The portion of a computer's central processing unit that makes decisions for the microprocessor based on mathematical and logic functions.

arpanet. The first wide-area network and the predecessor of today's Internet as developed by ARPA, or the Advanced Research Projects Agency of the U.S. Department of Defense.

array. A group of light-sensitive recording elements often arranged in a line. Used as a scanner image-sensing device.

array processor. The portion of a computer designed to allow any machine instruction to operate on a number of data locations simultaneously.

art. (1) Hand-drawn originals used for photomechanical reproduction. (2) Flat graphic images that are reproduced in the printing process. Some examples include paintings, photographs, and computer-generated diagrams and charts.

art assembly. Preparing comprehensives and keylines with black-and-white stats, or color images, and type.

art knife. A tool with a small, sharp blade used for lightly cutting tracing paper, screen printing stencil films, and other materials.

Art knife

art paper. A coated sheet used in printing halftones.

art type. Typefaces, designs, and individual characters screen-printed onto gummed acetate sheets. The type or designs are cut from the acetate sheet and pressed or rubbed against the copy area. Alternative term: *rub-down type.*

art type, preprinted. Sheet containing the complete letters of the alphabet, numbers, punctuation marks, and figures. The characters are transferred onto the layout by burnishing (dry transfer) or adhesion.

artifact. A visible defect in an electronic image, caused by limitations in the reproduction process (hardware or software). Aliasing patterns are an example of artifacts.

artwork. A general term for photographs, drawings, paintings, and other materials prepared to illustrate printed matter.

artwork, comprehensive. Design produced primarily to give the customer an approximate idea of what the printed piece will look like. Alternative terms: *comprehensive; comp.*

artwork, separated. Design that indicates each area to print in a color on a different layout.

ASA rating. A scale approved by the American Standards Association that is used to identify the relative sensitivity of photographic films.

ascender. The portion of a lowercase character that extends above the height of the main body of the character. Some examples include "h," "k," "l," "b," and "d." See also: *descender.*

ASCII file. A text file containing no special formatting.

ASCII protocol. A simplified method of text file transfer with no allowances for error or flow control.

aspect ratio. The relationship between the height and width of a displayed object. A 1:1 aspect ratio means the object will appear undistorted.

aspheric. Photographic lenses ground solely to reduce distortions.

assemble draws. Collecting two or more groups of gathered signatures to form a complete book.

assembling. Collecting individual sheets or signatures into a complete set with pages in proper sequence and alignment. Assembling is followed by binding. See also: *collate; gathering; insert.*

assembly. Placing film or paper elements together in order on a suitable substrate. See also: *makeup.*

assembly language. Low-level computer language that is translated directly into machine code by an assembly program.

assignable cause. The identifiable variation in quality.

astigmatism. An optical error that prevents photographic lenses from focusing sharply on both horizontal and vertical lines.

asymmetrical digital subscriber lines (ADSL). A communications mode being promoted by the cable television and telephone industries for their upcoming cable-based Internet services. ADSL provides a downstream bandwidth of 1.5 Mbps (from producer to consumer) and an upstream bandwidth of 640 Kbps (from consumer to producer). It is suitable for downloading web pages and uploading email and simple text commands at speeds exceeding that of 28.8-Kbps modems. See also: *high-bit-rate digital subscriber lines.*

asynchronous. A communications method in which data bits are sent one after another, with start and stop bits indicating the beginning and end of each data unit. See also: *synchronous transmission.*

asynchronous ink jet. See *drop-on-demand ink jet.*

asynchronous transfer mode (ATM). An electronic transmission method that breaks data into a series of 53-byte fixed-length packets or cells for transport at speeds ranging from 64 Kbps to 622 Mbps.

attenuation. (1) A decrease in the intensity of light as the distance from its source grows. (2) A decrease in the magnitude of current, voltage, or the power of a signal transmission between two points. (3) A specific decrease in the optical power of a fiber optic cable caused by absorption, scattering, and other radiation.

audit trail. An established method for tracing the changes made to pictorial or text data during each stage of processing.

authoring. In multimedia, the complete process of preparing a presentation, including writing and creating the sound, graphic, and video components.

authoring language. An application that provides the tools for creating instructional or presentation programs often with multimedia components.

author's alterations (AA). Changes requested by the author or author's representative after the original copy has been typeset. Alternative term: *author's corrections.*

author's proof. Prepublication copy sent to the author for approval. It is returned marked "OK" or "OK with changes."

autochrome. The first commercially successful screen plate for color photography, introduced in 1904 by Auguste and Louis Luminere in Lyons, France.

autokerning. The automatic reduction of unwanted white space between type characters.

automatic picture replacement. Scitex computer technology that enables the operator to replace for-position-only artwork with the actual images that will be used during printing. See also: *open prepress interface.*

automatic reject. A quality control feature on binding equipment that routes flawed products to a special tray without interrupting the production flow.

autopagination. Software capability that permits camera-ready pages to be generated from a typesetter, word processor, or desktop publishing workstation.

autopositive. Photographic films or papers that, unlike normal silver materials, produce a positive image from a positive original. See *direct positive.*

autoscreen. A photographic film with an internal mechanism that permits a halftone to be generated from a continuous-tone original without the use of a halftone screen.

autotrace. A feature found in some graphics programs that allows conversion of bitmapped images into an object-oriented format. See also: *bitmap; object-oriented.*

autotype. The material used to fill in or outline typographic characters in litho stripping.

auxiliary roll stand. A second cylinder on which a web of paper is held. It can be mounted above another such cylinder on a web offset press. The auxiliary roll stand reduces downtime by permitting one cylinder of paper (the first "stand") to be re-loaded while the other is still unwinding. It cannot be used to feed two webs at the same time unless it is converted to a dual roll stand.

azeotrope. A mixture of solvents that exhibits a constant maximum or minimum boiling point which is higher or lower than that of any of its components.

B

back cylinder. See *impression cylinder.*

back cylinder print. A press malfunction which causes the printed image to transfer to the impression cylinder and then to the press sheet.

back gray cloth. Cotton fabric material placed over the waterproof layer on top of the felt padding on the screen-printing table to prevent through-printed dyes from being absorbed into the felt padding. After printing, the back gray cloth can be discarded.

back margin. The distance between the fold edge and the edge of the body of the type (text matter) next to the fold. Alternative terms: *binding margin, gutter margin.*

back matter. Material printed at the end of a book, including the appendix, addenda, glossary, index, and bibliography. Alternative term: *end matter.*

back pressure. The force between the blanket cylinder and the impression cylinder that facilitates the transfer of the image from the blanket to the printing substrate. Alternative term: *impression pressure.*

back printing. Reproducing an image on the underside or second surface of a transparent sheet or film. Alternative terms: *reverse printing; second-surface printing.*

back spinner. The roller used to remove excess glue from the backbone of a book in order to meter glue thickness on a perfect binder.

backbone. (1) The portion of a bound book that connects the front and back covers. Alternative term: *spine.* See also: *rounding and backing.* (2) In electronic communications, a high-speed link to which network nodes and data switches are connected.

back-edge curl. In offset printing, a curve that develops at the tail end of a press sheet as a result of printing heavy solids close to this edge. Excessive dampening can also be a cause.

backer roller. In gravure printing, a steel roller used to push the rubber impression roll against the engraved cylinder in order to overcome deflection problems on very wide equipment where a relatively small diameter rubber roll is required. Alternative term: *backup roller.*

back-etching. Reducing the density of a continuous-tone negative; a color-correction technique.

background. The area of an illustration or photograph that appears behind the principal subject.

background processing. Procedure by which a computer can execute one function, such as printing, while the user simultaneously executes another function, such as word processing or image editing.

backing. See *rounding and backing.*

backing away (from the ink fountain). A condition in which an ink does not flow under its own weight or remain in contact with the fountain roller. It "backs away" and is not transferred to the ductor roller. Eventually, the prints become uneven, streaky, and weak. A conical ink agitator, which applies a finite amount of force to the ink, keeps it flowing or prevents it from backing up in the fountain while automatic ink leveling keeps the fountain full.

Ink backing away from roller

backing up. Printing the reverse side of a sheet that has already been printed.

backlap. In screen printing, a very heavy, rough application of color on one side of a print, which is caused by color pulling through the screen behind the squeegee at the beginning of the printing stroke.

backlighting. (1) Light shining on the subject from the direction opposite the camera, as distinguished from frontlighting and sidelighting. (2) The process of illuminating transparent artwork or screen-printed transparency films from behind. (3) Illuminating transparent or translucent copy from behind on a graphic arts camera.

backlining. The piece of paper, muslin, or other material that reinforces the backs of books after they have been rounded and backed.

backs. The negative flat or plate for the second side to be printed or printed sheets that are to be backed up.

backspace. To move back one space or character from the current position of a screen cursor or printing element.

back-trap mottle. Blotches and streaks in the solids and tones of an overprinted ink film on a press sheet due to the transfer of a printed ink film from the paper to the blanket of a subsequent printing unit. This trap problem occurs almost exclusively on sheetfed presses with four or more printing units. It has some of the same characteristics of poor trap and halftone and ink film mottle.

backup. The act of saving some or all of the information on a computer system to tape or disk for safekeeping.

backup registration. Correct relative position of the printing on one side of the sheet or web and the printing on the other side.

backward broadside. A printed page on which the text runs sideways.

bad break. In text composition, setting a hyphenated line as the first line of a page; ending a page with the first line of a paragraph or a single word or hyphenated word; or dividing a word incorrectly anywhere in the text.

balance. Placement of colors, light and dark masses, or large and small objects in a picture or layout to create harmony and equilibrium.

Baldrige Award. See *Malcolm Baldrige National Quality Award.*

ball mill. A rotating cylinder containing smooth pebbles or porcelain balls in which organic pigments or inorganic ceramic materials are ground in either a wet or dry state. See also: *paint mill.*

ballard process. A method of plating a shell of copper on a gravure cylinder with a material that can be stripped off easily.

band. The frequency spectrum between two defined limits.

banding. An electronic prepress term referring to visible steps in shades of a gradient.

bandwidth. A frequency measurement expressed in cycles per second (hertz) or bits per second (bps) of the amount of information that can flow through a channel.

bar code. A binary coding system using a numerical series and bars of varying thicknesses or positions that can be read by optical character recognition (OCR) equipment. Bar codes are used in printing as tracking devices for jobs and sections of jobs in production. Alternative term: *Universal Product Code.*

bareback roller. A form or ductor roller in a dampening system that operates without cloth or paper covers.

barrel mount. A simple tube in which a lens is mounted. It has no shutter, although an iris or other diaphragm may be supplied.

barrier coat. A coating applied to face material to provide increased opacity and/or prevent migration between the adhesive and face material. Alternative terms: *primer; sealer coat; tie coat.*

base. (1) All of the metal below the shoulder of a piece of type. (2) The wood or metal block upon which relief printing plates are mounted to make them type-high. See *block.* (3) Ink. Usually only one coloring matter, pigment, or dye, properly dispersed in a vehicle. The bases commonly used to manufacture offset inks are aluminum hydrate and a gloss white. (4) A flat sheet of paper or film that provides the support for a photosensitive coating or emulsion. (5) A modifying additive for screen printing inks. (6) The initial artwork or pasteup board to which all overlays are attached.

base alignment. Positioning different typefaces and sizes with their characters all on the same optical baseline. See also: *baseline.*

Al**phabet**

Base alignment

base color. A first color used as a background on which other colors are printed.

base cylinder. A rotogravure printing cylinder before copper plating, polishing, and etching.

base density. The small-value nonimage-area optical density of a transparent base after the photographic material has been exposed and processed. It consists of the density of the base material plus any overall slight fogging of the base by the photographic process or other influence.

base flash. In photography, the exposure that produces the shadow dot endpoint dot size without a main or bump exposure.

base sheet. The paper, index stock, paperboard, or plastic substrate upon which the image elements are assembled in precise position.

base white. A reducer added to ink to make a proof lighter in appearance.

baseband. A frequency band that uses the complete bandwidth of a signal. See also: *broadband.*

baseband transmission. Transfer of a digital or analog signal in its original form without modulation. See also: *broadband transmission.*

baseline. A typographic term for defining the imaginary line on which the bottom serifs of lowercase letters such as "x," "w," and "m" seem to rest.

baseline shift. A typesetting command used to set a character in a position different from its "normal" vertical position.

basic input/output system (BIOS). The code that controls basic hardware interactions, such as the keyboard and hard drive, on a computer system.

basis weight. The weight in pounds of a ream (500 sheets) of paper cut to its basic size in inches. Some basic sizes include 25×38 in. for book papers, 20×26 in. for cover papers, 22½×28½ in. or 22½×35 in. for bristol, and 25½×30½ in. for index. For example, 500 sheets of 25×38-in., 80-lb. coated paper will weigh eighty pounds. See also: *paper sizes, international.*

basis weight, actual. The basis weight of paper as actually measured under its existing environmental conditions. This may differ from its nominal basis weight because of manufacturing variations and the influence of variable moisture content on a paper's weight. See also: *size, basic.*

bas-relief. A special effect obtained by making a positive transparency from a negative, binding the two together slightly out of register, and printing from the combination.

batch processing. Automated execution of a set of instructions on a sequence of computer files.

bath. (1) Any chemical solution used in photography. (2) Inclusive term for chemical solutions (such as etchants) used in photoengraving, electroplating, and electrotyping.

baud. An expression of the number of signal events (usually data bits) transmitted per second over a communications channel.

baud rate. The speed of information transfer between electronic devices expressed in data bits per second or the maximum number of changes that can occur per second in an electrical circuit. Baud is often used interchangeably with bits per second but this is incorrect.

baudot code. A data transmission system in which five bits of equal length represent one character often with one start and one stop element added.

Baumé scale. Unit for measuring the density or specific gravity of the liquids used in the printing processes.

bayonet. On a saddle stitcher, the prong onto which the signature drops just before it is picked up by the chain pin. Alternative term: *sword.*

BBSs. See *bulletin board systems.*

beam splitter. An optical device used to split a single beam of light into two or more beams. Commonly used in color scanners in both input and output sections.

beard. In hot-metal typesetting, the beveled space below the printing surface of a type letter.

bearer. A hardened steel ring located at the end of the plate and blanket cylinders. The bearers are the true diameter of the cylinders. When the cylinders are in contact during printing, the bearers are forced together under a preload, or preset pressure, which is separate from the plate-to-blanket pressure, or squeeze.

bearer pressure. The force with which the bearers of opposed cylinders contact each other on an offset lithographic press.

bearer-contact press. A press that runs with the bearers of the plate and blanket cylinders in contact.

bearer-to-bearer. The cylinder arrangement in which the bearers of the plate and blanket cylinders contact each other.

beater. The original mechanical refiner, in which paper fibers suspended in water are circulated around an oval tub and passed between the refining surfaces of the rotating metal bars of the beater roll and the stationary metal bars of the bedplate.

beater-sized pulp. Papermaking furnish (mixture of fibrous and nonfibrous materials in a water suspension) to which sizing is added during beating. Alternative terms: *internal-sized pulp; engine-sized pulp.* See also: *sizing.*

bed. On a guillotine paper cutter, the flat metal surface on which the cutting is performed. Alternative term: *table.*

bed knife. A stationary cutting tool located in the frame of a sheeter.

Bekk smoothness gauge. An instrument used for measuring paper roughness by the flow rate of air between a metal cylinder with an open bottom and the paper.

bell character. A precedence code used to alert the typesetting machine that the character(s) that follow are to be interpreted as instructions (e.g., a line length change) or special characters (e.g., a copyright symbol).

bellows. (1) The folding portions of a press on which the plate or form is supported during printing. (2) The folding light-tight section of some cameras that connects the lens to the camera back.

bellows extension. The distance from the filmholder of a camera to the center of the camera lens: one of the distances that can be varied to change reproduction percentage (the other is copyboard extension).

belt press. A printing press that uses two continuous tracks for printing books in an in-line operation from a paper roll to a delivered book, ready for its binding at the end of the press.

bench micrometer. See *blanket thickness gauge.*

benchmark. A performance measure of equipment or procedures to be used as a point of reference in future tests of the same things.

Benday. Trademark process for applying a texture of dots or other patterns on line plates or in artwork by placing the etching resist or ink on an embossed texture film and then transferring the resist or ink to the desired areas on the plate or copy. Named after the inventor Benjamin Day.

Benday tints. A term used for simulated Benday screens that the artist applies from stock transparent sheets of printed patterns or screens pasted on top of artwork, or by using a patented drawing paper with invisible patterns, to which the artist applies a developing chemical. Halftone tints added to indicated areas by the stripper to give a tone in gray instead of solid are also sometimes erroneously referred to as Benday tints.

bender. (1) A paperboard that can be creased, scored, or folded without breaking. (2) A device that creases a printing plate in such a way that it fits precisely into the clamps of a press's plate cylinder.

benzidine yellow. See *diarylide yellow.*

Bernoulli. Brand name for removable storage media based on the principle of avoiding destructive physical contact between a read/write head and a rotating disk.

beta test. The first public release of computer software or other products for the purpose of eliciting review comments and fixing errors, or bugs. See also: *alpha test; bug.*

bevel. (1) In platemaking, the edges of a relief printing plate, (sometimes undercut) trimmed at a downward angle for attachment to a base. (2) In electrotyping, a slug cast with a beveled edge to provide a beveled flange on the plates. (3) In bookbinding, paring or sanding off the head, front, and foot edges of coverboards.

bezier curve. A vector graphic, named after Pierre Bezier, that is defined mathematically by two endpoints and two or more other points that control its shape.

Bezier curve

bible paper. A very thin, lightweight, bright, strong, opaque paper made from rag and mineral fiber pulp.

bichromated colloids. Various substances (albumin, glue, gum arabic, shellac) used as plate coatings in photoengraving and lithography and rendered light sensitive by adding ammonium bichromate.

bi-cutter. A stencil knife with two adjustable-width blades used to cut parallel lines simultaneously.

bimetal plate. A lithographic printing plate made from two metals, one forming the ink-receptive image area (usually copper) and one forming the water-receptive nonimage area (chromium, stainless steel, aluminum, zinc, etc.).

bimetal varnish. A term used by printers to describe a viscous varnish in the ink that is used to toughen the dried ink film. See also: *binding varnish.*

binary. A choice or condition with two possible values or states.

binary code. A representation of information using a sequence of zeros and ones. See *bit* and *byte*.

binary digit (bit). The most basic unit of information in the binary numbering system. Binary information is stored as a series of zeros and ones, indicating low (off) or high (on) electrical current. See also: *bit; byte*.

binary file. Information stored as binary digits; in other words, in machine-readable form. Images transported over the Internet are encoded as binary files.

bind. To join pages of a book together with thread, wire, adhesive, crash (a coarse fabric), or other materials, or enclose them in a cover.

bind margin. The gutter or inner margin of a book, from the binding to the printed area.

binder. (1) The portion of the vehicle in an ink composition that, in combination with the pigments, forms the film, or the adhesive components of an ink that hold the pigment to the printed surface. (2) In paper, an adhesive component used to cement inert filler, such as clay, to the sheet. (3) Carriers or vehicles that fix the pigments in screen printing dyes onto the fibers of the fabric being decorated. (4) A person or machine that binds books. (5) A cover designed to hold loose pages and/or pamphlets, e.g., three-ring and post-style binders.

binder's board. One of the stiffeners (a high-grade pulp board) often used when making book covers. About 0.070-in. thick, it is used under cloth or paper binding materials.

binder's creep. The slight but cumulative extension of the edges of each inserted spread or signature beyond the edges of the signature that encloses it. This results in progressively smaller trim size on the inside pages. Alternative terms: *pushout; shingling*.

binder's die. A piece of brass for cover stamping.

bindery. A facility where finishing operations such as folding, joining signatures, and covering are performed.

binding. Joining the assembled pages of a printed piece together. Binding takes many forms including saddle-stitching, adhesive binding, mechanical binding, loose-leaf binding, and Smyth sewing. Binding is also used as a generic term to describe all finishing operations.

binding, cleat-laced. A method of repairing casebound books by first removing the case and cutting off the spine. Grooves are cut into the spine in a diamond pattern, thread is laced into the grooves, and the book is reattached to the original case, but it will no longer lie flat when open. Alternative term: *oversewing.*

binding, mechanical. Clasping individual sheets together with plastic, small wire, or metal rings. Two examples are three-ring binding and spiral binding. See also: *spiral binding.*

binding, spine-see. A form of mechanical binding in which a continuous wire (corkscrew or spring coil) is run through round holes punched in the binding edge of the sheets. Spine-see bindings can be exposed, semiconcealed, or concealed. See also: *binding, mechanical.*

binding agent. A substance that holds the emulsion of a photographic material to the base during coating, developing, fixing, and washing.

binding dummy. Blank pages of assembled signatures stitched and trimmed to show the amount of compensation needed for creep.

binding lap, low folio. Approximately ⅜ in. (10 mm) of extra paper on the low page number (folio) side of a folded signature, as required for mechanical feeding (saddle binding).

binding varnish. A viscous varnish used in the composition of inks to toughen the film. See also: *bimetal varnish.*

BinHex. A method of encoding binary files in ASCII for transfer over the Internet. BinHex is used frequently on Macintosh computers.

bit. The smallest unit of information used in a computer file. It has one of two possible values—zero or one—used to indicate "on" or "off" or "yes" or "no" in the storage and transfer of electronic information and images. See also: *binary digit; byte.*

bit error rate. The number of errors that are actually written or read during data transfer, particularly in fiber optics.

bit pad. The two-dimensional surface on which a designer plots the x-y coordinates of a drawing with a stylus when executing an electronic design.

bite. (1) A surface characteristic of paper that causes it to accept ink, pencil, or other impressions. (2) Subjecting a metal photoengraving to the etchant. See also: *rollup.*

bitmap. An image represented by an array of picture elements, each of which is encoded as a single binary digit. Alternative term: *bit image.* See also: *line art; object-oriented; raster; vectors.*

Bitmap

bitmapped graphics display. A computer system that can control individual pixels, allowing the monitor to show high-resolution graphics (an accurate reproduction of arcs, circles, or other curved images), in addition to text.

bits per inch. A reference to data density on magnetic media.

bits per second (bps). The speed at which data is transferred over a computer modem and telephone line.

black. (1) The absence of all reflected light; the absence of color. (2) An ink that appears to absorb all wavelengths of light. It is used as one ink in the four-color printing process.

black, full-scale. A black separation negative with dots throughout the full tonal range of the image. Unlike a half-scale, or skeleton, black, a full-scale black will print in all tonal areas of the reproduction from the highlight to shadow. See also: *skeleton black.*

black, skeleton. See *skeleton black.*

black, three-color. The color that would be produced if solids of ideal magenta, cyan, and yellow process-color inks were overprinted. Since each process-color ink absorbs some of the two components of white light that it should completely transmit, overprinting solids of three typical printing inks usually results in a brown. Many color control bars include a three-color patch.

black light. (1) A light source rich in ultraviolet and low-frequency blue radiation. (2) A common name for ultraviolet rays that have a wavelength between 320 and 400 nanometers.

black printer. (1) The plate that prints black ink in four-color process printing. (2) The halftone film used to burn the plate that will print black ink or the printing screen used in process-color reproduction to print the color black and add detail to the print. The letter "K" is often used to designate this color. Alternative term: *key plate*. See also: *black, full-scale; skeleton black*.

black-and-white (B/W, B&W). Originals and printed material comprised only of black and white with tones of gray.

black-and-white art. Line art usually produced on smooth or textured board with pen or brush and black ink or generated using a computer.

blackbody. (1) An ideal body whose spectral energy distribution depends only on its temperature. Used to establish a set of standard spectral energy distribution curves associated with blackbody temperatures. (2) A material that absorbs all incident light and reflects none. See *color temperature*.

blade. The flexible edge of a squeegee used in screen printing. It may be made from various elastomers of polyurethane, neoprene, or rubber.

blade coater. A device that first applies a surplus coating to a paper web and then evenly levels and distributes it with a flexible steel blade.

blade coating. A method of coating paper using a flexible blade set at an adjustable angle against the web in manufacture. The web is usually supported by a soft-surfaced backing roll.

blade streak. A wider indentation than a blade scratch, also caused by a large particle lodged behind the blade during coating.

bladeless ink fountain. A disposable sheet of polyester foil that is held in contact with the fountain roller by a series of small cylinders parallel to it.

blank. (1) A thick paperboard, coated or uncoated, produced on a cylinder machine and designed for printing. Thickness ranges from 15 to 48 points (0.380 to 1.220 millimeters). (2) An unprinted page or sheet side. (3) Unprinted cardboard, metal sheets, or other substrates used for making displays and signs.

blank dummy. A full size, serviceable model of a display without printing or artwork. Alternative term: *mock-up*.

blanket. (1) In presswork, a sheet of cork, felt, or rubber used on a press platen or impression cylinder to cushion the impression in printing. (2) In lithography, a rubber-coated fabric mounted on a cylinder that receives the inked impression from the plate and transfers (or offsets) it to the paper. Such blankets are also mounted on the impression cylinders of sheetfed gravure presses. (3) In stereotyping and electrotyping, a yielding resilient material for backing the mat or lead sheet that is pressed into the printing form to produce the mold. (4) Sheet of wool or rubber used in newspaper and poster work on the tympan of cylinder presses to secure a smooth but not too hard printing surface.

blanket, compressible. A blanket with a specially manufactured layer designed to "give" or compress, under pressure from the plate and impression cylinder. Compressible blankets resist smashing and usually print a sharper halftone dot. These blankets most often print with a plate-to-blanket squeeze of 0.004–0.006 in. (0.10–0.15 mm). Some produce optimum highlight and shadow detail with a squeeze as high as 0.008 in. (0.20 mm).

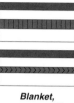
Blanket, compressible

blanket, conventional. A hard, noncompressible blanket that bulges out on either or both sides of a nip under pressure.

blanket compressibility. The extent to which blanket thickness reduces under pressure, such as during a printing impression.

blanket compression set. The reduction of blanket caliper or thickness after several thousand impressions.

blanket creep. The slight forward movement or slip of the part of the blanket surface that is in contact with the plate or paper.

blanket cylinder. The cylinder that carries the offset rubber blanket, placing it in contact with the inked image on the plate cylinder and then transferring the inked image to the paper carried by the impression cylinder. The blanket cylinder has a gap where the blanket clamps are located. The outer ends of the cylinder house the bearers.

Blanket

←Clamps

Blanket cylinder

blanket piling. Piling develops when poorly bonded paper surface fibers, coating from coated paper, or slitter dust accumulates on the blanket surface. It may occur in the image and nonimage areas. A large degree of piling can distort the ink transfer, leading to poor print quality.

blanket smash. Areas of low ink density in the press sheet image. The caliper of the blanket in these areas is too low to develop sufficient impression pressure against the plate or paper or both. Alternative term: *blanket low spots.*

blanket thickness gauge. A special micrometer for measuring the offset blanket under uniform pressure. See also: *Cady gauge; micrometer, dead-weight.*

blanket wash. An oil-based solvent used for cleaning the blanket and rollers on the press.

blanket-to-blanket. A cylinder configuration on a perfecting press whereby two blanket cylinders, each acting as an impression cylinder for the other, simultaneously print on both sides of the paper passing between them. Most commonly used in web press designs. Alternative term: *perfecting press.*

bleaching. (1) A chemical treatment that further purifies chemical pulps, bringing them to a white state and improving their chemical stability and permanence. Also a chemical treatment of mechanical pulps to alter or remove some of their coloring substances and to improve their brightness. (2) Whitening of photographic images during intensification, or removing the image entirely.

bleachout process. Method of making line drawings on photographs and silverprints with waterproof inks. The image serves as a guide to the artist and is removed by bleaching afterwards, leaving only the drawing on the surface of the paper.

bleed. (1) A printing area that extends to the edge of the sheet or page after it is trimmed. See also: *extended color; full bleed.* (2) A slight extension or thickening of printing detail, usually of the lighter color or tint, to produce color overlap zones, so that a white gap will not show in printing when slight variations in register occur throughout the pressrun. (3) Condition that results when a solvent causes a pigment color to spread or run.

bleed tab. A bleeding ink square at the edge of a page that functions as a guide for locating specific material.

bleeding. Diffusion or migration of color from an ink film to the surrounding substrate, another surface with which it comes in contact, or into a succeeding application of ink or coating.

bleedoffs. Pictures, lines, or solid colors that extend beyond the edge or edges of a page so that when margins are trimmed, the image is trimmed even with the edge of the page.

blend. Joining two colors so smoothly that there is no perceptible line at the intersection. In digital painting, the quality of the blending process is an indication of the quality of the electronic prepress system.

blind folio. A page number counted but not actually expressed (printed).

blind image. In lithography, an image that is firm on the plate but has lost its ink receptivity and fails to print, usually because of excess moisture or chemical contamination.

blind keyboard. A keyboard that inputs data without providing the operator with a display of the keystrokes on paper or a screen.

blind stamp. A design impressed into a surface without foil or ink, to give a bas-relief effect. Alternative term: *emboss.*

blister. (1) In printing, an oval-shaped, sharply defined, bubblelike formation that bulges out on both sides of the web. (2) In binding, an area where the cover material is not firmly glued to the stiffening or boards. (3) In process photography, blisters occur when excess acid is used in the short stop or fix bath. Alternative terms: *air bells; blow; bubbles.*

block. (1) A group of related characters or words considered to be a unit in page layout applications. (2) In engraving, the wood or metal base upon which relief plates are mounted to make them type-high. (3) British term for a photoengraving. (4) A wood cut. (5) To mount a plate on a base. (6) In bookbinding, to form or emboss the entire impressed or relief design in one operation. (7) In art preparation, to mask, cover, opaque, or paint out portions of a copy or negative to modify the printing areas.

block colors. Colors printed solid, i.e., with near identical opacity and density over the entire surface and without gradations, tints, or shading.

block letters. Type cut from wood, or type that resembles letters cut from wood (Gothic or sans serif letters).

block printing. Printing from wooden or linoleum blocks with the printing image cut in relief. Used before the invention of movable type, and now limited to special art reproductions, and decorative wallpaper and fabric printing.

blocking. (1) Condition that occurs when printed sheets stick together because a wet ink film continues to hold them together after the ink should be dry. Blocking can also occur within rolls. (2) Mounting or nailing printing plates on permanent wooden supports.

blockout. (1) In screen printing, liquid masking material used to cover nonimage areas of the screen around the perimeter of the stencil. It seals the fabric of the printing screen against leakage in the nonimage areas between the design to be printed and the extreme edges of the frame. Alternative terms: *blockout compound; blockout filler.* (2) Etching or routing a halftone plate to eliminate the background and create a silhouette or outline. Alternative term: *cutout.* (3) To opaque, mask, or spot out an area on a negative or positive so that it will not transmit actinic light.

bloom. (1) Solid material exuding from the base and migrating to the surface of a substrate. (2) Powder, usually talc, found on the surface of a new offset blanket.

blow back. Reversing the action of a vacuum printing frame to aid in removing the printed substrate more quickly.

blow-downs. A series of air holes, located near the top of the delivery, that assist in dropping the sheet onto the delivery table. Alternative term: *sheetfed fan delivery.*

Blow-downs

blow-up. (1) Enlarged photomechanical line reproduction, which is produced from a proof of a smaller halftone, particularly a newspaper (coarse-screen) halftone, and shows highlight effects and accented contrast. (2) Any photographic enlargement of an original.

blue. See *additive color process; additive primaries.*

blue copy. See *blue printer.*

blue key. A blueprint on glass or a vinyl plastic sheet, which contains all elements with register marks, and is used as a guide for stripping a flat of photographic elements of other colors to register.

blue printer. The negative or positive representing all of the cyan values of the print.

blueline. (1) A drafting surface mounted on metal or board, coated with an iron sensitizer, exposed (contacted) to a negative and developed in water, producing a non-photographic blue image. (2) A blueprint on an offset plate, which is used as a guide in applying tusche or crayon handwork. (3) A blue-on-white print made by exposing sensitized paper to a negative in contact. It is used as a final proof before platemaking. See also: *brownprint; silverprint; Van dyke.* (4) Nonreproducible blue guidelines or images, usually printed photographically on a set of glass, metal, plastic, or paper sheets.

blueline flat. One of a set of flats for color reproduction, each with identical blueline images. A group of negatives (or positives) for a selected printing color is registered to the blueline image when attaching (stripping) them to the film flat.

blueprint. (1) Originally, a blue photoprint produced by the diazo process; now any print used as a proof to check image element positions in type layouts. (2) A photographic print, usually produced in contact with a negative, on paper, glass, or metal, which serves as a guide for an artist "keying" art for multicolor work. (3) A method of securing a copy of unit negatives or a flat to check layout and imposition. (4) Ozalid prints made from photographic positives.

blue-sensitive emulsion. A photographic material that can be exposed by blue light, but is not changed by green light and red light. It is only sensitive to blue light.

blur. In electronic prepress, softening the detail of an image feature. The reverse process is known as sharpening.

BNC connector. A bayonet-type connector used for joining screened co-axial cables, especially in local-area networks using thin-wire Ethernet.

board. A heavy, thick sheet of paper or other fibrous substance, usually with a thickness greater than 6 mil (0.006 inch).

body. (1) The relative term describing the consistency of an ink or varnish, referring mainly to the stiffness or softness of an ink, but implying other things including length and thixotropy. (2) A viscosity increase caused by polymerization of drying oils at high temperatures. (3) The printed text of a book not including endpapers or covers. (4) The size of type from the top of the ascenders to the bottom of the descenders. (5) The thickness of a linecasting slug.

body gum. Linseed oil that has been heat-polymerized to a heavy, gummy state. It is commonly used as a bodying agent in inks. Alternative term: *#8 varnish.* See also: *bodying agent.*

body size. A hot-metal typography term denoting the measurement from the top to the bottom of a piece of type. In phototypesetting, the body size is identical to the point size of the character.

body stock. (1) The paper substrate to which coating is applied during the manufacture of coated printing papers. (2) Any paper, film, fabric, laminated or foil material suitable for converting. See also: *face material.*

body type. Text set in paragraph or block form, as distinguished from heads and display type matter. Alternative term: *body matter.*

bodying agent. A material added to an ink to increase its viscosity and drying time.

bodyline capacity. The maximum number of lines of copy that can be contained on a page.

boilerplate. Standard text that is stored electronically and can be rearranged and combined with fresh information to produce new documents.

boldface type. A version of a typeface that is heavier than the normal weight in the type family. Boldface type is used for emphasis.

bond paper. A strong, durable, writing paper with a smooth, uniform finish, originally used for printing stocks and bonds, now also used for letterheads, stationery, and business forms.

bonding agent. An ink additive used to enhance adhesion.

bonding strength. (1) An ink film's ability to resist picking, splitting, and delaminating during printing. (2) The force with which paper fibers adhere to each other. (3) The strength with which an applied surface coating adheres to the substrate after drying.

bone folder. A hand tool used for folding and creasing printed material.

bonus-color concept. Obtaining an extra color or shade by overprinting two or more transparent or translucent inks instead of running the job through the press again to obtain a third color.

book. A set of written, printed, or blank sheets bound together as a volume.

book block. A book that has been folded, gathered, and stitched but not cased-in.

book cloth. A starch-filled, plastic-coated or impregnated cotton cloth used for book covers.

book paper. A term used to describe a group of papers of a higher grade than newsprint, which are used primarily for book and publication printing and a wide variety of commercial printing applications. Book papers, as a class, include coated and uncoated papers in a wide variety of basis weights, colors, and finishes.

booklet. Any pamphlet sewed, wired, or bound with adhesive. It contains very few pages and is not produced for permanence.

boot. To start up a computer. During the boot-up sequence, the computer carries out hardware diagnostic tests, determines what peripherals are connected, and loads the operating system.

border. A printed line or design surrounding an illustration or other printed matter.

bottom printing. Printing a clear ink film with a laterally reversed design so that the printing reads through the back of the film.

bounce. In lithography, an abnormal reaction to compression, which results in erratic rotational movement of the press cylinders, causing missed or imperfect impressions.

Bourges artist's shading sheets. A trademark name for more than 200 patterns of transparent plastic sheets with opaque, halftone, Benday, and other character effects in black-and-white, which are available for use on line copy, in contact screen printing, and over photographs and photographic negatives.

box. (1) A term papermakers use to refer to a container for water or other intermediate products. (2) An item of type or other graphic matter ruled off on all four sides by a border, or otherwise segregated from the body copy—for example, by overprinting the designated area with a pale tint. Alternative terms: *box rule, sidebar.*

brainstorming. A technique that groups use to generate ideas about a particular subject or causes of a particular outcome. It can be conducted in a structured fashion where each person, in turn, provides an idea, or in an unstructured fashion, where people provide ideas as they think of them. The process continues until no more ideas are forthcoming.

brayer. A small hand roller used to distribute ink, on a test slab or proof press.

break. (1) In artwork, to separate and mark the areas to be printed in different colors. See also: *color break.* (2) An interruption in the flow of text. See also: *bad break.* (3) A weakness in a web of paper that causes it to crack, thereby interrupting the flow of the web through a press.

breakacross. A photo or other image that extends across the gutter onto both pages of the spread. Alternative terms: *crossover; reader's spread.* See also: *spread.*

breakthrough. Complete penetration of an image from the printed to unprinted side of the sheet.

bridge. (1) The unit that interconnects two or more local-area networks that use the same logical link control protocol but may use different medium access control protocols. The term can also refer to the equipment used in a connection of local loops, channels, or rings to match circuits and facilitate data transmission. (2) The area (wall) around or between the etched cells even with the surface of the cylinder on which the doctor blade rides during gravure printing.

bridge roller. A component of combination continuous-flow dampening systems on sheetfed offset presses. This roller contacts the dampening form roller and the first ink form roller and transports dampening solution from the dampening system into the inking system.

bridging. The ability of a direct-emulsion stencil material to fill the gaps between screen threads and retain solidity after exposure and washout.

bright enamels. Papers that have been coated on one side and highly polished and calendered.

bright plating. A process used in gravure that produces an electrodeposit with a high degree of specular reflection in the as-plated condition.

bright-field illumination. Illuminating a negative or film positive directly from behind so that the light strikes the image at right angles to the surface, allowing the viewer to check halftone dots through a magnifier. See also: *dark-field illumination.*

brightimeter. An instrument used to measure TAPPI brightness, and the fluorescent component of brightness, of a paper.

brightness. (1)The subjective perception of luminous intensity from any light sensation, running the gamut from lightness and brilliance to dimness or darkness.

(2) With paper, the percent reflectance of blue light only, centering on the wavelength of 457 nm.

bristol. A heavyweight paper, usually six points or more in thickness, used for printing.

bristol board. A laminated cardboard with a smooth finish, which is used as a drawing surface.

broadband. A frequency band that can be divided into several narrower ones to support simultaneous transfer of voice, video, and data. See also: *baseband.*

broadband transmission. Using analog signals, carrier frequencies, and multiplexing techniques to permit more than one node on a network to broadcast at a time. See also: *baseband transmission.*

broadcast. The simultaneous transmission of data to more than one destination.

broadside page. A book page with text positioned sideways, requiring the reader to rotate the book 90° to read it.

brochure. A pamphlet folded or bound in the form of a booklet.

bromide. A photographic contact print or enlargement made on paper sensitized with a silver bromide emulsion.

bromide paper. Photographic paper with a light-sensitive orthochromatic emulsion, which is used to produce positive prints of copied, enlarged, reduced, and screened images.

bronzing. (1) In process-color printing, the effect that appears when the toner in the last color (often black) migrates to the surface of the printed ink film, causing a change in the spectral aspect of surface light reflection. (2) Applying bronze metallic powder to the press sheet, usually with a special bronzing machine. Alternative term: *bronze dusting.*

brownprint. A photographic contact print made on a thin paper sensitized with a silver and iron compound. Brownprints require intense light for exposure and were once widely used for proofing flats. Sepia prints or black photographs, which have been chemically converted (toned) to a brown color are not considered brownprints. See also: *silverprint; Van dyke.* Alternative term: *brownline.*

browse. To search the Internet's World Wide Web or another computer network or database for information.

browser. See *Internet Explorer; Netscape Navigator; World Wide Web.*

brush dampener. A system on a lithographic press that uses a rotating brush to transfer small amounts of water from the fountain to the dampener roller train.

brush plating. A method of electroplating gravure cylinders by applying the plating solution with an anode pad, which is moved over the cathode to be plated.

bubble jet. Ink jet technology in which drop emission is produced on demand by a thin film of boiling ink in a tubular chamber. Alternative terms: *asynchronous ink jet; thermal ink jet.* See also: *drop-on-demand ink jet; valve jet.*

buckle folder. A bindery machine in which two rollers push the sheet between two metal plates, stopping it and causing it to buckle at the entrance to the folder. A third roller working with one of the original rollers uses the buckle to fold the paper. Buckle folders are best suited for parallel folding.

Buckle folder

buckram. A heavy, coarse book cover cloth.

buffer. (1) A device that separates the other devices in a system. (2) An intermediate area for the storage of electronic data. (3) On a digital printing device, the area in which an image file is given the format and other properties suitable for input.

buffer capacity. (1) The ability of a solution to resist a change in pH when a strong acid or base is added. (2) A measurement of the amount of data that can be stored in a frame buffer in a computer system.

buffering agent. A dampening solution ingredient used in lithography to neutralize acids and bases, thereby regulating the acidity or alkalinity of the solution.

bug. A computer program error.

building-in. Placing cased-in books in a press while the adhesive is drying. See also: *casing-in; covering.*

build-up. A raised surface, smaller than the inside dimensions of the screen-printing frame, upon which the stencil and screen rest while the stencil is adhered to the screen.

bulk. (1) The thickness of a pile of an exact number of sheets under a specified pressure. (2) The apparent specific volume of a sheet of paper when in a pile under definite pressure.

bulking dummy. Blank sheets of the actual stock, folded and gathered to show the thickness of the book.

bulletin board systems (BBSs). Small, often local or regional repositories for electronic files and text messages related to a very specific topic. A certain BBS may or may not be accessible through the Internet or may require a long-distance phone call via computer modem to establish contact.

bullets. (1) Solid square or circular patches exposed onto phototypesetting film or paper so that the image density can be evaluated with a densitometer. (2) Large dots used to precede listed items or to add emphasis to particular parts of a text.

bump exposure. A brief exposure without a screen that supplements the main exposure, which is made with a screen, in halftone photography. The bump exposure compresses the screen density range without flattening the highlights. Alternative term: *no-screen exposure.*

bump-up process. Method of etching and treating halftone plates in premakeready.

Buna-N. A synthetic rubber used in the manufacture of flexo plates and rollers.

burn. Exposing the image on a printing plate with any light source high in ultraviolet radiation.

burn out. To overexpose a press plate in such a way that the finest highlight dots are not reproduced on the plate.

burn twice. Producing the same image on opposite ends of the plate by exposing the film flat twice consecutively.

burning in. (1) Re-exposing part of an image projected on an enlarger easel to make that area of the print darker. (2) Heating a developed glue print on copper or zinc to bake the enamel image and make it resistant to acids or mordants. (3) In etching, applying heat to a plate dusted with etching powder to fuse or melt the applied powder.

burnish. (1) Rubbing an image element backed with adhesive to adhere it to a base sheet. (2) Rubbing photoengravings to increase the dot size in relief printing by spreading the metal or to correct and darken local areas. (3) To brighten book edges. (4) To brighten bronze printing by passing the sheets between metal rollers. (5) In steel die engraving, to print blind over gold or silver printing to increase its brilliance. (6) In platemaking, to rub and polish small rough areas on the surface of the plate. (7) The act of reducing cell size or making repairs on a gravure cylinder with an engraver's hand tool.

burnisher. A blunt instrument with a smooth surface, which is used to apply rubdown and dry-transfer photomechanical materials. A burnisher can also be used to make minor plate corrections.

burnout mask. An assembly of cutout image masks that are used to crop image size and to minimize the number of unwanted images (e.g., cut lines) that have to be corrected. Any printing form with a number of pages will have cut lines in the margins that must be eliminated.

burr. Thin ridge or shoulder of metal left on a printing plate by a graver, saw, router, or cutter.

burst. (1) A short period of intense activity on an otherwise quiet data channel. (2) A sequence of signals counted as one unit according to a specific measure. (3) See *air shear burst.*

burst binding. A special perforating device on web presses that slits the spine edge so that glue can penetrate the pages during perfect binding. With this method, it is not necessary to mill the spine off the book at the perfect binder, thus allowing for an additional ⅛ in. of trim.

bursting strength. How well a paper resists rupturing under pressure.

bus. A facility for transferring data among several devices, located between two end points with transmission restricted to one device at a time. Also the interconnection of a series of computer processors.

bus topology. A local-area network (LAN) configuration, such as IBM's Ethernet, that requires all of the network terminals to be linked by a single backbone cable with signal terminators at each end. See also: *local-area network; topology.*

business forms bond. A paper manufactured for the specific requirements of producing continuous business forms with web printing and converting methods.

business paper. A stock classification that includes bond, duplicator, ledger, safety, and thin papers.

bustle wheel. A mechanical device used to compensate for paper expansion in web offset printing.

butt. (1) To adjoin two pieces of film or two colors of ink without overlapping. (2) The unusable portion of a roll of paper on a web press.

butt splice. The end-to-end joining of two similar materials, such as webs of substrates.

byte. A single group of bits (most often eight) that are processed as a unit. Also the smallest addressable unit of main storage in a computer system. See also: *binary digit; bit.*

C

C. (1) On PCs and PC clones, the default letter assigned to the first hard drive. (2) A computer programming language.

C++. A high-level, object-oriented programming language used extensively by software vendors and by Apple Computer.

C print. Any reflective color print. Originally, the term was used to describe a particular Eastman Kodak integral tripack color print material.

cache. Small portion of high-speed memory used for the temporary storage of frequently used data.

cadmium red. An inorganic red pigment that is composed principally of cadmium sulfide and cadmium selenide. It resists contamination by light, heat, and soap.

cadmium yellow. An inorganic yellow pigment that is composed principally of cadmium sulfide and, in lighter shades, zinc sulfide. Cadmium yellow also resists contamination by heat, light, and soap.

Cady gauge. Tradename for a dead-weight bench micrometer used to measure the caliper (thickness) of blankets, plates, and packing in the center and on all edges. See also: *blanket thickness gauge; micrometer, dead-weight.*

calender. (1) A set or stack of horizontal cast-iron rollers at the end of a paper machine. The paper is passed between the rollers to increase the smoothness and gloss of its surface. (2) A similar configuration of heated rollers used for flattening one or both sides of synthetic screen-printing fabrics. Alternative term: *machine calender.* See also: *calender rollers; calendering.*

calender rollers. Heavy cast-iron rollers that compress and smooth the paper at the end of a papermaking machine.

calendering. (1) A method of producing a very high gloss surface on paper stock by passing the sheet between a series of rollers under pressure. (2) A process for smoothing paper by running it between polished metal rollers. See also: *calender; calender rollers.*

calibrate. To adjust the scale on a measuring instrument such as a densitometer to a standard for specific conditions.

calibration. A process by which a scanner, monitor, or output device is adjusted to provide a more accurate display and reproduction of images.

calibration bars. On a negative, proof, or printed piece, a strip of tones used to check printing quality.

California job case. An open box with compartments in which individual type characters are separated for the hand compositor.

California job case

caliper. The thickness of a sheet of paper or other material measured under specific conditions. Caliper is usually expressed in mils or points, both ways of expressing thousandths of an inch.

calligraphy. Various styles of elegant handwriting, many based on classic examples from the fourteenth through the eighteenth centuries.

callout. A portion of text, usually duplicated from accompanying text, enlarged, and set off in quotes and/or a box to draw attention to what surrounds it.

calotype. The earliest process of making photographic negatives and prints on sensitized paper. Alternative term: *talbottype.*

camel's hair brush. A large, soft brush that is used to dust photofilms or plates. It is also used in some etching processes.

camera. A light-tight photographic device that records the image of an object formed when light rays pass through a lens and fall on a flat, photosensitive surface. In addition to the lens, other camera components include automatic or manual focus and size adjustments, a film- or paper-holding mechanism, and an area for previewing the final image. A light source and metering device may also be included. See also: *darkroom camera; camera, process.*

camera, adjustable. A graphic arts camera with variable distance settings, lens openings, and shutter speeds that can be set and reset manually or automatically to suit a given job.

camera, automatic. A camera with a built-in exposure meter with a self-regulating mechanism that adjusts the lens opening, shutter speed, or both, for proper exposure.

camera, digital. A photographic system using a charged-coupled device to transform visual information into pixels that are assigned binary codes so that they can be manipulated, compressed, stored, or transmitted as electronic files. Alternative term: *electronic camera.*

camera, process. A camera designed especially to create halftone images and color separations for photomechanical reproduction and similar work.

camera, vertical. A space-saving graphic arts camera that is housed entirely in the darkroom or an adjacent light-tight room. The copyboard and filmholder are perpendicular to the optical axis of the camera's lens (i.e., the copyboard is at the bottom and the camera back at the top).

Camera, vertical

camera angle. The level or direction (high, medium, or low; left, right, or straight on) defined by the position of the subject matter in relation to the camera lens. Alternative term: *viewpoint.*

camera back. The portion of a graphic arts camera that secures the photosensitive paper or film in place. Located in the darkroom, the camera back is comprised of a hinged vacuum filmback and a ground glass plate.

camera bed. The base of the graphic arts camera that supports the other camera elements and movable guide rails, which are used to adjust focusing and reproduction size.

camera exposure. Producing a latent image on photosensitive material from the light rays that a subject reflects or transmits when photographed under controlled conditions of time and intensity.

camera extension. The distance between the lens diaphragm and the surface of the film or plate at any definite scale of reproduction. See also: *copyboard extension.*

camera film. A high-contrast, silver-based orthochromatic graphic arts film designed specifically for exposure using a graphic arts camera. Alternative term: *lith film.*

camera lens. An arrangement of circular pieces of glass with concave or convex surfaces that controls incoming light rays by focusing them on ground glass or film.

camera lucida. An optical viewer used to obtain the correct proportion and perspective from an original photograph or actual scene. The subject is projected onto drawing paper, enabling the artist to directly trace its outlines and detail.

camera mount. The base on which the camera is secured to eliminate vibration. Alternative term: *camera stand.*

camera scaling. A process camera equipped with devices that size images correctly on a focusing screen without exact measurements.

camera-back masking. A single-stage color correction process where photographic masks are made and placed over unexposed separation film in the camera back before creating separation negatives on a process camera.

camera-ready copy. All printing elements prepared to be photographed on the graphic arts camera: text type set in the correct point size and properly mounted to the page grid; headlines, copy blocks, and screened prints; keylines showing the exact size and position of halftones or four-color photographs to be stripped in; and spot color elements mounted to acetate overlays, properly registered over the black copy, and marked for screen percentage and colors. Manual pasteup techniques or computer-based pagination systems may be used to create the layout. Alternative term: *camera-ready art.*

cap height. The height of a capital letter from the baseline to the top of the letter in a particular typeface.

capillary film. A presensitized, uniformly coated stencil film that is adhered to the wet screen fabric under slight pressure.

caps. Capital or uppercase letters.

caps, small. A second size of uppercase letters made on the same body size as regular capital letters. Small caps are usually close in size to the lowercase characters in the font.

caption. The descriptive text accompanying a photo, illustration, chart, or table that explains or identifies the content. Alternative term: *cutline; legend.*

captured keystrokes. Data that is received via telecommunications (modem) or on disks, diskettes, or magnetic tape and transferred directly into a computer or typesetting system without any need for rekeying.

carbon arc. A light source consisting of two closely spaced carbon rods that generate a controllable electrical current when an electric discharge passes across the gap between them. The emitted light is extremely high in actinic value. In the graphic arts, carbon arc lamps have been replaced by pulsed-xenon and quartz-halogen lamps, which are considered safer sources of illumination. See also: *arc lamp.*

carbon black. An intensely dark, finely divided pigment obtained by burning natural gas or oil with a restricted air supply. The resulting black pigment consists mostly of elemental carbon, a small percentage of ash (mineral matter), and a somewhat higher percentage of volatile matter. Carbon black is commonly used in formulating black inks.

carbon print. A photograph made on a gelatin-coated dyed or pigmented paper material.

carbon tissue. (1) A light-sensitive, gelatin-coated paper used in the conventional gravure process to convert the image on a photographic positive to an image that will print from the copper cylinder. Carbon tissue also serves as a mask that controls the etching depth and size of gravure cylinder cells in the conventional method. (2) A dyed or pigmented gelatin-based photographic material coated onto a paper support, which is exposed, developed, and adhered to the screen printing fabric. In this process, special screen printing stencils that print detailed designs on various surfaces are created.

carbonizing paper. An uncoated grade of paper made from bleached or unbleached chemical pulps or mixtures of unbleached chemical and mechanical pulps. Its significant properties include uniformity of surface and caliper, freedom from pinholes, close formation, high density, strength, nonporosity, and the ability to accept carbon inks without penetration and release them subsequently under pressure or impact.

carbonless paper. A specialty paper that produces duplicate copies of hand-written, typed, or otherwise impact-printed sheets without the use of carbon paper. To achieve this, NCR paper is coated with two different microencapsulated chemicals—one on the face and the other on the reverse side of the sheet. When pressure is applied to two attached sheets of paper, the encapsulated chemicals break and mix, producing a visible image similar to that formed by carbon paper. Originally manufactured by the National Cash Register Corp. Alternative term: *NCR (no-carbon-required) paper.*

carbro print. A photographic print made by superimposing red, yellow, and blue layers of gelatin on a bromide-based paper to create the tones of an image. Alternative term: *carbros.*

carbro process. A chemical action in a special bleach bath that tans the pigmented gelatin on bromide paper, producing a carbro print.

cardboard. Layers of paper laminated into sheets that are at least 0.006 in. (0.15 mm) or more in thickness.

carrier. (1) The tone with a fixed frequency and amplitude that is established between two communications connections. (2) A gravure term for film flat. Alternative terms: *cab; backing sheet.*

carrier sense multiple access with collision avoidance (CSMA/CA). The network access method in which a sending computer requests permission from a receiving computer before sending data. Transmission begins only after the receiving computer acknowledges the permission request.

carrier sense multiple access with collision detection (CSMA/CD). The network access method controlling a computer's access to the communications channel. If two or more computers try to send data at the same time, they abort their transmissions and attempt to resend the data after a short period of time.

case. (1) In typography, a portioned receptacle or tray used to store type and other hand-composition materials. The California job case is a well-known example. (2) In electrotyping, the base plate that is covered with a layer of molding wax and pressed into the form to create the mold. (3) In bookbinding, inserting and attaching a book into prepared (hard) covers.

case, three-piece. A binding method in which one piece of material is used to form the spine and a portion of the front and back of the cover and a different material is used for the balance of the cover's front and back. There is a slight overlap where the pieces meet. The actual binder boards constitute the third piece of material.

case, two-piece. A book covering made with two different materials that are applied to the binder boards separately. First, a standard case is made with a single piece of material. A second material is added over the first, covering the complete spine and partially wrapping around the front and back of the case.

case binding. The process that produces a hardcover book. Printed covering material is glued to rigid board material and then affixed to the book with endpapers. See also: *casebound book.* Alternative term: *edition binding.*

casebound book. A book bound with a stiff, hard cover. Alternative term: *hardbound book.*

casein. A sizing and adhesive used in manufacturing coated papers. It was also used in place of albumin as a sensitizer in early plate coatings and as a binder in aqueous dispersions of pigments.

casemaker. A machine that produces hardcovers for casebound books.

casing-in. Applying adhesive and combining a sewn and trimmed text with a cover (case). See also: *covering.*

Casing-in

cassette. (1) A portable housing or container for daylight transportation of either exposed or unexposed photographic materials, which makes it possible to operate a phototypesetting machine in a daylight environment. (2) In magnetic tape applications, a plastic cartridge that contains tape which is ¼ in. or narrower, takeup reels, and a read/record head pressure pad.

cast. See *color cast.*

cast coater. A device that applies a wet coating to a paper web before it contacts a highly polished, heated cylinder drum.

cast-coated. A high-gloss, ink-absorbent paper with an enamel finish. Cast-coated paper is dried under pressure against a polished cylinder during manufacture.

Cast coater

casting. A method of producing hot-metal type. Molten metal is forced into molds called matrices (mats). The resulting lines of type are called slugs.

cast-off. (1) An estimate of the number of characters to be typeset. (2) To estimate the final length of a printed manuscript. (3) A procedure used in calculating the format and space requirements of tabular matter. See also: *copyfitting.*

catalyst. A substance that alters (initiates or accelerates) the velocity of a reaction between two or more substances without changing itself in chemical composition.

catch-up. A condition that occurs in lithography when insufficient dampening causes the nonimage areas of the plate to become ink-receptive and print as scum or when excessive ink reaches the plate. See also: *scum.*

cathode-ray tube (CRT). An electronic vacuum tube containing a heated cathode that generates electrons and multiple grids for accelerating the electrons to a flat screen at the end of the

Cathode-ray tube

tube. The screen coating fluoresces wherever the electrons strike it, giving off light. CRTs are used as monitors in video display terminals (VDTs) and as an output light source in third-generation phototypesetters.

cause-and-effect diagram. A quality tool that illustrates the situations leading to various symptoms by analyzing a process. It is the logical outcome of a brainstorming session whereby the causes of a particular problem, such as paper waste in the press-room, are organized and summarized into meaningful groups, usu-ally related to staffing, materials, methods, machines, measurement, and environment. See also: *brainstorming.* Alternative term: *fishbone diagram.*

Cause-and-effect diagram

CCD array. A group of light-sensitive recording elements often arranged in a line (lin-ear array) and used as a scanner image-sensing device. See also: *charge-coupled device.*

CD-ROM (compact disk—read-only memory). An optical data storage device that consists of a platter in which data is etched as a series of pits and lands (the space between the pits) in a continuous spiral. Derived from the compact audio disk (CD), a typical CD-ROM holds 650 MB of digitally encoded computer data, which the user can retrieve (but not alter) using a laser-based reader. See also: *Photo CD™.*

cell. A small, etched depression in a gravure cylinder that carries the ink. In conven-tional gravure, cell depth may vary.

cell, quadrangular. An engraved depression with four walls and a flat bottom, typically found on an anilox roller used in flexography.

cell count. The number of engraved cells per linear inch (or linear centimeter) on an anilox roller.

center spread. Facing pages in the center of a newspaper section or a signature. See also: *double spread.*

centered. A typographic form in which various line lengths of type are symmetrically divided by a common vertical axis. The longest line of type represents the line length.

centerline. A line or mark added to copy, a page negative, or a film flat to denote the center of trim margins on a page or form. The centerline is also used as a registra-tion mark.

centipoise. A measure of the viscosity of water at room temperature.

central impression cylinder. See *common-impression cylinder.*

central processing unit. The silicon chip that interprets and carries out the instructions necessary to operate a computer. See also: *microprocessor.*

CERCLA. See *Comprehensive Environmental Response, Compensation, and Liability Act of 1980.*

chain transfer. A method of conveying sheets from one impression cylinder to the next by using sets of grippers riding on a chain to support the sheets.

chalking. Poor adhesion of ink to printing surface. This condition results when the substrate absorbs the ink vehicle too rapidly. The ink dries slowly and rubs off as a dusty powder.

character compensation. Reducing the width value of each printed symbol, which, in turn, decreases the white space between characters for tighter fit. See also: *kerning.*

character definition. A term used to describe the fidelity or resolution with which alphanumeric symbols are reproduced.

character generation. Constructing typographic images electronically as a series of dots, lines, or pixels on the screen of a cathode-ray tube (CRT).

character generator. A cathode-ray tube that displays characters on the screens of phototypesetters and word processors.

character master. A photographic or digitized font used to create images in a phototypesetting unit.

character memory. A mechanical or electronic buffer in a typesetting system that stores one or more characters, while previously transferred characters are processed.

character recognition. The function of systems that automatically read or recognize typed, printed, or handwritten characters or symbols and convert them to machine language for processing and storing in electronic systems. See also: *optical character recognition.*

character set. The particular array of character designs available on a typesetter, word processor and printer, or typewriter. Alternative term: *type font.*

character spacing reference line. In optical character recognition, a vertical line that is used to evaluate the horizontal spacing of characters. It can be a line that equally divides the distance between the sides of a character boundary or that coincides with the centerline of a vertical stroke.

character width systems. The amount of horizontal space a character occupies in relation to adjacent characters.

characteristic curve. A graphical representation of the relationship between exposure and density for any given photographic material developed under fixed conditions. The chart has a vertical density (D) scale and a horizontal logarithm-of-exposure (log E) scale. Alternative term: *D log E chart.*

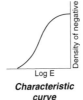

*Characteristic
curve*

characters-per-pica. System of copyfitting that utilizes the average number of characters per pica as a means of determining the length of the copy when set.

charge corotron. (1) A unit that produces coronae as needed in the electrophotographic printing process. (2) Material used in electrophotographic printing to generate the initial charge on a photoconductive medium.

charge transfer. (1) The process where the toner particles are conveyed from the photoconductor to the paper through a transfer corona. (2) The movement of electrical charges from one surface to another in an imaging system (e.g., from photoconductor to paper).

charge-coupled device. A component of an electronic scanner that digitizes images. A CCD consists of a set of image-sensing elements (photosites) arranged in a linear or area array. Images are digitized by an external light source that illuminates the source document, which reflects the light through optics onto the silicon light sensors in the array. This generates electrical signals in each photosite proportional to the intensity of the illumination. See also: *CCD array.*

charging bar. A corona discharge unit.

chase. (1) A rectangular, heavy metal frame into which type forms and cuts are locked together after handsetting in letterpress printing or for molding duplicate printing plates. (2) A metal frame with adjustable clamps used to position and hold the negative (or positive) on a step-and-repeat machine in platemaking. (3) To groove or cut a design into the surface of a plate, book, or other material. (4) A screen printing frame with a fabric attachment that holds and tensions the fabric. Based on the floating bar principle, it is usually made of aluminum and adapted to mount on a screen printing press.

check copy. A proof sent to a customer to okay all printing and binding instructions. It is also used as a master guideline in the bindery.

check sheet. A simple data recording device custom-designed by the user to allow for readily interpreted results. It is typically used to capture a record of how frequently events (e.g., downtime or defects) occur over a given period of time.

chemical fog. Cloudy areas that appear during development on the parts of a film not exposed to light.

chemical ghosting. Latent images that appear on the reverse side of a printed sheet when different inks chemically interact during critical drying phases. Alternative term: *fuming ghosting.* See also: *ghosting, gloss.*

chemical reversal. Converting a negative to a positive (or vice versa) by treating the photographic image with certain active elements.

chemical vapor drying. Hardening and setting the surface of a printed ink film with a gaseous mixture of elements instead of with heat.

chemicals, hazardous. An EPA designation for any hazardous material requiring an MSDS under OSHA's Hazard Communication Standard. Such substances are capable of producing fires and explosions or adverse health effects like cancer and dermatitis. Hazardous chemicals are distinct from hazardous waste. See also: *waste; waste, hazardous; waste, industrial.*

chemistry. The supplies used to expose and develop photosensitive materials.

chill rolls. On a web offset press, the section located after the drying oven where heatset inks are cooled below their setting temperature. Alternative term: *cooling rollers.*

Chill rolls

China clay. A natural white mineral pigment used in paper coatings and as an ink extender. Alternative term: *kaolin.*

Chinese brushes. Writing brushes used to apply an etch of ferric chloride solution on a surface.

chip. A wafer-shaped medium of specially formulated silicon or a similar substance used for micromanufactured electronic circuits, principally in computer systems.

chisel-point pencil. A tool for drawing lines that represent text type in a comprehensive layout. The tip is shaped into a four-sided wedge, and the lead is shaved to a uniform thickness that matches the x-height of the type to be set.

choke. A camera or contacting process whereby various images are made thinner without changing shape or position. The image area remains essentially the same except for a narrow reduction around its perimeter. Chokes are used to provide a printing overlap between a color or tinted background and display matter, to outline letters, or to achieve other special effects when preparing negatives. A contact positive is made from the choked negative to expose the background. Alternative term: *"skinny."* See also: *spread (fatty); trapping.*

Choke

chopper fold. Conveying a signature from the first parallel fold in a horizontal plane, spine forward, until it passes under a reciprocating blade that forces it down between folding rollers to complete the fold. Alternative terms: *cross fold, right-angle fold, quarterfold.*

chroma. A term used in the Munsell system of color specification to indicate the extent to which the color is diluted by white light. The intensity or strength of a color. Its saturation, or degree of departure from black and white.

chromatic aberration. The failure of a photographic lens to converge rays of different colors to the same focal point.

chromaticity. A color specification indicated by dominant wavelength and purity.

chromaticity diagram. A graphical representation of two of the three dimensions of color. It is used for plotting light sources rather than surface colors. Alternative term: *CIE diagram.*

chromatone. A photographic color print process.

chrome green. A fairly light-resistant, opaque green pigment made by mixing freshly precipitated iron blue and chrome yellow.

chrome yellow. A light-resistant, inorganic yellow pigment composed essentially of lead chromate.

chrominance. The color part of an electronic signal relating to hue and saturation but not to brightness (luminance). Neutral grays have no chrominance but any color is a combination of luminance and chrominance.

chromium. A blue-white metallic element, compounds of which are used as bleaching or hardening agents in photosensitive processes.

chromolithography. Obsolete lithographic color printing process in which a separate litho stone is required to print each color.

chuck. The mechanism on a paper roll stand that centers and grips the roll core.

cicero. The continental typographic measure equivalent to 12 points Didot, or 4.511 mm. See also: *Didot point system.*

CIE chromaticity coordinates. The ratios of each of the tristimulus values of a color to the sum of the tristimulus values. In CIE systems, they are designated by x, y, and z. Alternative terms: *trichromatic coefficients; trilinear coordinates.*

CIE diagram. See *chromaticity diagram.*

CIE L*a*b. Scales adopted by the International Commission on Illumination (CIE) to serve as a world-wide standard for color measurement.

CIE tristimulus values. The sum of the three reference or matching stimuli required to match with the color stimulus considered in a given trichromatic system.

circular screen. A round halftone screen that can be rotated to select different screen angles without repositioning copy.

circumferential register. The alignment of successive ink films on top of each other on the printed sheets, usually accomplished on a rotary printing press by moving the plate cylinder toward the gripper or tail. See also: *misregister.*

cissing. A defect in which a wet ink or varnish recedes from small areas of the surface, leaving either no coating or an attenuated one.

clamshell press. (1) A machine with two platens positioned directly over each other and hinged together on one side. Such platens are found on heat-transfer and diecutting equipment. (2) A flatbed screen-printing press designed with the screen carriage hinged to the printing table at one end.

clay-coated. Paper or board with an earthy material added to one or both sides to improve the quality of the printing surface.

Clean Air Act. U.S. federal guidelines for air quality and emission controls affecting all manufacturing concerns.

Clean Water Act. U.S. federal guidelines for water quality and controls affecting all manufacturing concerns.

cleanup. (1) Washing a lithographic plate during the pressrun to make the non-image areas ink repellent again. (2) After a pressrun, removing the plates and washing the entire press and surrounding area. Alternative term: *washup.*

client. A networked personal computer or workstation that requests information or applications from a centralized server.

client/server environment. A network system that uses a designated computer for centralized resource access.

clip art. Previously developed designs and graphics used in composing new artwork. Most clip art, which can be purchased in booklets or in electronic form, is in the public domain (copyright free) and can be used over and over again by anyone for any purpose once the initial purchase is made. Other clip art is purchased on a fee-per-usage basis.

clipboard. A temporary electronic storage area in a computer software program where text or graphics can be held for reuse.

cloning. A retouching function available on a color imaging system. It is normally used to remove image defects by replacing pixels in the defective areas with duplicate pixels from adjacent, nondefective areas. It can also be used to duplicate sections of an image. Alternative term: *pixel swopping.*

close register. Term used to describe jobs with smaller register tolerances. Alternative term: *tight register.*

closed loop. A process in which all control functions have been automated, including sensing output errors and correcting the input to compensate for the error.

close-up. A photograph taken with a special camera lens that is used to produce a detailed shot of a subject or scene, or a photograph taken very near a subject or scene.

close-up lens. An attachment placed in front of the built-in camera lens to produce more detailed photographs of a subject or scene than the camera normally could.

clothbound. A casebound book with a fabric cover.

CMOS. See *complementary metal-oxide semiconductor.*

coarse mesh. A screen printing fabric with large openings or apertures between the woven threads or strands.

coarse screen. Any halftone screen ruling of 120 lines per inch or lower. Using a coarse screen ruling results in a reproduction of low resolution, such as the 65-line screen ruling used for many newspaper halftones.

coater. A tool with a rounded, sometimes slotted edge used to spread sensitized emulsion evenly on a screen printing fabric. Alternative terms: *emulsion applicator; spreader.*

coating. (1) An unbroken, clear film applied to a substrate in layers to protect and seal it, or to make it glossy. (2) Applying waxes, adhesives, varnishes, or other protective or sealable chemicals to a substrate during the converting process. (3) The mineral substances (clay, blanc fixe, satin white, etc.) applied to the surface of a paper or board. (4) In photography and photomechanics, applying varnishes and other mixtures to plates and negatives; or applying light-sensitive solutions to plate surfaces.

coating, plate. Applying light-sensitive solutions to plate surfaces.

coating binder. A natural or synthetic material that promotes cohesion between the pigment and body stock, enhancing pick and water resistance, ink receptivity, flexibility, gloss, and blister resistance.

coating mottle. A small variation in gloss that can be detected on a coated, calendered sheet by viewing it at an angle to check for specular reflection from the surface.

cobalt drier. A liquid drier used in lithographic inks to accelerate oxidation and polymerization of an ink film.

cobwebbing. (1) Fine filaments of ink that appear between the screen fabric and the substrate during screen printing. (2) In gravure, a filmy buildup of dried ink on the doctor blade, the ends of impression roll, or printing cylinder.

cockle. (1) The effect of uneven moisture absorption on paper. The paper swells in the areas of greatest absorption, which causes a slightly bumpy surface contour. (2) A finish produced by air-drying bond and onionskin papers.

coder-decoder (CODEC). A device used to convert analog signals into their digital counterparts and vice versa.

cold color. A bluish or greenish hue.

cold curing. Treating an ink or coating at the normal atmospheric temperature.

cold enamel. A solution of bichromated shellac used as a photoengraving sensitizer for metal plates.

cold end. The intake section of a conveyor dryer where heat is used to promote drying.

cold flow. The partial fusing of individual particles of thermosetting plastic powder after the mass of the powder has been subjected to a high temperature, but not one high enough to melt the material.

cold type. Characters produced on paper or film for photomechanical reproduction without the use of metal type. The term originally applied to any method of preparing text by direct-impression from typewriter mechanisms. Today, it usually refers to phototypeset galleys, laser-printed proofs, or paginated films generated from imagesetters. See also: *hot-metal.*

cold-setting inks. Solid inks that are melted and applied as liquids through a heated press cylinder. These inks solidify again on contact with the unheated substrate.

collate. The process of sorting the pages of a publication in the proper order. See *assembling; gathering; insert.*

collating mark. A distinctive, numbered symbol printed on the folded edge of signatures to denote the correct gathering sequence.

Collating mark

collator, automatic. A mechanical device that collects document sheets into a desired sequence.

collimator. An optical instrument that produces a beam of parallel light rays or forms an infinitely distant virtual image that can be viewed without parallax. In printing, a collimator is used to check register and alignment between two or more photographic images separated from each other, such as superimposed flats.

collodion. A viscous solution of pyroxylin used especially as a coating for photographic films. A collodion emulsion, used as an adhesive, contains a silver halide in suspension.

colloid. Water-soluble, very fine noncrystalline substances, such as gelatin, glue, or albumin, that become light-sensitive when a bichromate is added. These materials, which are used as vehicles in photomechanical sensitizers, will not diffuse or pass through a parchment membrane if dissolved in water.

colloid mill. A machine that disperses pigments during the manufacture of some printing inks, by producing intense shearing stresses in the liquid to which the solid pigments have been added.

collotype. A photomechanical printing process in which a bichromated gelatin-coated plate is exposed through continuous-tone negatives. This process is used most often for short runs of fine art prints. Alternative term: *photogelatin printing.*

colophon. (1) Traditionally, the printer's signature and the date of completion written at the beginning or end of a book. (2) The publisher's trademark printed on cover or title page. (3) A modern colophon at the back of book often includes information about the paper, typeface, and typesetting method used, how the illustrations were produced, and what printing process was employed.

color. A visual sensation produced in the brain when the eye views various wavelengths of light. Color viewing is a highly subjective experience that varies from individual to individual. In the graphic arts industry, lighting standards and color charts help ensure the accuracy of color reproduction.

color, HiFi. A special high-fidelity color reproduction process based on the Küppers model that uses seven basic colors instead of four to expand the color gamut of printing. The basic colors are cyan, yellow, magenta, orange, green, violet, and black. Because seven colors are used, color separations are made using stochastic screening technology to prevent moiré, which would occur if conventional halftone screening technology was used. See also: *stochastic screening.*

color balance. (1) The correct combination of cyan, magenta, and yellow needed to reproduce a specific photograph without an unwanted color cast or color bias. (2) The specific combination of yellow, magenta, and cyan needed to produce a neutral gray in the color separation process. (3) The ability of a film to reproduce the colors in an original scene. Color films are balanced during manufacture to compensate for exposure to specific light sources.

color bar. A device printed in a trim area of a press sheet to monitor printing variables such as trapping, ink density, dot gain, and print contrast. It usually consists of overprints of two- and three-color solids and tints; solid and tint blocks of cyan, magenta, yellow, and black; and additional aids such as resolution targets and dot gain scales. Alternative terms: *color control strip; color control bar.*

color blindness. (1) A deficiency in vision that permits a person to see only two hues in the spectrum, usually yellow and blue. (2) Term sometimes used to describe an emulsion that is only sensitive to blue, violet, and ultraviolet light.

color break. Indicating on tissue overlays attached to the mechanical what image areas will print in what colors (usually line and screen tints). This is done so that a different plate can be prepared for each color in a multicolor job.

color burn-out. An objectionable change in the color of a printing ink that may occur either in the bulk or after the ink has been applied to the substrate. When the problem occurs in the bulk, it is usually caused by a chemical reaction between certain components in the ink formula. After the ink has been applied to the substrate, heat generated in a pile of freshly printed material during drying may cause color burn-out to occur.

color cast. Modifying a hue by adding a trace of another hue to create such combinations as yellowish green or pinkish blue. Color casts can be undesirable as in the contamination of the desired hue by a second hue. For example, a gray intended to appear as a neutral can under some conditions have a red, yellow, or blue cast or appearance. Other colors can have a cast as well, e.g., reds with a yellow or blue cast or blues with a red or yellow cast, etc.

color chart. A printed reference card that contains a range of overlapping halftone tint patches in various combinations of the process colors. This chart helps in selecting proper ink, paper, and film combinations. It is also helpful in testing the effect of color filters and the specific sensitivity of photographic plates. Printers should reproduce color charts in their own plants under the same conditions that they would print an actual job.

color circle. (1) A GATF diagram used to plot and visualize the hue error and grayness characteristics of a given ink. (2) A round group of color blocks arranged to illustrate the relationships between different colors.

color compensating filter. A transparent transmission device used to correct the color balance of transparencies.

color computer. The analog or digital device in the color scanner that determines the amount of each process ink necessary to reproduce the color in the original image. A digital color computer uses lookup tables to determine the dot percentages, while an analog color computer typically uses masking equations to determine the percentages.

color control strip. See *color bar.*

color conversion. Producing a color transparency from a color reflection original so that a flexible copy of the original can be color-separated on a rotary-drum scanner. Color conversions are also made for other duplication purposes.

color copy. The original color artwork, transparencies, photographs, keylines, or other materials furnished for reproduction.

color correction. (1) A photographic, electronic, or manual procedure used to compensate for the deficiencies of the process inks and color separation. (2) Any color alteration requested by a customer.

color deficiency. An inherited abnormality in which viewers cannot distinguish between various colors, red and green in particular. This condition is more prevalent in men of all races than in women of any race.

color density. The opacity, purity, or brilliance of a color.

color difference. The apparent distinction between two colors viewed under standard conditions.

color duplicating. Producing an identical transparency from an original transparency for image assembly, or for retouching or adjusting the color cast, density range, or reproduction scale. Alternative term: *dupes.*

color electronic prepress system. A computer-based image manipulation and page-makeup system for graphic arts applications. CEPS replaces manual correction techniques previously accomplished with duplicate transparencies and emulsion stripping.

color fidelity. How well a printed piece matches the original.

color filter. See *filter.*

color gamut. The range colors that can be formed by all possible combinations of the colorants in a color reproduction system. See also: *palette.*

color guide. Supplementary visual instructions that indicate the hues to be reproduced in a given job.

color harmony. Properly blending hues, shades, and tints to produce a pleasing effect.

color hexagon. A trilinear plotting system used as a color control chart to detect changes in the hue of two-color overprints.

color iteration. The process of generating halftone films that match color proofs.

color management system. An electronic prepress tool that provides a way to correlate the color-rendering capabilities of input devices (e.g., scanners and digital cameras), color monitors, and output devices (e.g., digital color proofers, imagesetters, and color printers) to produce predictable, consistent color. Color management consists of three primary steps: (1) calibration of input devices, monitors, and output devices to known specifications, (2) characterization, which is a way of determining the color "profile" of a particular device, and (3) conversion, which performs the "color correction" function between color-imaging devices.

color match. Condition resulting when no significant difference in hue, saturation, and lightness can be detected between two color samples viewed under standard illumination.

color notation. A system for identifying colors by symbols or numerical values. The Munsell system, accepted by the U.S. Bureau of Standards, is one example.

color OK sheets. The printed colors approved for ink/color matching.

color overlay. Transparent film sheets, usually made of acetate, that are superimposed over each other to represent each color in a reproduction.

color patch. Small samples of the inks that will be used for a process-color job. They are printed on the required paper stock and attached to the original art to serve as a reference in the color separation process.

color photography. Reproducing a subject or original scene in its natural colors with specialized films.

color primaries, additive. The three basic colors, which, when properly selected and mixed, produce any hue. In the visual spectrum, the three primary colors are green, red, and blue. When combined, these colors form white light. In the printing process, the three primary (process) colors are yellow, magenta, and cyan.

color process, fake. A method of producing halftone color plates from a photograph or other monochrome original. The color effects on the various plates are achieved by skillful retouching, reetching, and finishing. Photographic masking techniques and tint sheets may also be employed to approximate the proportional color printing values on each fake color separation or printer.

color process work. See *process color.*

color proof. See *proof; proof, progressive.*

color reference. An established set of process inks printed to specific densities on the actual substrate that will be used for a job. The color reference sheet is compared against sheets printed during the run and color is adjusted accordingly.

color rendering index. A measure of the degree to which a light source influences color perception. Objects are illuminated under a nonstandard light source (such as fluorescent light) and then under a standard source (such as 5,000 Kelvin) and the differences in color are compared. Alternative term: *color quality index.*

color reproduction guide. A test image containing examples of solid primary colors, secondary colors, three- and four-color images, and tint areas. The guide should be reproduced under normal in-plant printing conditions with the same press, inks, and paper that will be used for the actual job. It then serves as the standard for correcting defects in printing ink pigments and the color separation process.

color retention. The ability of a color to resist fading or otherwise deteriorating after exposure to light. Alternative term: *colorfast.*

color scanner. A device incorporating a digital or analog computer that separates colored originals electronically by using the three additive primary colors of light in the form of blue, green, and red filters, plus a preprogrammed black printer correctly balanced with the color separations. A light beam moves over the image point by point, generating a separate, color-corrected, continuous-tone intermediate or screened halftone film negative or positive representing each of the process colors and black. See also: *electronic color scanner.*

Color scanner

color sensitive. An emulsion or other light-sensitive material that is receptive to other light waves in addition to blue, violet, and ultraviolet. See also: *orthochromatic; panchromatic.*

color sensitizing. Increasing the receptivity of an emulsion or other light-sensitive material to light waves in addition to blue, violet, and ultraviolet by adding certain dyes or other chemicals.

color separation. Using red, green, and blue filters to divide the colors of a multi-colored original into the three process colors and black. The four resulting film intermediates are used to prepare the yellow, magenta, cyan, and black printing plates. Color separation is most often accomplished with an electronic color scanner, but film-contacting and process-camera methods are also employed on occasion.

color separation, direct-screen. In this method, a process camera, contact printing frame, or enlarger is used to make color separation exposures through a photographic mask and a halftone screen onto high-contrast panchromatic lith film so that color-corrected halftone separation negatives are produced in one step and the need to screen tone values separately is eliminated.

color separation, indirect. A two-step process in which continuous-tone separations are produced from full-color originals, and halftone negatives or positives are made from the continuous-tone separations. In the first step, the color values are separated; in the second step, tone values are screened.

color sequence. The order in which colors are printed on a substrate as indicated by the order in which the inks are supplied to the printing units on the press. Color sequence determines how well the inks will trap on the substrate. Alternative term: *color rotation.*

color space. The three-dimensional area where three color attributes, such as hue, value, and chroma, can be depicted, calculated, and charted.

color standard. An ink sample, printed proof, or press sheet to which another similar material is compared.

color strength. (1) The relative amounts of pigment in an ink film. (2) The concentration or dilution (attenuation) of a color. Alternative terms: *chroma, intensity,* and *saturation.*

color swatch. A small, printed solid used for color matching or measurement. It represents what an ink color might look like after it is printed.

color temperature. The degree (expressed in Kelvins) to which a blackbody must be heated to produce a certain color radiation. For example, 5,000 Kelvin is the graphic arts viewing standard.

color theory, additive. See *additive color process.*

color toner. An ink formulation mixed with another formulation to affect the appearance of the final print. Toner colors are not intended to be printed alone.

color transform. An equation used to transfer color from one space to another, as in moving data from RGB color space to CMYK color space. See also: *color space.*

color transparency. A positive color photographic image on a clear film base. It must be viewed by transmitted light.

color triangle. A diagram used to indicate the range of pure colors that can be produced from a set of process inks.

color variation. A term used to describe changes that occur in the density of a color during printing as a result of deviations in the amount of ink accepted by paper or the amount of ink fed to the paper.

color vision, abnormal. Defective color vision, which may take the form of protanopia (confusion of red and bluish green); protanomalous (a deficiency in the red response to certain color mixtures); deuteranopia (confusion of red and green); deuteranomaly (a deficiency in the green response to certain color mixtures); tritanopia (confusion of blue and yellow); and monochromatism (inability to discern different hue and saturation values). Alternative term: *color blindness.*

color volume. The capacity of all the mesh openings in one square meter of stretched screen fabric to hold ink.

colorant. An ink, pigment, toner, or dye that modifies the natural color of a substrate.

color-blind emulsion. A photographic material that is only sensitive to blue wavelengths and can be handled safely under yellow, orange, or red light during processing. It is suitable for any job that does not require color separation.

color-corrected lens. A complex assembly of optical components designed to bring all colors to a sharp focus at the same focal plane and to produce an image of exactly the same size and position in each color. See also: *apochromatic lens.*

colorfastness. How well a printed substrate retains its color under normal storage conditions and resists change as it ages or is exposed to light, heat, or other environmental influences. Alternative terms: *color permanence, color retention, color stability.*

colorimeter. An instrument that measures and compares the hue, purity, and brightness of colors in a manner that simulates how people perceive color.

colorimetry. The science of determining and specifying colors.

Color-Key. Trademark for a color proofing system that generates a set of process-color transparent film positives from separation negatives so that registration and screen-tint combinations can be checked before actual press proofs are produced.

column. A vertical arrangement of text characters, numbers, or other symbols.

column inch. A unit of measurement that is one inch deep and one column wide.

column rule. A line used to separate vertical arrangements of text in printed matter.

coma. A lens aberration affecting the rays that are not parallel to the lens axis. Image areas near the edges of the picture appear as ovals pointing toward the center.

comb, plastic binding. A curved or rake-shaped plastic strip inserted through slots punched along the binding edge of the sheet.

comber. A press or folder component that fans the sheets to improve separation and feeding accuracy.

*Comb,
plastic binding*

combination. (1) Line and halftone matter merged onto a single film or plate. (2) A stripping layout containing a variety of different printing forms instead of a group of identical forms as in a step-and-repeat assembly.

combination dampening. A system that incorporates features of the plate- and inker-feed dampening systems.

combination plate. A plate made from several different negatives, usually, but not always, requiring a multiple exposure of each negative. Alternative term: *photo-composed plate.*

command-line interface (CLI). Use of keyboarded instructions rather than a mouse and graphical elements to direct computer operations.

commercial online services. For-profit corporations that distribute information over their own computer networks and provide links to other computer networks, including the Internet's network of networks. America Online and CompuServe are two examples of commercial online services.

common gateway interface (CGI). A standard that describes how World Wide Web servers access external data and return it to the user as an automatically generated web page. CGI scripts are used to create interactive forms and other tools that respond to user-supplied data. See also: *practical extraction and report language (perl)*.

common-impression cylinder (CIC). A cylinder configuration used in both web and sheetfed press designs. The common impression cylinder is in contact with several blanket cylinders that are, in turn, in contact with plate cylinders. This configuration is used to print more than one color on one side of the sheet or web, in one printing unit. The CIC configuration saves space and reduces the chance of doubling. Alternative term: *central impression cylinder*.

common-impression press. A flexo or sheetfed or web offset press that has one large-drum impression cylinder, which holds or supports the substrate, and several color stations positioned around it.

common-line mask. A cover used to ensure proper alignment when adjoining film flats have images that share a border line along one side. Alternative term: *common cropper*.

compact disk, photo storage. See *Photo CD*™.

compact disk read-only memory. See *CD-ROM*.

comparative weight. The size-to-weight ratio of paper in a size that is larger or smaller than its basic size.

comping. Indicating type in a comprehensive layout. For text type, single lines or pairs of lines are drawn to the correct line length. The thickness of the single lines, and the distance between pairs of lines, are equal to the x-height of the type to be set. For headline type, a sample of the typeface is duplicated in the correct size, usually by tracing.

complementary colors. Any two opposite (or contrasting) colors that produce white or gray when combined. In printing, complementary colors neutralize or accentuate each other, diminishing or enhancing the attention value of the print.

complementary image assembly. Combining the detail of each color from different film flats by double printing during platemaking. The combined exposures will produce the complete printed image if each flat is exposed successively in register onto the sensitized surface.

complementary metal-oxide semiconductor (CMOS). A computer chip that stores the basic system configuration of a motherboard.

compose. Setting text in the proper order and form.

composing. The process of setting type.

composing machines. Typesetting machines used to cast and compose type in justified lines. Intertype, Linotype, and Monotype machines are some examples.

composing room. The area in a printing plant where type is set.

composing stick. With movable type, a small, hand-held tray where type is assembled and justified after it is hand-selected from the type case. Alternative term: *job stick; stick.*

composite. A single film carrying two or more images (usually line, halftone, or screen tint) as a result of photocombining (contacting) two or more separate film images. Alternative term: *one-piece film.* See also: *montage; surprint.*

composite negative/positive. See *montage.*

composition. (1) Setting or assembling type. (2) Formatting typeset text before printing. Alternative terms: *pagination* and *page makeup.* See also: *phototypesetting; typesetting.*

composition rollers. Inking cylinders with resilient or somewhat elastic covers.

compositor. A person who sets type.

comprehensive. A precise layout, prepared by the graphic designer, that shows the final position of all type and illustrations. Alternative terms: *comp* and *mock-up.*

Comprehensive Environmental Response, Compensation, and Liability Act of 1980 (CERCLA). U.S. federal program enacted and designed to clean up identified environmentally damaged sites. Commonly referred to as the

"Superfund Program," it involves remedial investigations, feasibility studies, and implementing corrective measures.

compressibility. The extent to which the thickness of a substance reduces under pressure, such as blanket compressibility during printing impression.

compression. Reducing the size of a file for storage purposes or to enhance the speed of data transfer by eliminating the redundancies and other unnecessary elements from the original. See also: *data compression; tone compression.*

compression set. A permanent reduction in blanket thickness or the thickness of any of its component parts.

computer graphics. Producing graphic material from computer systems. This process also often involves integrating text and art and completing page layout on the computer before outputting it to a laser printer or imagesetter.

computer graphics interface. A hardware-independent link between a device driver and higher level graphics programs. Alternative term: *virtual device interface.*

computer graphics metafile. A hardware-independent data structure for storing and transferring two-dimensional graphic information.

concatenation. To link two or more units of information, such as data files, as one unit.

concept creation. Selecting images and generating and approving ideas from thumbnails and rough layouts during the graphic design process.

condensed. A typeface in which the height is proportionally greater than its width.

condenser enlarger. A device that uses undiffused light to produce high-contrast and high-definition photographic prints, or a series of lenses used to refocus light onto a negative or positive. Any scratches and blemishes on the original film will become more apparent.

condenser lens. A photographic lens used to focus light from one source to project negatives or positives onto photographic material or lithographic printing plates.

conditional match. Colors that resemble each other under present illumination and viewing conditions, but may not match under differing conditions.

conditioning. Exposing paper to the proper combination of temperature and humidity to prepare it for printing.

conductivity. The measurement of a solution's ability to conduct electricity, based its concentration of ions. The measurement is expressed in micromhos. Conductivity is the most accurate method of measuring fountain solution concentration due to the increased use of buffering agents to control pH levels.

cones. The sensors in the eye that permit color vision.

configuration. A group of machines that are inter-connected and programmed to operate as a system.

conjugate foci. (1) The distance from the lens to the copyboard and from the lens to the image or focal plane at any scale of reproduction. (2) A lens or optical arrangement employed to concentrate light rays.

console. The computer system workstation where operators per- form specific tasks by executing commands through a keyboard. Modern presses have consoles that control inking, dampening, and plate register moves. The results of the operator's commands can be reviewed on a nearby monitor.

Console

contact film. Blue-sensitive, continuous-tone film with a relatively high maximum density, excellent resolution, and a special antihalation backing that allows exposure through its base without loss in quality. This film has been designed specifically to re-produce a same-size reverse (positive) image from an original negative, or a negative image from a film positive as the films are held together in a vacuum frame. Darkroom (high-speed) contact films may be handled under red or yellow safelights while room-light (slow-speed) films may be handled under yellow fluorescent or subdued white lighting. Alternative term: *color-blind film.*

contact frame. A device that holds the imaged and the photosensitive materials together for exposure. Alternative term: *vacuum frame.*

contact halftone screen. A photographically produced film consisting of vignetted dots, used in contact with unexposed film to create halftones.

contact negative. An inverse impression of tones from the original reproduced when light-sensitive film is exposed as it is held against a film positive in a vacuum frame.

contact photography. A photographic process used to reproduce images by exposing a light-sensitive material as it is held against a transparent or translucent (transmission) original in a vacuum frame. See also: *diffusion transfer.*

contact positive. A light-sensitive film exposed as it is held against a film negative in a vacuum frame. The rendition of tones on a positive are similar to those on the original.

contact printing. Producing a photographic print by exposing sensitized paper, film, or printing plates held against a negative or positive in a vacuum frame. The resulting contact print is a same-size negative or positive reproduction.

Contact printing frame

contact printing frame. A device used in contact printing to hold a negative against photographic paper or film with vacuum pressure. Light from an external source exposes the paper or film.

contact screen. A photographic film with a dot structure of varying density that is placed in contact with unexposed film to convert a continuous-tone image into patterns of small, solid-tone dots that vary in size (a halftone). See also: *halftone screen.*

contaminant. Any physical, chemical, biological, or radiological substance or matter that has an adverse effect on air, water, or soil.

continuous discharge. A routine release into the environment that occurs without interruption, except for infrequent shutdowns for maintenance, process changes, etc.

continuous feeder. A paper-supply mechanism that can be reloaded without stopping the press.

continuous form. A series of connected sheets that feed sequentially through a printing device.

continuous improvement. Process of business management based on data tied to customer satisfaction. See also: *total quality management.*

continuous jet. A nonimpact printing technology in which a steady stream of ink is forced at high pressure through a small nozzle and dispersed as small droplets through a charging field. The stream of charged droplets then passes between high-voltage deflection plates. Because the plate voltage varies, only selectively charged droplets form the desired shape or pattern on the substrate. Excess droplets are diverted and recirculated.

continuous pulping. Using uninterrupted pressure from a continuous digester to extract water from wood during papermaking. Alternative term: *batch digester.*

continuous tone. A photographic image or art (such as a wash drawing) that has not been screened. It has infinite tone gradations between the lightest highlights and the deepest shadows.

continuous-tone gray scale. A scale of uniform tones, from white to black or transparent to opaque, without a visible texture or dot formation.

continuous-tone negative. An inverse impression of tones from the original reproduced on sensitized film without using a halftone contact screen.

continuous-tone proof. An illustration without halftone dots, which is produced on a computer screen at view file or fine file resolutions with the red, green, blue (RGB) color parameters.

contour. A typographic form in which type is set to create "shapes" other than blocks. Line lengths are individually calculated to ensure that the type fills a prescribed image or nonimage area.

contouring. A printed image defect in which shade and density variations are in evidence as visible steps.

contrast. The relationship or degree of tonal gradation between the lightest and darkest (highlight and shadow) areas in an original, reproduction, or negative.

contrast grade. A rating of 0–5 that designates the tonal differences among various photographic papers. A paper with a grade of 0 has the lowest contrast, and one with a grade of 5 the highest. Grade 0 paper is used with high-contrast negatives, and grade 5 paper is used with low-contrast negatives.

contrast gradient. The rate at which exposure to light will change the density on a given photographic emulsion after processing under fixed conditions.

contrast ratio. (1) A measure of a paper's opacity, ranging from 100% in a totally opaque stock to a minimal percentage in transparent stock, such as tracing paper. (2) The total reflectance of a dry ink or coating film printed on a black substrate with a reflectance percentage of 5% or less when compared against the reflectance percentage of the same material applied in an identical manner over a substrate with 80% reflectance. See also: *opacity.*

control chart. A trend diagram with an average line and statistically determined upper and lower control limits. The control limits represent the natural variation to be expected in the particular process, such as fountain solution pH and conductivity readings taken over a specific period of time. Various methods of interpretation are used to determine when the process is operating in a

An x̄ control chart

state of statistical control (with only natural or common variation present) and when it is operating out of statistical control (with assignable or special causes of variation present). Alternative term: *x̄ chart*. See also: *trend chart.*

control strips. (1) Continuous or step wedges (film) with graduated densities that are preexposed under exacting conditions and used to test development solution in automatic processors. (2) Any test image printed on the trim edge of a sheet and used to visually assess ink settings.

convection drying. Hardening and setting the ink film on a printed substrate by circulating hot air continuously and uniformly around it in a contained area.

converting. Any manufacturing or finishing operation completed after printing to form the printed item into the final product. Bagmaking, coating, waxing, laminating, folding, slitting, gluing, box manufacture, and diecutting are some examples. Converting units may be attached to the end of the press, or the operation may be handled by a special outside facility.

converting paper. A paper product designed to be processed into envelopes, carbon-base paper, and business forms bond.

conveyor dryer. An ink drying system that incorporates a drying chamber with a belt conveyor. Some additional features may include an exhaust system, a cooling chamber, and a UV lamp. Belting materials may be made of metal or heat-resistant synthetics.

cool colors. Blues, grays, and greens. Colors that suggest water, ice, and the sky.

cooling rollers. See *chill rolls.*

cooling zone. The portion of a drying system in which the heated substrate is cooled before removal.

copier. A machine that makes reproductions directly from graphic materials by the electrophotographic (xerographic) process or another nonimpact method.

copper etching. Producing line and halftone images in relief by applying corrosive acid to a metal plate with a design cut into it.

copper twisted-pair. The most basic network cabling available. Its unshielded version is only suitable for voice networks or entry-level LANs. When insulated, it can better withstand interference and its speed improves, topping out at 4 Mbps. Copper twisted-pair cabling is also sometimes referred to as ordinary telephone wire.

copy. (1) Any material given to the printer for reproduction, particularly text and artwork. Alternative term: *original.* (2) To duplicate a photograph by contact printing.

copy, hard. Printed machine output of a photographic proof or text.

copy, soft. Text or images viewed or previewed on a video display terminal. See also: *proof, soft.*

copy area. The portion of an image carrier containing text, graphics, and photos.

copy block. Segments of a job, which may include line and halftone copy as well as text, paginated as a unit on a phototypesetter, imagesetter, or desktop publishing system. Alternative term: *area composition.*

copy density range. The difference in density from the highlights to the shadows of a photograph.

copy modification. Stretching, slanting, outlining, expanding, condensing, or otherwise changing the original copy to fit the design, pattern, or mood of a piece.

copy preparation. Specifying the size and location of type and illustrations and positioning them properly on a page.

copyboard. The glass-covered frame at the end of a process camera that holds the original to be photographed. Its other components include back and front lighting capabilities and variable (tilt-to-vertical) loading positions. Alternative term: *copyholder.*

copyboard chart. A card printed with solid patches of tricolor inks, a gray scale, and register marks to serve as an aid in three- and four-color photography.

copyboard extension. The distance between the lens and copyholder on a graphic arts camera. Along with the bellows extension, it can be varied to change the reproduction percentage. See also: *camera extension.*

copydot technique. Photographing halftone illustrations and associated line copy without rescreening the illustrations. The halftone dots of the original are copied as line material.

copyfitting. Adjusting copy to the allotted space, by editing the text or changing the type size and leading.

core. A transportable, hardware-independent interface for two- and three-dimensional graphical output as well as interactive input.

corner box. A simple gauge for maintaining register while mounting thin sheets to heavy stock.

corner marks. Lines indicating the final size of a job. Alternative term: *crop marks.*

corona. Small, thin wires that supply an electrical charge that fuses toner particles to the substrate in a nonimpact printing process.

corotron. An electrical device without a screen that creates a corona discharge.

corrugated board. A laminate made from flat sheets of paper and paper stock with a fluted, ridged, or grooved surface.

cost recovery. A legal process by which potentially responsible parties who contributed to contamination at a Superfund site can be required to reimburse the Trust Fund for money spent during any cleanup actions by the U.S. federal government.

couch roll. A paper machine cylinder with a perforated shell. Water is removed by applying vacuum to the shell before the web is transferred to the press.

counter. (1) In metal type, the hollow parts around and within the lines of the face of the type. (2) Any area in the face of a letter that is less than type-high and enclosed by the strokes.

counter-etch. The acid solution applied to grained metal plates in lithography to render the surface sensitive or receptive to litho ink.

counter-stacker. A bindery device that gathers and piles books, newspapers, or printed signatures in predetermined quantities for storage or shipment.

cover sheet. A clear transparent overlay used to protect artwork during handling.

covering. The process of pasting endpapers to a hardback book and drying them under pressure. See also: *casing-in; building-in.*

covering power. (1) The maximum ability of a lens to form a sharp, focused image. (2) The ability of an ink to obscure the substrate and produce a uniform, opaque surface. See also: *opacity.*

cradle-to-grave system. A procedure in which hazardous materials are identified and followed as they are produced, treated, transported, and disposed of by a series of permanent, linkable, descriptive documents (e.g., manifests). Alternative term: *manifest system.*

crash. A coarse fabric used to strengthen the joints of casebound books.

crayoning. A method of retouching lithographic plates by hand.

crease score. A fold made by pressing a groove into paper stock without cutting its fibers.

creasing. (1) Pressing lines into a book cover during binding. (2) Crimping or indenting along the binding edge of sheets or pages so that they will lie flat and bend easily. (3) Indenting bristol or boxboard to guide subsequent folding or forming.

creep. (1) Movement of the blanket surface or plate packing caused by static conditions or by the squeezing action that occurs during image transfer. (2) The displacement of each page location in the layout of a book signature as a result of folding the press sheet. Alternative terms: *thrust; pushout.* See also: *shingling; wraparound.*

Creep (2)

crocking. Ink that smudges or rubs off.

Cronak process. Treating zinc plates with moist sodium bichromate and sulfuric acid to improve tone reproduction and reduce oxidation.

crop. To opaque, mask, mark, cut, or trim an illustration or other reproduction to fit a designated area.

crop marks. Small lines placed in the margin or on an overlay, denoting the image areas to be reproduced.

cropping. (1) Indicating what portion of the copy is to be included in the final reproduction. (2) Trimming unwanted areas of a photograph film or print.

cross-direction. The position across the grain, or at a right angle to the machine direction, on a sheet of paper. The stock is not as strong and more susceptible to relative humidity in the cross-direction.

crossfeed. The side-to-side motion of a reading or writing head, such as the exposure head of a film plotter, as it moves across a cylinder or other device holding the original.

cross-grain. Folding at right angles to the binding edge of a book, or at a right angle to the direction of the grain in the paper stock. Folding the stock against the grain.

cross-hatch test. A method used to determine how well an ink adheres to a substrate. Officially, the ASTM D3359 Ink Adhesion Test.

cross-laminated. Layers of coating applied at right angles over previously applied coating layers.

crossline screen. A glass halftone screen with opaque lines crossing each other at right angles, forming transparent squares, or screen apertures. See also: *halftone screen.*

cross-machine direction. A position perpendicular to the direction of web travel through the paper machine.

cross-machine tension burst. A web break caused by an abrupt change in cross-machine paper caliper or by winding the roll too tightly.

crossmarks. Register symbols used to accurately position images and superimpose overlays onto a base or to each other.

crossover. See *breakacross; spread.*

cross-perforation. A series of holes or slits pierced at a right angle to the direction of web travel to prevent the signature from bursting during folding. Cross-perforating also prevents gusseting.

cross-web. The position at a right angle to the grain or machine direction of a web of flexible material.

cryptography. The science of coding messages so that they cannot be read by anyone other than the recipient. See also: *encrypt.*

crystal base. A water-clear additive used to modify the viscosity of transparent screen-printing inks in halftone screen printing.

crystallization. Ink that fails to adhere (trap) properly over a previously printed, dried ink film.

CSMA/CA. See *carrier sense multiple access with collision avoidance.*

CSMA/CD. See *carrier sense multiple access with collision detection.*

cure. The process of drying ink sufficiently so that it does not adhere to the printer or press. Inks are also cured to prevent blocking and setoff.

curing oven. A chamber in which a freshly printed ink surface is dried to improve adhesion, solidify the film, or otherwise alter it without solvent evaporation (oxidation).

curl. Uneven warping of the edges of a sheet aggravated by moisture and affected by the direction of the paper fibers.

cursor. The blinking line approximately the length of one character that, as displayed on a computer screen, marks the current working position in a file and can be moved to any other point in the file by shifting the position of the mouse and clicking on the new position, by clicking on a command in a dialog box, or by executing function key commands.

curtain coater. A machine that spreads an even thickness of a low-viscosity liquid (usually clear or adhesive) across a flat sheet or surface.

curved screen. Special mesh barriers mounted on flexible frame and often used to print on rounded surfaces or objects.

cut. (1) To dilute or thin an ink, lacquer, or varnish with one or more solvents or clear base. (2) A term originally referring to a woodcut but now generally used to denote a zinc etching, halftone engraving, or other illustrative matter. See also: *engraving.* (3) To trim book edges during the binding process. (4) Any incision or shearing of paper stock with a knife blade or automated machine, such as a guillotine. (5) To etch or reduce negative density or dot size in graphic arts photography. (6) An opening in goldenrod or masking paper; the area cut open to expose the image to the printing plate.

cut score. A crease formed when the paper stock is partially slit.

cut sheet. (1) Paper that has been trimmed on a guillotine or rotary cutter. (2) A fine paper with dimensions of 16×21 in. or less. The most common cut size is 8½×11 in. (3) Paper that has been cut into sheets in predetermined dimensions and sold in packaged reams.

cut-in head. Type larger than body text located in a white space in the side of a typeset page and often used to introduce a new subsection of a chapter.

cutline. See *caption.*

cutoff ink level. A screen-printing term describing the top surface of a printed ink film as it sits on the upper surface of the stencil fabric after the squeegee passes in a printing stroke, but before the printing screen is lifted from contact with the substrate.

cutoff length. (1) The distance between corresponding points of repeated images on a web. (2) The circumference of the plate cylinder.

cutout. The area of the printing form that has been sliced off or perforated for subsequent removal; for example, corner cuts and binder holes.

cut-size paper. Paper sized specifically for printing, copying, or duplicating, such as 8½×11-in., 11×14-in., and 11×17-in. paper.

cutter. (1) A machine for cutting paper stock. (2) A reciprocating or rotary blade for cutting a paper web into sheets. (3) A device for cutting rules to a desired length. (4) The operator of a cutting machine.

cutter and creaser. A fully automatic press that slices and/or scores lightweight paperboards.

cutter dust. Small fiber particles chipped off as the paper is cut. Cutter dust can cause printing difficulties.

cutting reducer. A subtractive chemical that removes equal quantities of silver from the high-, intermediate-, and low-density areas on a photographic negative. Useful for treating fogged or overexposed images.

CWT. Hundred weight; the specified cost of one hundred pounds of a particular paper.

cyan. A blue-green color, complementary to red. Along with yellow and magenta, one of the three primary subtractive colors, or process colors used in the printing process. Cyan reflects blue and green light, while absorbing red.

cyan printer. (1) The plate used to print the cyan ink in process color reproduction. (2) The negative or positive film or color proof that indicates what image areas will print in cyan.

cyberspace. The alternative world inhabited by frequent users of the Internet and commercial online services. The term was popularized by novelist William Gibson in his book *Neuromancer.*

cyclic redundancy check (CRC). Automatic error checking method used in data communications, file compression, and MS-DOS data copying. See also: *XMODEM-CRC.*

cylinder. (1) A roller with grippers that hold and press the sheet against the inked form roller on a printing press. (2) Any roller or drum with a continuous or screened circumference used in papermaking. (3) Any of the principal rollers on an offset printing press: plate, blanket, and impression cylinders. See also: *drum.*

cylinder gap. The space between the lead and tail edges of the gripping mechanisms on press cylinders.

cylinder guide marks. Lines on an offset press plate that match corresponding lines on the press's plate cylinder, ensuring that each plate will be positioned identically on press.

cylinder machine. Papermaking equipment that forms a web of paper on a cylindrical-shaped mold revolving in a vat of water-suspended fibers.

cylinder press. (1) A basic press design in which the form is held on a reciprocating flatbed that moves alternately under the ink rollers and a large rotating cylinder. The cylinder carries the paper, pressing it against the form. (2) A screen printing press in which the substrate, wrapped around a rotating drum, contacts the printing surface of a moving screen and is discharged onto a conveyor after printing. (3) A press used for diecutting.

cylinder undercut. The difference between cylinder body radius and bearer radius.

cylindrical printer. A mechanical arrangement for screen printing bottles, metal drums, etc.

D

D log E chart. In graphic arts photography, a characteristic curve illustrating a vertical density (D) scale and a horizontal logarithm of exposure (log E) scale. Alternative term: *H and D chart* (from the names of its originators, Hurter and Driffield).

daemon. The UNIX computer program that routes electronic mail or performs some other routine task.

daguerreotype. A positive image produced on a silver-coated copper plate. The first practical photographic process, it was invented by Louis J. M. Daguerre in 1839. The image is developed by exposing the plate to metallic mercury vapors.

Dahlgren dampening system. A trademark name for a type of continuous-flow dampening system.

daisy-wheel printer. An impact printer in which the type elements are mounted at the ends of arms that extend from a center point. See also: *impact printer; strike-on.*

dampener covers. Molleton, paper, or fiber sleeves over dampening rollers that aid in carrying the dampening solution.

dampener roller endplay. Undesirable side-to-side movement of dampener rollers caused by space between bearings and roller brackets or hangers.

dampener roller setting. The pressure required between rollers in the dampening system and between these rollers and the plate to consistently transfer an even film of water to the plate.

dampeners. Paper, cloth, or rubber-covered rollers that distribute water to the printing plate in the lithographic process.

dampening. Moistening nonimage areas of lithographic plates with water-covered rollers.

dampening fountain. A pan on the press that holds the solution used to wet the plate. Alternative term: *water pan.*

dampening refrigeration unit. A reservoir that cools the dampening solution to a constant temperature lower than the pressroom temperature while recirculating it through the dampening system. Alternative term: *recirculator.*

dampening solution. A mixture of water; gum arabic; an acid, neutral, or alkaline etch; and isopropyl alcohol or an alcohol substitute used to wet the lithographic press plate. Alternative term: *fountain solution.*

dampening system. A series of rollers that moisten the printing plate with a metered flow of a water-based solution containing such additives as acid, gum arabic, and isopropyl alcohol, or other wetting agents.

Dampening system

dampening system, continuous-flow. A mechanism for distributing a thin, even film of dampening solution to the lithographic plate without interruption. Alternative term: *continuous-feed.*

dampening system, conventional. A mechanism in which a ductor roller transfers dampening solution intermittently to a series of rollers and then to the plate.

dampening system, inker-feed. A continuous-feed dampening system in which the first ink form roller is a combination inking/dampening form roller.

dampening system, plate-feed. A continuous-feed dampening system that has separate inking and dampening form rollers.

dancer roller. A weighted or spring-tensioned controlled roller positioned between a paper roll and a press unit on a web. It senses and removes web slack by controlling the paper reel brake.

dandy roll. The hollow, wire-covered cylinder on a papermaking machine that improves paper formation or presses a watermark into the wet, newly formed web.

dark reaction. In an unexposed light-sensitive emulsion or coating, the slow chemical change that occurs when the material is stored in an unlighted area.

dark spot. A concentration of pigment in one area caused by a depression in the printed substrate.

dark-field illumination. A method of inspecting the halftone dots on film negatives placed against a dark background and lit indirectly (from behind). Using a hand-held magnifier, it is easy to examine the amount of fringe around a dot. See also: *bright-field illumination.*

darkroom. The light-tight chamber in which photographic materials are handled and processed.

darkroom camera. A graphic arts camera constructed so that the rear element, film holder, ground glass, and focusing controls are within the darkroom, permitting the film to be loaded directly without holders.

Darkroom camera

dash. A typographical character or sign. Dashes are classified according to the following four criteria: weight, design, width of image and allotted space, and vertical position. Some examples include the em and en dashes.

data. Text, audio, video, and images stored in a form the can be understood by a computer.

data blocks. The maximum size of continuous data blocks that can be recorded as a single block of data. Larger data blocks transfer and store data more efficiently.

data compression. A software or hardware process that reduces the size of images so that they occupy less storage space and can be transmitted faster and easier. This process is accomplished by removing the bits that define blank spaces and other redundant data, and replacing them with a smaller algorithm that represents the removed bits. Data must be decompressed before it can be used. See also: *compression; tone compression.*

data conversion. Technique of changing digital information from its original code so that it can be recorded by an electronic device using a different code. Data created in one software format may be converted to another before printing. Data must also be converted for various output devices, such as when RGB colors are converted to CMYK.

data field. Within a database the area designated for the entry of specific information.

data file. Text, graphics, or pictures that are stored electronically as a unit.

data processing. (1) Changing raw data or information into a usable format by using a computer. (2) The systematic manipulation of information; for example, handling, merging, sorting, computing.

data transfer rate. The sustained speed at which data can be written or read and conveyed by a device, generally given in kilobytes per second (KBps) or megabytes per second (MBps).

database. An electronic program that is used to efficiently organize, store, retrieve, and modify information, such as a mailing list. The data can be quickly rearranged and sorted or searched alphabetically or numerically.

daylight camera. A self-contained graphic arts camera that does not have to be operated in a darkroom.

daylight fluorescence. The phenomena of increased color brilliance where the wavelengths of other colors in the spectrum converge.

DCS. See *desktop color separation.*

dead matter. Typeset material not to be used again.

dead-weight micrometer. See *micrometer, dead-weight; blanket thickness gauge; Cady gauge.*

debossing. A technique for impressing a design or texture into a substrate.

deburring. Using mechanical, chemical, or electrochemical means to remove the thin ridge or irregular sharp edges that develop on a gravure cylinder when it is engraved before printing.

decal. A design screen-printed on a special paper for transfer to a substrate. Pressure-sensitive markings and water-slide transfers are two examples of decals that are externally processed before application to the end-product. Alternative term: *decalcomania.*

decal, duplex. A heavy backing paper laminated with a very high grade of tissue paper, which, in turn, is coated with the decal solution to receive a screen-printed image.

decal, heat-release. A decal printed face down on a special release paper to be transferred from the carrier paper to the substrate with applied heat and pressure.

decal, simplex. A design printed on a special paper that is highly water absorbent and has a coating of water-soluble adhesive on one face. The design is printed on the adhesive surface and dipped in water to release the image from the adhesive so that it will slide into position from the paper surface. Alternative term: *decal, (water) slide-off.*

decal, varnish-on. A clear lacquer printed on duplex paper, followed by a design screen-printed in reverse, and another coat of lacquer. An adhering varnish is then applied to the substrate before the decal is positioned.

decal adhesive. A clear, screen-printable, water-soluble compound printed over the face surface of decals so that they adhere face down and can be viewed through a transparent substrate.

decal varnish. A specially formulated quick-setting lacquer used to adhere decals that will be exposed to the weather.

decalcomania paper. An absorbent paper made of cotton fiber mixed with chemical wood pulps. The finished paper, which is coated with decal solution to receive a screen-printed image, has a smooth, uniform surface with good wet strength.

deck. A single unit on a multicolor printing press.

deckle. (1) The removable, rectangular wooden frame that forms a raised edge against the wire cloth of the paper-forming mold and holds the stock suspension on the wire when handmade paper is produced. The resulting untrimmed, irregular edge on a sheet of paper forms where the pulp flows and sets against the frame. This is referred to as *deckle-edged paper.* (2) On a fourdrinier papermaking machine, the arrangement on the side of the wire that keeps the stock suspension from flowing over the edges of the wire. (3) The canvas webbing wound around the ends of cylinders on papermaking equipment to control the width of the sheet. (4) A term indicating the width of the web of paper formed on a papermaking machine.

decompress. To return compressed data to its original size and condition.

dedicated equipment. A word processor, typesetter, or other device permanently assigned, either by configuration or software, to one task.

dedicated telephone lines. Specially leased lines than provide constant and direct access to a network at high speeds (1.544 or 45 Mbps).

deep etch. (1) A lithographic platemaking process in which the ink-receptive printing areas are slightly recessed below the surface of the plate. (2) In photoengraving, increasing the depth or clearance below the printing surface in the nonimage areas to improve printing properties and reduce routing, particularly in combination plates and plate duplication.

deep line cut. A method of cutting screen-printing overlays so that trapping is improved.

deep-etch plate. A positive-working printing plate in which the image area is etched into the plate's surface.

deep-etch solution. A light-sensitive coating used to prepare deep-etch offset plates that may be used as a resist in the direct-transfer gravure process.

deep-well exposing unit. A table or bench equipped with a flexible, transparent top that can be molded around a direct printing screen by vacuum for exposing.

default. A method or value that a computer (or photocomposition system) will use in processing information unless the operator/programmer specifies otherwise.

definition. (1) How well a photographic lens projects distinct (sharp) images of a subject. (2) Image resolution, sharpness, or fidelity. The clarity of detail.

deflection. In flexography, the condition that results when fountain roll pressure against the anilox roll causes both to bend or bow slightly. Excessive bending of both or either one will result in uneven ink metering and subsequent nonuniform printing.

deflection gauge. An instrument used to measure how a screen bends at the center when it is stretched.

deflection plates. (1) In ink jet printing, image carriers charged with high and varying degrees of voltage. They steer, or deflect, charged droplets of ink onto a substrate. (2) An electrostatic deflection grid used to steer continuous ink-jet droplets on a substrate.

degradation. Decrease in quality or loss of ability to perform up to standards.

degradee. The French term for fade. In the graphic arts, a degradee is a halftone tint that varies from a given small dot size to a given large dot size. See also: *vignette.*

deinking. Treating wastepaper with heat and chemicals to soften the ink and remove it, coatings, and other contaminants from the paper fibers so that the paper can be recycled.

delamination. The continuous splitting, or separation, of the paper's surface caused by the tack of the ink and the rubber blanket.

delete. A proofreader's mark indicating printing matter to be removed.

delimiter. A code in the form of a space, tab, or comma that is used to separate data into fields for import or export in a database program.

delivery. (1) The section of a printing press that receives, jogs, and stacks the printed sheet. (2) The output end of bindery equipment.

Delivery (1)

delivery, dual pocket. A two-tray system on a three-knife trimmer in which a counter activates a switch that directs a specified number of signatures into one tray or the other.

demand printing. A method of producing a select number of documents at a given time by storing a publication electronically. It is easier to update and modify documents more frequently and print additional copies at a later date without incurring new start-up costs. Excessive inventories are also eliminated. Production usually takes place on some sort of electronic, nonimpact printer. See also: *nonimpact printer.* Alternative term: *on-demand printing.*

demographic edition. A printed job, usually an advertisement or sections of a magazine, that is targeted toward a specific consumer group within a defined geographic area. See also: *ink-jet printing.*

dense. A film negative that is too dark.

densitometer. An instrument for measuring the optical density of a negative or positive transparency, or of a print. Reflection densitometers measure the amount of light that bounces off a photographic print at a 90° angle. Transmission densitometers measure the fraction of incident light conveyed through a negative or positive transparency without being absorbed or scattered. Combination densitometers measure both reflection and transmission densities.

densitometer response. A photometric response in which accuracy of the attenuation of light level is determined and specified and a spectral response in which the sensitivity or measurement of each wavelength is compared to a standard such as ANSI PH2.18.

densitometry. The procedure of measuring optical density and using such measurements to control factors in graphic reproduction.

density. (1) The light-stopping ability of an image or base material, sometimes referred to as *optical density.* (2) A photographic term used to describe the tonal value of an area. A darker tone has a higher density than a lighter tone. A dry ink film has a higher density than a wet one. (3) The specific gravity or weight per unit volume of paper.

density, apparent. Weight per unit volume.

density, printing. The amount of type per unit of line length.

density, unwanted. A measure of the extent to which an ink absorbs the colors it should reflect.

density capacity. The theoretical maximum density that a given photographic emulsion can produce. Alternative term: *contrast capacity.*

density difference. (1) A measure of density, relative to a target, or specified value. (2) The distinction between test and copy densities.

density range. The measured difference between the maximum and minimum densities of a particular film negative or positive.

density range, basic. The BDR of a screen is expressed as the difference between a full-range continuous-tone original's tone density in the area of the original that produces the smallest printable dot (with a given screen) and the tone density that produces the largest nonsolid-printing dot.

densometer. An instrument that measures the air resistance of paper in terms of the time required for a specific volume of air to pass through a given area of the paper under a constant pressure.

deplate. To electrolytically remove a metal deposit from the surface of a gravure printing cylinder by reversing the negative and positive poles. The anode becomes the cathode, and the cathode (the cylinder) becomes the anode.

depth. (1) On relief printing plates, the vertical difference between the actual printing surface and the bottom of etched or engraved areas. (2) Vertical measurement, as in the depth of a page, a figure, or a table.

depth gauge. An instrument that measures the vertical difference between the actual printing surface and the bottom of etched or engraved areas on a plate or cylinder. It measures the depth between the dots on letterpress engravings in thousandths of an inch and the depths on a gravure embossing cylinder.

depth of field. The distance range between the nearest and farthest objects that appear in acceptably sharp focus in a photograph.

depth of focus. The distance range over which the film can be shifted at the film plane inside the camera and still have the subject appear in sharp focus.

depthometer. A calibrated gauge used to micrometrically measure the depth of letterpress printing plates. Alternative term: *halftonometer.*

desaturated color. A color that appears faded, printed with too little ink, or as though white had been mixed with the colorant.

descender. The portion of a lowercase type character that extends below the common baseline of a typeface design, such as in "g," "j," "p," "q," and "y." See also: *ascender.*

descriptor. In a database, the word used to classify a record so that all records containing this word can be retrieved as a group.

desensitize. (1) To chemically treat the nonimage areas of a lithographic plate to make them water-receptive and ink-repellent. (2) An agent or dye used to treat exposed photographic plates and films to permit development in brighter light.

design motif. A distinctive feature, shape, figure, or other thematic element in a work of art. A dominant idea or central theme. A single or repeated design element or color.

design of experiments. A branch of applied statistics dealing with planning, conducting, analyzing, and interpreting controlled tests to evaluate the factors that control the value of a parameter or group of parameters, such as the impact of oven temperatures, press speed, and ink tack on ink drying and setoff.

desktop. The space in a computer represented on the display screen (as in a Macintosh environment) by document, folder, file drawer, and printer icons, etc. The electronic equivalent of an office desk, it is used to create, edit, and store documents.

desktop color separation (DCS). A color file format that creates five PostScript files for each color (CMYK) and a data file about the image.

desktop publishing. The creation of fully composed pages with all text and graphics in place on a system that includes a personal computer with a color monitor; word processing, page-makeup, illustration, and other off-the-shelf software; digitized type fonts; a laser printer; and other peripherals, such as an optical image scanner. Completely paginated films are output from an imagesetter. See also: *electronic publishing.*

detackifier. An additive used to improve ink flow and shear.

detail. (1) The defining power of a photographic lens. (2) The minute, individual features in originals and photographic reproductions.

detail enhancement. See *unsharp masking.*

detectors. The devices on a web press that sense web breaks.

detergent resistance. How well an applied ink or coating withstands the effects of chemicals.

develop. See *development.*

developing agent. The chemical compound within the developer that renders the latent image visible. Alternative term: *developer.*

developing ink. A nondrying, greasy liquid applied to lithographic plate images to protect the image and keep it ink-receptive while the plate is developed, etched, and gummed.

developing pad. A plush-covered wooden or plastic block used to distribute the developing solution over the surface of deep-etch lithographic plates to remove the unhardened image areas.

developing sink. A fixture designed especially for developing photographic film. It is composed of partitioned trays to hold solutions and a water-mixing faucet with or without temperature controls. Some also come with built-in light tables for visually examining the results. Alternative term: *darkroom sink.*

developing tank. A lighttight container used for processing film.

developing tray. Large, shallow plastic or stainless steel container used to process films manually.

development. (1) The process of converting a latent photographic image on film or paper to a visible image. (2) In lithographic platemaking, removing the unhardened coating from the plate surface.

dial indicator. A watch-like instrument used to measure concentricity, run-out, deflection, and the relative position of mechanical components.

dialog box. Window appearing on a computer screen requiring the user to provide additional information before a command can be completed.

dial-up connectivity. Linking to a computer network via modem and regular telephone lines.

diaphragm. A perforated plate or adjustable opening mounted behind or between the elements of a camera lens. It is used to control the amount of light that reaches the film. Openings are usually calibrated in f-stop numbers. See also: *iris diaphragm.*

diaphragm control. Devices on process cameras calibrated to various aperture ratios to accommodate all optical factors of line and halftone photography and any selected camera extension and screen ruling.

diapositive. A European term designating a photographic or manually produced film positive.

diarylide yellow. A strong organic pigment used as a colorant in yellow process inks.

diazo process. A photographic procedure in which a group of light-sensitive compounds are applied to paper, plastic, or metal sheets. The substrate is then exposed to intense blue and/or ultraviolet light and developed with ammonia vapors or an alkaline solution to form an image. The diazo process is used to produce proofs from positive film flats and color-pack natural color proofs. It is also used to coat presensitized press plates. Alternative terms: *dyeline; diazoprint; direct-positive; ammonia-process print; whiteprint.*

dichroic filter. An optical device that stops certain wavelengths of light, while allowing certain others to pass through.

dichroic fog. A chemical cloud on a film negative that appears red in transmitted light and green in reflected light. It is caused by an exhausted bath that should be changed or by an excess of hypo, ammonia, or sulfite in the developer.

didot point system. A European method of printing measurement. Twelve didot points equal the didot pica or cicero. The didot point is equal to 0.0148 inch; the cicero is 0.1776 inch.

die. (1) A pattern of sharp knives or metal tools used to stamp, cut, or emboss specific shapes, designs, and letters into a substrate. (2) A plate cut, etched, or embossed in intaglio to provide a raised impression on paper.

die, embossing. A heated or cold brass or steel tool that impresses a design in relief into a paper substrate. Unlike a cutting die, the edge is not sharp.

Die, embossing

die board. The plywood base into which the steel rule dies are inserted.

die press. (1) A manually operated press that forms steel rules. (2) A machine that cuts the shape of the die into the substrate.

diecut. A printed subject cut to a specific shape with sharp steel rules on a press.

diecutting. (1) Using sharp steel rules to slice paper or board to a specific shape on a printing press or a specialized stamping press. (2) Engraving dies used in stamping or finishing. Alternative term: *die sinking.*

dielectric ink. A printable compound that insulates the substrate as it dries.

dielectric printing process. A nonimpact printing technique in which paper with a conductive base layer is coated with a nonconductive thermoplastic material. A set of electrode styli apply an electric charge to areas of the substrate corresponding to the latent image of the original. Following the charging step, the paper is imaged by a toner system similar to that used in electrostatic copying devices. Alternative term: *electrographic printing.* See also: *electrostatic paper.*

dielectric-coated paper. A printing substrate that has been electrostatically charged in a dot pattern in the image areas and then passed through a liquid toner suspension of charged particles. The toner particles adhere to the paper wherever a charge exists, resulting in a permanent, high-contrast image.

dieresis, diaeresis. A mark placed over a vowel to indicate that the vowel is pronounced as a separate syllable.

dies, male and female. The convex and concave dies, respectively, used for forming cutting dies.

diesis. See *pi characters.* Alternative term: *double dagger.*

die-stamping. Use of a die of brass or other hard metal to stamp the case of a book. The case may be stamped with ink or metallic foil. If the impression is without color, the case is said to be *blind-stamped.*

differential letterspacing. See *spacing, proportional.*

diffraction grating. An optical device composed of fine lines that create a color spectrum by separating white light into its component parts.

diffraction theory. In halftone photography, dot formations that occur as the result of deflected light.

diffuse. Not sharply defined. The reflection of light from a rough surface or the appearance of an object through translucent glass.

diffuse highlight. The highlight tone that carries the smallest printable dot.

diffuse opacity. See *opacity.*

diffuse reflection. Scattering light in all directions away from a surface.

Diffuse reflection

diffuse transmission. The process by which incident light that passes through an object is redirected or scattered over a range of angles.

diffuser. A roughened sheet of plastic placed between a transparency and the photographic film when making unsharp masks.

diffusion. Softening the detail in a print with a diffusion lens/disk or other material that scatters light.

diffusion disk. Flat glass with a pattern of lines or concentric rings that break up and scatter light from an enlarger lens, softening the detail in a print.

diffusion transfer. A process used to produce positive screened prints and line prints on paper, film, or lithographic plates by physically transferring the image during processing from an exposed special light-sensitive material (a negative sheet with a silver emulsion) to a sheet of paper, film, or aluminum (the receiver sheet). Alternative term: *photomechanical transfer* (PMT™ 3M). See also: *contact printing.*

diffusion-condenser enlarger. A device that combines scattered light with a system that produces more contrast and sharper detail on the final print than a diffusion enlarger, but less contrast and blemish emphasis than a condenser enlarger.

diffusion-transfer base stock. A paper with a high degree of wet strength and a smooth surface to which a silver-halide emulsion is applied. The paper must be free from iron, copper, and sulfur, and must resist yellowing from contact with caustic solutions.

digital. Method of representing information in numerical (binary) code. Unlike analog signals, digital ones are either "on" or "off." See also: *analog.*

Digital Data Exchange Standards (DDES). An established set of protocols, formats, and values that allows the exchange of data between equipment made by different manufacturers.

digital device. A scanner, computer, or other equipment that uses discrete electronic pulses, signals, or numerical (binary) codes to represent information. The values are stored as a series of ones and zeros.

digital dot. An imaging spot created by a computer and output by a laser printer or imagesetter. Digital dots are uniform in size; halftone dots vary in size.

digital hard proof. See *direct digital color proof.*

digital photography. See *camera, digital.*

digital plotter. A device that accepts discrete pulses and control signals as input and produces graphs, charts, and drawings as output.

digital signal stream. A succession of bits used to communicate image information in binary code.

digital soft proof. See *copy, soft.*

digital transmission. A communications mode in which the data to be transferred is represented as discrete (and discontinuous) electronic pulses or signals, the values of which are stored as a series of zeros and ones, otherwise known as binary digits.

digital type. Characters composed of dots.

digitalize. See *digitize.*

digitize. To convert an image or signal into binary form. Alternative term: *digitalize.*

digitized information. Text, photographs, and illustrations converted into digital signals for input, processing, and output in an electronic publishing system.

digitizing tablet. A device using a stylus and an x-y coordinate system to trace or draw images for input to a computer graphics systems.

digraph. A group of two successive letters forming a singular phonetic sound and often joined with a small line in typography; for example the "oa" in float and the "sh" in shall. See also: *diphthong.*

dilutent. A solvent that is added to reduce viscosity.

dimension marks. The lines placed outside the image area on the copy to be reproduced that are used to indicate the size of the reproduction or enlargement.

dimensional stability. How well an object maintains its size. How well a sheet of paper resists dimensional change when changes occur in its moisture content.

DIN rating. A European system of identifying the relative sensitivity of photographic films.

diphthong. Combining two characters into a single graphic and single sound, such as "ae" and "oe" in words of Greek origin.

œ æ

Diphthong

direct access. A continuous connection to a network over high-speed, leased telephone lines instead of via a less-powerful modem and regular telephone lines.

direct digital color proof (DDCP). Proof printed directly from computer data to paper or another substrate without creating separation films first. Proof made with computer output device, such as laser or ink-jet printer.

direct drive. A rack-and-gear drive mechanism on some screen printing presses that synchronizes movement of the surface to be printed with the movement of the screen/squeegee.

direct emulsion. A liquid polymer used as a screen printing stencil after it has been photosensitized, coated onto a stretched screen, exposed to actinic light, developed, and washed out.

direct halftone. A color separation halftone negative produced by exposing a color subject directly through a halftone screen and filter with an enlarger and a film positive.

direct infeed system. A press feeder in which the front guides stop the sheet and move out of the way at the proper time. No intermediate transfer device is used.

direct lithography. A lithographic process in which the plate and printing surface are brought into contact.

direct photography. Producing halftone images by actually photographing the object to be reproduced instead of rephotographing a continuous-tone picture of the object.

direct positive. Copy reproduced without creating intermediate negatives, as in the diffusion transfer process. A Photomechanical Transfer (PMT) is one example.

direct transfer. The method of printing an image with a single screened positive onto a gravure cylinder coated with a light-sensitive resist. No continuous-tone positive is required.

direct-entry phototypesetter. A phototypesetting device in which the typesetting unit, keyboard, and visual display (if any) are combined into a single machine, with all elements physically interlinked. Some such devices are also capable of accepting input from separate auxiliary keyboards or editors.

direct/indirect printing screen. A gelatin-coated plastic sheet adhered to the underside of a screen fabric with a sensitized emulsion that is applied from the upper side through the fabric. After drying, the screen is exposed through a positive, developed, and the plastic support sheet stripped away. Alternative term: *direct/indirect photostencil.*

directory. A computing term that describes a method of cataloging the contents of a data storage system.

direct-screen color separation. The process by which the colors of original copy—reflection or transmission—are photographically divided into the primary printing color components as positives or negatives, which are used to produce printing plates.

direct-to-plate technology. Those imaging systems that receive fully paginated materials electronically from computers and expose this information to plates in platesetters or imagesetters without creating film intermediates.

disappearing guide. A register stop that mechanically retracts into the printing table on an automated screen printing press during the printing cycle.

discharge permit. A document required by regulatory agencies before a printing plant may release an effluent into the environment.

discharge printing. Pattern-printing darkly dyed textile substrates with a color-removing chemical to produce a design into which lighter hues may be printed.

discoloration. Any change from the original color, or an unintended inconsistency of color.

discretionary hyphen. A code used to indicate a possible hyphenation point in a word. The operator of a computer or typesetter with this capability may insert such hyphens several times within a word. The machine will then recognize the hyphen yielding the tightest possible fit and disregard the others.

dished roll. A web of paper with progressive concave or convex edge misalignment, which is noticeable immediately after the roll is unwrapped.

disk, floppy. A thin, flexible, removable magnetic disk used to store computer data. An example is a high-density 3½-in. computer disk.

Disk, floppy

disk, hard. A platter-like magnetic storage device permanently encased in a computer system.

disk, magnetic recording. A rotating circular component on which information is recorded in a computer system. It may be permanently installed in the computer or removable.

disk, rigid. A precision magnetic disk used to store computer data and programs. Alternative term: *disk, hard.*

disk drive. The mechanism that rotates the magnetic disk and positions the read/write head(s) at the desired location.

disk refiner. A device that rubs, rolls, disperses, and cuts pulp fibers during papermaking.

disk storage. A method of retaining magnetic data on and retrieving it from the tracks and sectors on a floppy or rigid computer disk. See also: *random access.*

disk track. One of several concentric circular recording bands where data is stored on a magnetic disk. Each track may consist of several sectors with a fixed memory capacity.

disperse dye. A water-insoluble textile colorant.

dispersing agents. Materials added in small amounts to aid in separating a pigment in a liquid medium. See also: *wetting agent.*

display device. Most commonly the cathode-ray tube (CRT) or light-emitting diode (LED) that produces a visual image of type characters or other graphic designs and symbols on a computer or typesetting monitor. See also: *monitor screen.*

display type. Those type styles and sizes designed mainly for use as headline and advertising matter, instead of as straight text or body composition. Alternative term: *display matter.*

distortion. In camera lenses, any departure from the proper perspective of an image. In photography and platemaking, a departure in size or change in the shape of a negative or reproduction when compared to the original.

distortion camera. A copying, stat, or other graphic arts camera equipped with cylindrical lenses and tilting copyboards that produce a variety of optical special effects for type or design purposes.

distortion copy. Copy intentionally altered during preparation to compensate for the effects of the dimensional changes that will occur naturally during processing or other production operations. Flexo rubber printing plates require such allowances to compensate for shrinkage, stretching, etc.

distributing rollers. In an offset inking system, the series of cylinders that moves the ink from the ductor roller and works it into a thin, uniform layer before transferring it to the form rollers.

dithering. (1) A digital pixel averaging technique used to add detail or minimize the difference between pixels. This is accomplished by filling in a gap between two pixels with another pixel that is the average of the other two. The result is less jagged edges. See also: *anti-aliasing.* (2) Injecting a small electrical signal into an electromechanical device to eliminate static friction. (3) An electronically controlled nonimpact printing method used to produce color shades with an ordered "jitter" of ink drops.

divergent lens. A camera lens that bends light rays away from its axis. Alternative term: *negative element.*

D-max. The maximum density that can be achieved in a given photographic or photo-mechanical system.

D-min. The lowest density that can be achieved in a given photographic or photo-mechanical system.

doctor blade. (1) A steel blade that wipes the excess (surface) ink from a gravure cylinder before printing, or the excess coating from the cylinder during finishing operations. (2) A steel or wooden blade used to keep cylinder surfaces clean and free from paper, pulp, size, or other material during papermaking. (3) A long metal knife blade used to apply or remove ink or coating on a printing press or finishing system. A doctor blade is also used on some flexographic presses to remove ink from the surface of the anilox roll. Alternative term: (in screen printing) *flood bar.*

doctor roll. The fountain cylinder on a flexographic press.

doctoring. To add something to an ink to obtain better results during printing.

document. A carrier, such as magnetic tape or disk, that contains a representation of stored electronic information.

document reader. An OCR device that converts typewritten alphanumeric characters into electronic bits and bytes.

dodge. (1) To withhold light from a portion of the image projected on an enlarger easel during basic exposure time to make that area of the print lighter. (2) To partially restrict the light reaching a section of a film flat during exposure. A fixed or movable mask is used to reduce the relative exposure to this section of the flat in platemaking.

dog-ear. A corner or other portion of a page that is misfolded to such a degree that it cannot be corrected by trimming.

domain name service (DNS). An Internet program that provides a seamless translation of the alphabetical web site or email addresses that humans use into the corresponding numerical Internet protocol (IP) addresses that computers use during information transfer. The actual computer that handles this is called the domain namer server. See also: *Internet protocol (IP) address; server; transmission control protocol/Internet protocol.*

dominant wavelength. A colorimetric quantity used to designate hue. It is one of the three quantities used in the CIE specification of color.

dongle. A small piece of hardware that plugs into a computer port to allow access to restricted areas of a network or to copy-protected software.

dot. The individual element of a halftone. It may be square, elliptical, or a variety of other shapes.

dot, elliptical. A halftone screen dot with an oval, rather than circular shape, which sometimes produces better tonal gradations. See also: *elliptical dot screen.*

dot, hard. A photographic term denoting excessive contrast or a halftone dot with a sharp distinctive edge.

dot, soft. A halftone dot with insufficient density for platemaking. See *fringe.*

dot area. In photomechanical reproduction, a screen breaks the wide tonal range found in the original into discrete intervals (from 1% to 99%), creating a halftone dot pattern. The value of each increment, or interval, in the halftone is expressed as the percentage of dot area covered.

dot area, apparent. The ratio of the absorptance of a tint area to the absorptance of the corresponding solid (100%) tint area. In theory, the area of a printed dot that would create the correct tonal perception if reproduced on a perfect reflection or transmission surface.

dot etching. A manual technique of altering the dot size on halftone films to correct colors or adjust the hues of individual tonal areas.

dot formation. (1) The arrangement and size of dots on halftone negatives and positives and printing plates. (2) In dot etching, the photographic construction of individual dots to provide a proper density gradient suitable for dot size reduction.

dot fringe. See *fringe*.

dot gain. The optical increase in the size of a halftone dot during prepress operations or the mechanical increase in halftone dot size that occurs as the image is transferred from plate to blanket to paper in lithography. Alternative terms: *dot spread; ink spread*.

dot gain, equivalent. The apparent dot area of a reproduced tint area minus the actual dot area of the film used to create that tint.

dot gain, physical. An increase in dot area caused by liquid absorption or ink dot spread. This increase over the physical film dot size area is known as the *add-on increase*. That is, a dot gain of 10% to a 50% film dot results in a physical dot area of 60%. This is observed through a magnifying system.

dot leaders. Evenly spaced dots at the baseline between typographic elements on a line, as between chapter title and page number in a table of contents listing. Other typographic characters may be used as leaders, such as the hyphen (hyphen leaders) or the dash (dash leaders).

dot pattern. The design formed by the dots in a halftone screen or a screen-printing stencil. The light and dark tones produced by the dots, which vary in size, compose the image.

dot range. The difference between the smallest printable halftone dot and the largest nonsolid-printing dot.

dot slurring. Smeared or elongated trailing edges on halftone dots.

dot spread. See *dot gain*.

dot values. The size of dots in a halftone reproduction, usually expressed as a percentage.

double burn. Photoprinting different line and halftone negatives in register and in succession, on the same photosensitive surface.

double column. A page consisting of two vertical sections of printed type separated by a rule or blank space.

double etch. Preparing a gravure cylinder or plate in a two-step process using a single carbon tissue laydown or transfer, or two separate laydown or transfer operations. Double etches have been used to etch type and line work separately from tone work or illustrations.

double exposure. (1) Two pictures taken on one frame of film. (2) Two images printed on one piece of photographic paper. (3) A supplementary exposure given the main image to obtain special effects.

double image. The appearance of extra, unwanted dots in the image area. Not to be confused with slur or doubling in which desired image dots are distorted.

double overlay masking. See *masking, two-stage.*

double score. Two parallel creases made in close proximity on a substrate.

double spread. A printing image that extends across and fills two pages of a brochure, book, or folder. If located in the center of a book or folder, it is called a center spread. Alternative terms: *spread, double-page spread, double truck.*

double-black printing. A method of improving black coverage by printing the same area twice with two separate specially prepared negatives. Alternative terms: *double hitting, double-bump black.* See also: *duotone, double-black.*

double-dot halftone. Combining two halftone negatives to reproduce a superior halftone range; one halftone made to reproduce highlights and shadows, the other for expanded middletones.

double-fan binding. A binding method in which a stack of single sheets or four-page signatures are securely clamped at the face instead of the spine. Glue is applied to the fanned sheets in two different directions, resulting in a book that lies flatter than a traditional side-sewn book.

double-sheet detector. A device that can be set to stop the feeding action where the sheet-separation unit picks up two or more sheets simultaneously. Alternative terms: *two-sheet detector; two-sheet caliper.*

Double-sheet detector

double-sided roller coater. A machine that can coat both faces or sides of a sheet simultaneously.

double-sixteen. A folder that takes a thirty-two page form and folds it as two separate or inserted sixteen-page forms.

double-thick cover stock. Two sheets of 65-lb. paper stock laminated together.

double-thirty-two. A folder that takes a sixty-four-page form and folds it as two inserted or separate thirty-two-page forms.

doubletone ink. A printing ink that produces the illusion of two-color printing with a single impression. These inks contain a soluble toner that bleeds out to produce a secondary color.

doubling. A printing defect in the halftone imaging process that appears as a faint second image slightly out of register with the primary image.

dowel. A short plastic or metal pin used for plate and film position register.

download. To transfer a file or files from a remote computer to a local computer's hard drive. See also: *upload.*

downtime. The period of time in which a device is not working because the system is malfunctioning or maintenance is being performed.

draw. (1) In lithographic printing, a register problem that occurs when the halftone dot is enlarged toward the tail end of the sheet. (2) Gathering the signatures of a book together.

drawdown. (1) A method of determining ink shade by placing a small amount of ink on paper and then using a spatula to spread it and produce a thin ink film. (2) The duration of time required to remove air from a vacuum frame to allow the original film and the contact film to achieve uniform contact before exposure.

drier. A class of substances added to ink to accelerate drying.

drift. (1) The continued deformation of a rubber flexo plate under strain. (2) The change in a given durometer reading after a specified period of time.

driving side. The side of a press on which the main gear train(s) are located. The opposite of the operating side. Alternative term: *gear side.*

drop folio. See *folio, drop* and *footer.*

drop initial. Typographic style in which an oversize initial is placed so as to "drop" below the top alignment of the accompanying text setting.

drop shadow. A dark outline in or around portions of typeset letters. The shadow effect is separated from the main body of the letter by space.

drop writer. See *ink-jet printing.*

drop-on-demand ink jet. A nonimpact printing method in which ink droplets are emitted only when required for imaging. Alternative terms: *asynchronous ink jet; intermittent ink jet.* See also: *bubble jet; valve jet.*

dropout. (1) The loss or elimination of very small highlight dots in a halftone print. (2) Eliminating highlight dot formations in halftone negatives with a supplementary or modified exposure that causes the highlights to print as clear white. Alternative terms: *highlight print; facsimile halftone.* See also: *knockout.*

dropout ink. On scanner forms, those reflective colors producing lines and instructions visible to the human eye, but not to optical scanners. See also: *nonread color; nonread ink.*

dropout mask. A mechanical or photomechanical covering that enables the photographer or film assembler to eliminate highlight dots from certain areas of the film negative or positive.

drum. (1) An oscillating metal ink distribution roller. (2) A synonym for cylinder in many press applications. See also: *cylinder.*

drum scanner. Color separation equipment on which the original transparency is wrapped around a hollow, plastic rotary cylinder. See also: *scanner.*

dry dusting. A preliminary pass of the sheets under pressure through the press to remove excessive spray powder, surface material, or other debris.

dry finish. Paper or paperboard with an unglazed, rough surface.

dry laydown. Method of transferring carbon tissue to the gravure cylinder or plate when the tissue is not wet. During the laydown process, water is applied between the gelatin side of the tissue and the copper face of the cylinder or plate. The water softens the gelatin while the pressure applied by a rubber roller causes carbon tissue to adhere to the copper surface.

dry method. Preparing carbon tissue screen printing plates by sensitizing the tissue and then letting it harden before exposure.

dry offset. Printing from relief plates by transferring the ink image from the plate to a rubber surface and then from the rubber surface to the paper. Printing with this process on an offset press eliminates the need to use water. Alternative terms: *indirect letterpress; letterset; relief offset.* See also: *offset printing.*

dry printing. Multicolor printing in which each successive ink color is applied after the previous ink color has been allowed to dry on the sheet.

dry retouching. Correcting continuous tone, line, or halftone negatives with red or black dyes.

dry silver process. Developing a photographic image by using heat to darken dry silver particles that have been exposed to light.

dry trapping. The ability of a dry, printed ink film to accept a wet ink film over it.

dry-back. The change in color, gloss, or density of an ink film as it dries and penetrates the substrate.

dryer. (1) A unit on a web press that hardens the heatset ink by evaporating the solvent ingredient in it. (2) Any conveyor or static oven used to hasten drying of a wet material by subjecting it to heat generated by gas flame, electricity, or air circulated at an ambient temperature. Dryers may also be used to cure solid inks, such as plastisols.

drying agent. An ink additive, such as a salt of cobalt or manganese, that acts as a catalyst in converting a wet ink film to a dry ink film.

drying in. Condition that occurs when ink dries prematurely in the meshes of a (screen) printing screen, blocking and clogging the stencil openings. This causes a lack of detail in the printed image.

drying stimulator. A catalytic agent—e.g., cobalt chloride—that complements the drier in the ink.

drypoint positive. A film with tones similar to those in the original produced by scratching lines into sheet plastic and then filling them with opaque ink. Drypoint positives are used in making photostencils for screen printing.

dry-transfer lettering. Special type symbols, characters, and display fonts that can be transferred letter-by-letter from wax-backed sheets to the pasteup by applying pressure or rubbing the sheet against the pasteup. Alternative term: *rub-down type.*

dry-transfer print. A photographic color print made by transferring three transparent dye images to a gelatin-coated paper from three different gelatin-coated relief positives.

dry-up. The problem that occurs when ink appears in the nonimage areas of the plate if it is insufficiently dampened. Alternative term: *catch-up*.

ductor roller. A cylinder that alternately transfers ink from the ink fountain roller to the ink distribution rollers or dampening solution from the water fountain roller to the dampening rollers on an offset press.

ductor shock. The vibration sent through the inking system when the ductor first contacts the oscillating roller.

dummy. (1) A preliminary layout showing the position of illustrations, text, folds, and other design elements as they are to appear in the printed piece. (2) A set of blank pages prepared to show the size, shape, style, and general appearance of a book, pamphlet, or other printed piece. (3) A diagram of each newspaper page, prepared by the editorial department, to guide compositors in placing and fitting stories and illustrations.

dump gate. A switch on binding equipment that diverts products from an automated line to a handwork station.

duotone. A special effects technique that consists of making a two-color halftone reproduction from a single-color original. In the most common type of duotone, the two halftones are printed in two different colors—one in a color (a normal halftone negative) and the other in black (to print the lighter-than-normal shadows). Alternative term: *duograph*.

duotone, double-black. Duotone printed from two halftones, one for highlights and the other for midtones and shadows. Both halftones are printed with black inks to increase the tonal range. Alternative term: *duotone black*. See also: *double-black printing*.

duotone, fake. Producing a two-color reproduction from a single halftone negative and a halftone screen tint, instead of producing a true duotone from two different halftone negatives.

duotone black. See *duotone, double-black*.

dupe. See *duplicate*.

duplex. (1) A twin, a double, or a "two-in-one" unit. (2) A perfecting press or electronic printer that allows two sides of a sheet to be printed in one pass. See also: *simplex*. (3) Paper printed with a different color on each side. (4) A typesetting term used to describe a method of simplifying character set-width determination.

duplicate. Photographic copies of an original film positive reproduced as a positive, or a negative reproduced as a negative, usually by contact printing. Alternative term: *dupe*.

duplicate plate. A relief plate made by reproducing an original plate through molding, plating, and casting techniques.

duplicate transparency. See *duplicating*.

duplicate-image contact. A print on film in which the tone values are the same as in the original film after contacting.

duplicating. (1) A photomechanical process in which an image identical to the original is formed on a photosensitive material. Alternative term: *duplicate transparency*. (2) Producing short runs of simple usually single- or two-color printed material on a small press. (3) Preparing identical printing plates to reproduce multiple versions of the same image.

duplicating (dupe) film. A photographic film used in contacting that, when exposed, produces a same-size reverse (positive) image from an original negative or a negative image from a film positive.

duplicator. Any press that is without bearers and smaller than 11×17 in. (279×432 mm). Duplicators are regularly used to print simple single- or two-color work, but can also be used to print multicolor jobs.

duplo. A scanner output configuration for exposing two color separations on one piece of film.

durometer. A measure of a roller or blanket's hardness or softness.

durometer gauge. Instrument used in printing to measure roller hardness. Alternative terms: *type-A durometer; Shore-A scale; plastometer*.

dusting. The accumulation of visible paper particles on the nonimage areas of the blanket. Alternative term: *powdering*.

dwell. The length of time the ductor roller is in contact with the ink and/or dampening pan roller.

dye. (1) A soluble coloring material, normally used as the colorant in color photographs. (2) Non-pigment coloring agents of mineral or vegetable origin with high penetration characteristics. Often used in decorating textiles.

dye emulsions. Screen printing inks in which dyes (liquids suspended in a viscous medium), rather than pigments (powders), contribute the color effects.

dye inks. Screen printing inks made by suspending dyes in specific vehicle formations using inert thickening agents. These inks are used in textile decoration. Alternative term: *dye pastes.*

dye pigments. Dyes that are naturally insoluble in water and can be used directly as colorants without any chemical transformation.

dye sublimation. A method of proofing in which the images are created by dyes secured to the substrate by heating.

dye transfer print. A continuous-tone color print in which the tones of the image are composed of three colored dyes (cyan, magenta, and yellow) held in suspension in a water-soluble base.

Dylux®. Du Pont trademark name for photosensitive polymer proof papers that produce dry proofs and require no processing.

dynamic balance. To maintain a constant equilibrium on a gravure cylinder base at top press speeds.

E

earth colors. Muted variations of more intense primaries prepared from various ores and oxides found in the earth, mostly iron or manganese oxides with aluminum silicates.

eccentricity. A roller or cylinder that does not rotate in a true concentric circle in relation to its axis. Alternative terms: *off center; out-of-round.*

edge acuity. The sharpness and absence of feathering on the edges of an image. Greater acuity is enhanced by uniform ink spread.

edge gilding. Coating the borders of pages with gold leaf.

edge staining. Coloring one or more of the trimmed ends of a book.

edit. To modify and/or rearrange information.

edition. The size of a print run, particularly limited runs of fine-art prints or serigraphs signed by the artist.

edition binding. See *case binding.*

effective aperture. In photography, the diameter of the lens diaphragm as measured through the front lens element; the unobstructed useful area of the lens. Alternative term: *f-number.* See also: *f-stops.*

effluent. Wastewater—treated or untreated—that flows out of a treatment plant, sewer, or industrial outfall. Generally refers to wastes discharged into surface waters.

eggshell finish. A paper with a relatively rough texture.

electric eye. The photoelectric cell used to control register on printing presses, exposures in photography, or the angle of cut on a guillotine paper cutter.

electric-eye line. The continuous solid mark etched around the circumference of a gravure cylinder. When printed on the web it activates a photoelectric cell that controls side-to-side register on the press.

electrical etching. Producing chemical changes by passing an electric current through an electrolyte. In relief printing, this is an inversion of electroplating.

electro-erosion. A process in which text and line graphics are created by passing an electric current through aluminized paper, to corrode the metal in the image areas. Alternative term: *electrosensitive printing.*

electrofax. An RCA trademark process in which paper coated with zinc oxide and other chemicals is used to develop images directly on copy paper.

electrographic printing/electrography. See *dielectric printing process.*

electrolyte. A nonmetallic electric conductor in which current is carried by the movement of ions.

electron beam coating. A clear film that dries by radiation-induced polymerization, leaving the stock with a glossy sheen.

electron beam curing. Quick method of drying inks by radiation-induced polymerization.

electronic camera. See *camera, digital.*

electronic color correction. The process of altering, retouching, cloning, combining, silhouetting, smoothing, sharpening, and adjusting tone and color balance or otherwise manipulating color images with an electronic (computer-assisted) imaging system.

electronic color scanner. Equipment that uses beams of light, electronic circuitry, and color filters to examine a color image, point by point, and separate it into films representing each of the three process printing colors (yellow, magenta, and cyan) and black. See also: *color scanner.*

electronic composition. Computer-assisted methods of copyfitting and pagination that output text and graphical elements in completed page form as paper galleys or film from an imagesetter.

electronic data interchange (EDI). A standard for the exchange of business documents, such as invoices and purchase orders.

electronic dot generation. Linking laser with digital technology to produce a halftone dot pattern without a contact screen. A separate digital computer in the laser scanner stores information about the halftone screen, its rulings, and screen angles.

electronic engraving. Printing forms produced by scanning the original optically and using the modified light signals generated to operate a tool that cuts into a metal or plastic plate and creates a relief or intaglio image.

electronic imaging systems. Computer-controlled equipment used to merge, manipulate, retouch, airbrush, and clone images, create tints and shapes, and adjust and correct individual color areas within an image that has been scanned, stored on magnetic disk, retrieved and displayed on the monitor, and positioned according to a predetermined layout.

electronic mail. Computer files and messages exchanged over computer networks or by using modems. Information may be transferred over short or very long distances. Alternative term: *email.* See also: *online.*

electronic manuscript/mechanical. A document, often with text and graphics merged, that is sent through the production process as a "soft copy" via modem, rather than as a "hard copy" (paper galley and pasteup board format).

electronic printer. See *nonimpact printer.*

electronic publishing. Any system using a computer and related word processing and design and page-makeup software to create paginated text and graphics, which are output to a laser printer with a PostScript interpreter and/or imagesetter at varying degrees of resolution from a minimum of 300 dots per inch to maximum quality levels exceeding 1,250 dots per inch. See also: *desktop publishing.*

electrophotography. In modern terminology, processes (including xerography and laser printing) that produce images by passing toner particles over an intermediate photoconductor drum, which receives an electrical charge that enables it to transfer and fuse the toner particles to plain (untreated) paper, forming the image.

electroplating. Depositing an adherent metallic coating upon an electrode to secure a surface (such as a gravure printing cylinder) with properties or dimensions different from those of the base metal.

electrosensitive printing. See *electro-erosion.*

electrostatic assist. Using electrical discharges that create enough force between the impression roller (positive) and the printing cylinder (negative) during gravure printing to achieve a more complete ink release from the etched cells. The static force tends to pull the ink from the cells and print fine dots on substrates with a relatively rough surface. An electrostatic assist reduces skips or snowflaking, as well as gaps or voids in the final print.

electrostatic copying. A process that uses an intermediate photosensitive plate or drum or a coated take-off sheet that is electrically charged to accept an image-producing agent in certain areas of the sheet.

electrostatic paper. A substrate with a photoconductive surface. See also: *dielectric printing process.*

electrostatic plate. An organic photoconductor that serves as an offset image carrier.

electrostatic printing. Printing method in which electrically charged, powdered colorant particles are transferred from the image carrier to a substrate moving in their path. The particles are fused to the substrate to form the permanent image.

electrothermosensitive. Those printing processes that rely on electricity to heat thermal printheads, which, in turn, are used to print on heat-sensitive paper or heat-sensitive ribbons that transfer the print to plain paper.

electrotype. A duplicate relief printing plate that is made by molding a sheet of hot plastic or wax mold against the original relief plate, electroplating the mold with a coating of copper or nickel, shaping the plate into a cylinder, and backing it with a plastic, wood, or metal support material.

elliptical dot screen. A halftone screen characterized by oval-shaped dots. Such screens are designed to avoid the sudden jump between midtone densities where the corners of square dots join. They also help to reduce image graininess. See also: *dot, elliptical.*

Elmendorf test. A measure of the tearing resistance of paper.

em. A printer's unit of area measurement equal in width and height to the height of the letter "M" in any selected type body size. Now commonly used as an abbreviation of pica-em, where the em is equivalent to 12 points (approximately one-sixth inch). See also: *en.*

Em

em dash. A line one em long that connects interrelated or parenthetical material in typeset text.

em space. A nonprinting fixed space equal in width to the point size of a font. It is used for indenting paragraphs and aligning type columns. Alternative term: *em quad.* See also: *en space; thin space.*

embossed finish. Paper with a textured surface resembling wood, cloth, leather, or other patterns. It is created by passing a web of paper between the nip of an engraved metal roll and a mating soft backing roll. The rolls may be engraved to produce various patterns.

embossing. (1) Using impressed dies to print text or designs in relief on any one of a variety of paper stocks. (2) The swelling of a lithographic offset blanket caused by ink solvent absorption. Alternative term: *blanket embossing.* (3) Undesirable condition resulting from heavy ink coverage in solid image areas on a press sheet. The ink pulls away from the paper as it is peeled from the blanket following impression, causing the solid image areas to appear as high relief images. Alternative term: *waffling.*

embossing cylinder. A steel roller that has been machine or chemically etched or milled and is used to impress a printed or unprinted sheet with a three-dimensional design effect.

embossing plate. An etched or engraved intaglio image carrier into which paper is pressed to form a raised design on the surface of the sheet.

emission. Pollution discharged into the atmosphere from smokestacks, other vents, and surface areas of commercial, industrial, and residential facilities or vehicle exhausts.

emulsification. Condition that occurs when a lithographic ink picks up too much dampening solution and prints a weak, snowflaky pattern. In extreme cases, the ink actually emulsifies in the water and shows up as small dots in the nonimage area. This is known as *tinting.*

emulsion. Photographic term for a gelatin or colloidal solution holding light-sensitive salts of silver in suspension. It is used as the light-sensitive coating on photographic film or plates in photomechanical printing processes.

emulsion side. The dull or matte side of a film. The side that bears the photosensitive coating.

emulsion speed. The rate of response of a photographic emulsion to light, determined under standard conditions of exposure and subsequent development.

emulsion stripping. Using chemicals to remove the emulsion from its base on a reproduction-size transparency, and assembling the transparency into a page format.

emulsion-action reversal. Pretreating a photographic emulsion to alter its normal (positive-to-negative, negative-to-positive) reaction to a light image in such a way that a positive results from a positive, or a negative from a negative. Alternative term: *image reversal.*

en. A printer's unit of area measurement equal to the same height but half the width of the em. The en is sometimes used to specify the area of composition as its value closely approximates the number of characters in the text. See also: *em.*

En

en dash. A line one en long that connects interrelated material in typeset text.

en quad. A nonprinting fixed typographic space that is one-half the em space; the width of an arabic numeral if the font does not contain a special figure space.

en space. A blank space half the value of the em space; usually equal to the width of a numeral in text sizes. It is used for alignment of figure columns and indentions. See also: *em space.*

enamel. A glossy paper surface coating material.

encode. To convert data to machine-readable form.

encrypt. To convert data into such a form that it cannot be read if intercepted by the wrong people. Only those who hold the key to an individualized encryption scheme can decrypt these messages. See also: *cryptography.*

end leaf. A strong paper manufactured for the specific requirements of combining and securing the body of a book to its case. One leaf is pasted against the book's front cover and one against the back cover. The remaining four, six, or eight pages (flyleaves), which are made of the same heavy stock, separate the case from the text pages. Endpapers are often marbleized or carry other ornamental printed designs. Alternative terms: *end sheet; endpapers; flyleaves.*

end matter. The material printed at the end of a book, after the text proper, including appendixes, bibliographies, glossaries, indexes, etc. Alternative terms: *back matter, reference matter.*

end product. The final package or printed piece ready for customer use after all folding, gluing, and other binding, finishing, and/or converting operations are completed.

endplay. Undesirable lateral movement caused by poor fit between the roller shaft and the roller bracket or bearing on a lithographic press.

end-point densities. The photographic highlight and shadow densities that yield the desired dot sizes at the extremes of the halftone range.

English finish. A grade of book paper with a smoother finish than machine-finish papers. It has a very uniform formation and a high filler content, and is calendered to achieve a very smooth, level surface.

engrave. To etch or cut a design into a printing plate so that the image area is raised above the nonimage area.

engraved blanket. A condition that results when ink ingredients cause portions of the surface of an offset blanket to disintegrate, which, in turn, makes the image area sink below the rest of the blanket surface.

engraved cylinder. An image carrier with recessed image areas that are filled with ink, which is then transferred to the substrate. Engraved, or intaglio, cylinders are often used in the gravure process.

engraving. (1) In the graphic arts, a metal plate with a relief-printing surface prepared by acid etching or electronic engraving. Line engravings reproduce only solid blacks and whites, while halftone engravings reproduce continuous-tone material as a series of very small dots. (2) An illustration prepared from a metal plate with a relief-printing surface that has been etched with acid or electronically engraved. Alternative term: *cuts.*

enlargement. A reproduction larger than the original itself. The degree of enlargement is specified as a percentage greater than 100%, or a ratio greater than one. Alternative term: *blowup.*

enlarger. A light source, lenses, bellows, and a film holder that are adjusted to project an image larger than the original from a film negative onto a sheet of photographic paper.

enlarger, diffusion. A device that scatters light before it strikes the negative, distributing the light evenly, to create a photographic print.

environmental assessment. An environmental analysis prepared pursuant to the National Environmental Policy Act to determine whether a federal action would significantly affect the environment and thus require a more detailed environmental impact statement.

environmental audit. An independent assessment of the current status of a party's compliance with applicable environmental requirements or of a party's environmental compliance policies, practices, and controls.

equalization. A process by which the range of gray or color shades in an image is expanded to make the image more attractive.

equipment, auxiliary. Web guides, ink circulating systems, antistatic devices, and other such things that are not standard on presses but are often incorporated for better control of the substrate.

equivalent weight. The term used to denote the respective weights of the same paper in two different sheet sizes.

ergonomics. The study of equipment design that improves convenience, ease of use, and operator comfort.

error correction protocol. These algorithms have built-in techniques to check the validity of data transmission. The simplest is the parity error check, where, for example, seven bits are transmitted and the eighth bit (of a byte) reflects whether the sum of the seven data bits is odd or even. If, after receipt, these two do not agree, the data is retransmitted.

error diffusion. In electronic scanning, smoothing a "rough" area of a digital image by averaging the difference of adjoining pixels.

escapement. The movement or act of various mechanisms in typesetters—commonly a prism, mirror, or electronic beam—that causes characters to be spaced horizontally across a line. In proportional spacing, the amount of escapement varies with each character, whereas monospaced characters have the same amount of escapement (width) for each letter, number, punctuation mark, space, etc.

estimating. The process of determining approximate cost, specifying required quality and quantity, and projecting waste.

etch. (1) To dissolve away with chemicals. (2) The function of increasing or decreasing the density of a continuous-tone image in one or more areas. It can be completed electronically or manually (with chemicals). (3) An acidified gum solution that reacts chemically with nonimage areas not protected by a resist. It is used to produce a relief image on an engraving plate. (4) In lithography, acidic substances, usually in a gum arabic solution, that are used to clean the plate and desensitize nonimage areas to ink, making them receptive to dampening solution (water) instead.

ethernet. A broadcast network standard, originally designed by Xerox, that transmits data throughout a network at 10 Mbps using the carrier sense multiple access/collision detection (CSMA/CD) access protocol to retransmit colliding data until the computers for which it is meant for acknowledge clear receipts.

exception dictionary. A list of words contained in a typesetting program, with indication of the points at which they may be correctly hyphenated. Ordinarily, a typesetting machine's hyphenation logic would have incorrectly hyphenated the words. The exception dictionary is accessible through the typesetter's operating routine, which checks the dictionary before hyphenating a word. If listed, the dictionary instructions for hyphenation are followed; if not listed, the word is hyphenated according to the underlying hyphenation logic housed in the unit's main program.

expansion card. An add-on electronic circuit board that enables a computer user to connect a modem, sound card, CD-ROM or other peripheral to a machine. See also: *peripheral equipment.*

expansion slot. The area on a computer where expansion cards are connected.

exposure. (1) The period of time during which a light-sensitive surface (photographic film, paper, or printing plate) is subjected to the action of actinic light. (2) The product of the intensity and the duration of the light acting upon a photographic emulsion.

exposure, line, basic. The exposure time required to produce an accurate reproduction of the original line copy.

exposure, main. The camera exposure made through the halftone screen to reproduce in the negative all areas of a photograph except the deeper shadows.

exposure, new main. The exposure time determined by multiplying the test exposure time by the exposure factor.

exposure index. A number assigned to a photographic material that is used in conjunction with an exposure meter to determine the correct aperture and exposure time.

exposure latitude. The range of exposures that will produce acceptable results from a specific film.

exposure meter. An instrument with a light-sensitive cell that measures the light reflected from or falling on a subject. It is used as an aid in selecting the proper exposure setting. Alternative term: *light meter.*

exposure setting. The lens opening and shutter speed selected to expose the film.

exposure test. Through a series of trials, establishing the quantity and length of time light is allowed to act on sensitized films or coatings as well as the distance from the light to the surface exposed.

extended binary coded decimal information code (EBCDIC). The 256-character, 8-bit code used as the system code on many IBM computers.

extended color. The extra color printed in the trim of a press sheet, to ensure that no white areas appear at the image edges if the paper is cut inaccurately. See also: *bleed; full bleed.*

extender. A transparent or white pigment or binder used to adjust the working properties and reduce the color strength of a printing ink without affecting its hue.

extension. (1) A three-letter suffix added primarily to DOS and Windows file names to describe the contents of the file. (2) The distance between the lens and the photo-sensitive material or between the lens and the copyholder in a camera.

extrusion. The production of a continuous sheet or film by forcing hot thermo-plastic material through a die.

F

fabric holder, adjustable. The movable part of a screen printing chase where the attached fabric is tensioned or register is controlled. Alternative term: *adjustable frames*.

fabric stretcher. A mechanical device used to spread the fabric over the screen printing frame.

fabric tensioning. Stretching the screen printing fabric in the warp and weft directions before securing it to the screen frame.

fabric thickness. The total average height of two crossing threads in a woven screen printing fabric, measured under tension.

fabrics, stencil. Woven webs of materials (natural and synthetic fabrics and fine wire) used as image carriers in screen printing.

face. See *typeface*.

face margin. See *trim margin*.

face material. Any paper, film, fabric, laminate, or foil material suitable for converting into pressure-sensitive decals that are attached to a support sheet. Alternative terms: *base material; body stock; face stock*.

fadeometer. An instrument used to measure the lightfastness of paper, inks, and other materials under controlled and reproducible conditions.

family. The variations of typefaces within the same design pattern such as Times Roman, Times Italic, Times Bold, etc.

fan delivery, sheetfed. See *blow-downs*.

fan delivery, web. A rotary unit with blades that form pockets which transfer individual folded signatures or newspapers from the folder to the conveyors that carry them to the delivery on a web press.

fan-out. An expansion of the sheet near the tail edge that occurs during printing due to pressure and moisture pickup.

FAQs. See *frequently asked questions.*

Farmer's reducer. A chemical solution (potassium ferricyanide and sodium thio-sulfate) that is used to reduce the density and increase the contrast of developed film negatives. A strong solution of Farmer's reducer is used in lithography to slowly dissolve the developed silver image on a photographic film or paper. It clears fog in the transparent areas of negatives or positives and reduces halftone dot size during tone or color correction. Named for its inventor Howard Farmer.

fast-scan direction. The raster direction designating the line element along which successive pixels are arrayed, perpendicular to the slow-scan direction.

FAT. See *file allocation table.*

fault tolerance. How well a computer system manages hardware problems without shutting down.

fax. Printed text, photographs, and other black-and-white or color images converted into electric signals and transmitted over telephone lines. The receiving unit automatically converts these signals back into a visible form, producing a replica of the original copy.

FDMA. See *frequency division multiplex access.*

feathering. A ragged edge on printed or handwritten type. It may be caused by poor ink distribution, a bad impression, excessive ink, or an ink not suitable for the paper.

feedboard. A platform or ramp on which the sheets to be printed are transported by tapes or vacuum belts to be registered [positioned] by the front stops and side guide, prior to insertion into the impression cylinder grippers by the infeed system. Alternative term: *feed table.*

Feedboard

feeder. (1) A mechanism which separates, lifts, and passes individual press sheets from the top of a pile table onto the feedboard to front stops. The sheets are laterally positioned on the feedboard by a side guide and then fed into the first printing unit. Alternative term: *feeding head; stream feeder.* See also: *sheet-separation unit.* (2) The device that forwards signatures or newspaper inserts, etc., through an in-line finishing system.

feeder foot. A lever that can be adjusted up or down to control height of the pile on a sheetfed press. It also blows a stream of air beneath the sheet lifted by the pickup suckers. Alternative term: *pressure foot.*

Feeder foot

feeler gauge. A thin strip of steel manufactured to a precise thickness. It is used to adjust the clearance between various press mechanisms and the sheet to be printed.

feet. The base of a piece of metal type.

felt side. The top side of the paper formed on the paper machine wire. It is the preferred side for printing. See also: *wire side.*

ferric chloride. A corrosive chemical dissolved in water and used to etch aluminum in preparation for copperizing.

ferrotype plate. A chromium-plated or black-enameled sheet of steel, or mirror-plated glass, used to dry photographic prints to a high-gloss finish. Alternative term: *glazing.*

festoon. A method of storing a relatively large amount of paper used for zero-speed splicing on a web press. The festoons also condition the paper, stretching it and removing the curl from the roll. See also: *flying paster.*

fiber. Wood particles used in the papermaking process.

fiber cut. A short, straight, fairly smooth slice in the web caused by a fiber bundle catching as the paper passes through the calender.

Fiber Distributed Digital Interface (FDDI). The standard for transmitting data at 100 Mbps over a fiber optic cable.

fiber puffing. Surface roughening of a coated paper containing groundwood fibers. Condition occurs during heatset drying.

fiber-optic cable. A network transmission media constructed from strands of glass or plastic and surrounded by protective insulation. It supports the nearly error-free transmission of multimedia data traffic encoded as pulses of light traveling at speeds in excess of 100 Mbps.

field. See *data field.*

file. A collection of digital information stored together as a unit on a computer disk or other storage medium and given a unique name, which permits the user to access the information. A file may contain text, images, video, sound, or an application program.

file, fine. A high-resolution electronic file that is used to image final halftone films. It is calculated after all corrections are made to the view file.

file allocation table (FAT). A hidden record of how files are stored in clusters on a hard or floppy disk.

file server. A workstation primarily responsible for redirecting resources across the network. Dedicated file servers require that the computer running the server software not be used for other tasks. Nondedicated servers permit the administrative tasks and the shared resources to be spread over various network nodes.

file transfer protocol (FTP). The tool used to retrieve information in the form of electronic files from any number of computer systems linked via the TCP/IP protocol. Users in effect transfer copies of information found on remote computers either directly to their own computers or to a service provider's network and then to their own computers.

filler. (1) Inorganic materials like clay, titanium dioxide, calcium carbonate, and other white pigments added to the papermaking furnish to improve opacity, brightness, and the overall printing surface. (2) Inert substance used in a composition to increase the bulk and strength, and possibly lower the cost.

filling up. A condition in which ink plugs up the areas between halftone dots and produces a solid rather than a sharp halftone print. This may also occur in the printing of type matter. Alternative term: *plugging.*

film. (1) Sheets of flexible translucent or transparent acetate, vinyl, or other plastic base materials that are coated with a photographic emulsion. (2) Any thin, organic, nonfibrous flexible material (usually not more than 0.010 in. thick) that is used as a substrate in flexography. Some examples include cellophane, polyethylene, Saran, acetate, and Mylar.

film, indirect. A polyester or plastic support coated with a light-sensitive emulsion. Alternative term: *transfer film.*

film, universal. A phrase used to describe color separation films used for lithographic and gravure publications printing. When exposed to offset printing plates or used to produce gravure cylinders under standard conditions, universal films should produce the same results.

film assembly. See *film image assembly*.

film base. The transparent material on which an emulsion is coated.

film coating. Applying a very lightweight mineral layer to paper; sometimes at the paper machine size press. Alternative term: *wash coating*.

film former. A resin that forms a tough, continuous film.

film image assembly. Positioning, mounting, and securing various individual films to one carrier sheet in preparation for platemaking. Alternative term: *film assembly*. See also: *imposition; stripping*.

film laminating. Bonding a plastic film with heat or pressure to a printed sheet for protection or appearance.

film leader. A length of protective film at the beginning of a roll of unexposed or processed film.

film plane. See *focal plane*.

film processors. Machines that treat and develop photographic films and papers with chemicals under controlled conditions to produce permanent visible images.

film speed. Numerical indicator of how sensitive a given film is to light. Films with higher numbers are more sensitive, or respond faster, to exposure.

filter. (1) A colored sheet of transparent material, such as gelatin, acetate, or glass, that is mounted over a camera lens to emphasize, eliminate, or change the color or density of the entire scene or certain elements in the scene. Photographic lenses absorb (filter out) certain wavelengths of light while allowing others to pass through. (2) A transparent material characterized by its selective absorption of certain light wavelengths and used in a variety of applications, for example, to separate the red, green, and blue components of an original when making color separation films.

filter, major. (1) The filter, the color of which is the complement of the subtractive process primary measured. (2) That filter, the color of which is mostly absorbed by any color when compared to the other additive filter primary colors. (3) Of the three primary color filters (red, green, and blue), the filter used to obtain the highest density reading. In most densitometric equations, the major filter reading is denoted by the symbol/letter "H."

filter, major-minor. (1) That additive primary filter (other than the major filter), the color of which is absorbed by any color, causing hue contamination. (2) Of the three primary color filters (red, green, and blue), the filter used to obtain the medium or middle density reading. In most densitometric equations, the major-minor filter reading is denoted by the symbol "M."

filter, minor-minor. (1) That additive primary filter, other than the major filter, the color of which is absorbed by any color, resulting in a gray or achromatic contamination, but not in hue contamination. (2) Of the three primary color filters (red, green, and blue), the filter used to obtain the lowest density reading. In most densitometric equations, the minor-minor filter density reading is denoted by the symbol/letter "L."

filter, neutral density. A device used to reduce the intensity of light reaching the film.

filter factor. The factor by which the standard exposure must be multiplied to compensate for the reduced light transmittance of a given filter.

fine-line copy. Copy with "tone" lines that are narrower than the dots produced by the screen. Fine-line copy is very difficult to reproduce.

fine-line developer. A chemical agent designed for the most accurate reproduction of line originals with fine and heavier line weights.

fineness of grind. The degree of dispersion of a pigment in a printing ink vehicle, usually measured on a grindometer or grind gauge.

finish. The surface characteristics of paper.

finishing. All forms of completing graphic arts production, including folding, trimming, and assembling sections; binding by sewing, wire stitching, or gluing; and diecutting or gold stamping.

firewall. The layer of security that protects internal computer networks from outside intrusions, particularly from the Internet.

fishbone diagram. See *cause-and-effect diagram.*

fit. (1) A term used to describe the horizontal spacing or relationship between two or more characters. Fit can be altered by kerning or modifying the horizontal width (set width) assigned to characters. Evaluating fit is generally subjective. (2) In regard to presswork, see *image fit.*

fix. (1) To stabilize the photographic image on film or paper after development by dissolving or neutralizing the remaining unexposed silver salts in the emulsion. (2) The chemicals used to "fix" or stabilize the image; the fixer.

fixed space. A typographic unit with a constant width instead of a variable width. The em and en are examples of fixed spaces.

fixed-focus lens. A camera lens with a stationary focus position determined by the manufacturer. The user does not have to adjust the focus.

fixer. A solution that makes the developed image on a film permanent. It does so by dissolving or neutralizing the remaining unexposed emulsion.

flagging. (1) Indicating a web splice so that the spliced product can be removed from the press folder and discarded. (2) Marking printed matter to indicate a change or correction. (3) Inserting small strips of paper into a skid of press sheets as needed to indicate segments of defective printed sheets.

flank. The working surface of the gear tooth below the pitch circle on a machine gear.

flap. A hinged section attached to a flat or film so that the individual printing detail is in register. Flaps are used to double print or surprint printing detail into a common exposure area.

flare. Stray, unwanted spread of light from the projected image that diffuses detail, increases fogging, and can reduce contrast. See also: *halation.*

flash. (1) A brief, intense burst of light produced by a bulb or an electronic unit, usually used where the scene lighting is inadequate for photography. (2) A phototypesetting function that is keyboard-controlled. Allowing flash will produce an exposed character—the normal function. Canceling flash will allow character escapement without the associated image—a feature often useful during typographic input. Virtually all phototypesetters have this function regardless of the light-source technology used.

flash exposure. The supplementary exposure given in halftone photography to strengthen the dots in the shadows of negatives, thereby lengthening the screen's tonal reproduction range.

flash exposure, basic. The time required for light to penetrate the openings of a contact halftone screen and produce a 90% dot on lith film.

flash lamp. An electric lamp attached to the front of a process camera and designed to transmit light through the lens during the flash exposure.

flat. (1) A sheet of film or goldenrod paper to which negatives or positives have been attached (stripped) for exposure as a unit onto a printing plate. (2) Description of a print or proof lacking contrast, color, or brilliance.

Flat (1)

flat color. An ink specially formulated to produce a desired hue, printed as a solid, tint, or halftone. Flat color inks are not designed to be overprinted with other inks, as process color inks are. The term may also be used to refer to an image that only contains color at a uniform density in any one segment. See also: *screen tint.*

flat etch. A chemical technique used to change the size of the dots over the entire halftone film image.

flatbed. (1) A printing press in which the form is held in a horizontal platen. Flatbed presses are often used as proofing presses. See also: *cylinder press; letterpress; platen press.* (2) A color scanner on which the original is mounted on a horizontal table instead of a rotary drum. See also: *color scanner.*

Flatbed-cylinder press (1)

flatbed cutter. A machine used to trim the edges of books.

flat-panel display. A computer monitor illuminated by liquid crystals, gas plasma, or electroluminescence.

flexographic ink. Quick-drying, fluid ink that is highly volatile.

flexography. A method of rotary letterpress printing characterized by the use of flexible, rubber or plastic plates with raised image areas and fluid, rapid-drying inks. See also: *letterpress; relief plate; relief printing.* Alternative term: *aniline printing.*

Flexography

flocculation. A mass formed when a number of fine, suspended particles group together.

flood coat. In screen printing, an even coating of ink, which covers the surface of the screen but is not forced through the image areas. This ensures that the entire screen receives the proper ink supply during impression.

flood stroke. The squeegee motion that deposits a thick layer of ink on top of the screen printing screen under light pressure. The excessive ink prevents the image areas from drying between printing strokes.

flooding. In lithography, excess water on the printing plate or in the ink caused by improper ink/water balance.

flop. To place a photographic film positive or negative with the emulsion facing up instead of down.

floptical. A 3½-in. high-density floppy diskette with closely spaced optical-servo tracks embedded into the disk by a laser, allowing the device to store 20 MB of information. The term "floptical" is a contraction of "floppy" and "optical."

flotation deinking. A method of removing ink and other contaminants from reclaimed paper by producing an ink-bearing froth that rises to the surface of the cells and is skimmed off.

floating point unit (FPU). The portion of a computer's microprocessor that enhances speed and mathematical precision.

flow. The smooth, uninterrupted movement of an ink.

flow chart. A pictorial representation of the steps in a process, such as the ways in which customer complaints are received, documented, addressed, and resolved. Flow charts are drawn to better understand how the various steps in a process are interrelated and how the overall process can be simplified.

Flow chart

flow control. A method of ensuring that data transfer does not overwhelm a network or modem.

fluff. Loosely bonded fibers projecting from the surface of a sheet of paper. Alternative terms: *fuzz; linting.*

flush. (1) Type composition set without paragraph indentions. (2) An ink wetting agent.

flush left. Lines of type composition aligned to the left margin, with a ragged right margin. Alternative terms: *quadded left; ragged right; unjustified text.* See also: *justification.*

flush right. Lines of composition aligned to the right margin with a ragged left margin. Alternative terms: *quadded right; ragged left.* See also: *justification.*

flushed colors. Dispersions of pigments in oil instead of water.

flushed pigment. A wet coloring processed in a mixer with a varnish.

flushing. A method of transferring pigments from dispersions in water to dispersions in oil by displacing the water with oil.

flying. A fine spray of ink thrown off rapidly moving ink rollers. Alternative term: *misting.*

flying paster. An automatic device that attaches a new roll of paper to an expiring roll without a press stop, while the paper is running at press speed and without the use of a festoon.

flying spot scanner. A device in which a spot of light moves over a surface in a series of narrow paths to dissect or assemble a photographic image or otherwise identify a sample of material.

focal length. The distance between the optical center of a lens and the point at which an object image is in sharp or critical focus.

focal plane. The light-sensitive film or plate on which camera images transmitted by a lens are brought to sharpest focus. The focal plane rests in a fixed position. Alternative term: *film plane.*

focal-plane shutter. An opaque curtain with a slit that opens in the front of the film in a camera, allowing image-forming light to strike the film.

focus. Adjusting the distance setting on a lens so that the subject is sharply defined.

focus lens, adjustable. A lens that has variable distance settings.

focusing magnifier. A lens through which the image on the ground glass is viewed for critical focusing.

fog. A photographic defect in which the image is either locally or entirely veiled by a deposit of silver. Fogging is caused by stray light or improperly compounded chemical solutions.

foil. (1) A thin metal or plastic membrane (less than 0.006 in. thick) that is often used as a substrate in the flexographic printing process. (2) A European term for polyester materials.

fold. Bending and creasing a sheet of paper as required to form a printed product.

fold marks. Guides on the pasteup that indicate where a printed piece will be creased.

fold plates. Two smooth, flat metal sheets that receive the paper that has come through the buckling mechanism on a folder during binding and finishing.

folder. Machine that creases and scores printed sheets of paper to particular specifications during binding and finishing. The process itself is called *folding*. See also: *folder, combination*.

folder, combination. A bindery machine or in-line finishing component of a web press that incorporates the characteristics of knife and buckle folders. See also: *folder*.

folder, quad. A machine that creases, scores, and delivers four sixteen-page signatures separately or as two thirty-two-page signatures from a single press sheet with sixty-four pages printed across it.

folder, ribbon. A folder on a web press used for publication work. It slits the web into multiple strips of the width required by the desired product size. Each ribbon is turned over an angle bar and guided into position so that all ribbons align with each other ahead of the jaw-folding section. The ribbons of paper are collated and brought down to the cutoff knives and folding jaws in either one or two streams. The press then simultaneously delivers either one or two sets of signatures of the same size. See also: *angle bar*.

folder dummy. A mockup that shows the placement of page heads, the binding edge, and the gripper and side-guide edges, as well as page sequence and signature arrangement. Alternative term: *folding dummy.*

folding endurance. The number of double folds a paper will withstand under tension and specified conditions before it breaks at the fold line.

Folder dummy

folding to paper. Bending and creasing sheets without regard to alignment of headers, footers, and other images throughout the signatures.

folding to print. Bending and creasing sheets so that the headers, footers, and other image areas are aligned throughout the signatures.

foldout. An oversize leaf, often a map, an illustration, or a table, folded to fit within the trim size of a book and tipped (pasted) in. See also: *gatefold.*

folio. (1) In printing, a page number, often placed at the outside of the running head, at the top (head) of the page. See also: *header.* (2) In descriptive bibliography, a leaf of a manuscript or early printed book, the two sides designated as "r" (recto, or front) and "v" (verso, or back). (3) Formerly, a book made from standard-size sheets folded once, each sheet forming two leaves, or four pages.

folio, blind. A folio counted in numbering pages but not printed (as on the title page).

folio, drop. In printing, a page number, often placed at the outside of the running head at the bottom (foot) of the page. See also: *footer.*

folio, expressed. Any printed folio.

folio lap. The additional paper on the side edges of a signature that extend beyond the trim size of the pages. Folio laps are included so that binding equipment can grab and insert the signature into a magazine or book. Alternative terms: *high folio; low folio.*

font. A complete collection of characters in one typeface and size, including all letters, figures, symbols, and punctuation marks. See also: *typefonts, "tuned."*

foot lambert. A measure of source brightness.

foot margin. The distance between the bottom edge of the body of type (text matter) on a page and the bottom edge of the trimmed page. Alternative term: *tail margin.*

footcandle. A unit in which light intensity is measured. It is equal to the intensity of a standard candle at a distance of one foot.

footer. A book's title or a chapter title printed at the bottom of a page. A drop folio (page number) may or may not be included. Alternative term: *running foot.* See also: *folio, drop; header.*

footnote. Reference material typeset at the bottom of a page in a smaller size than the body text.

foreground. The area between the camera and the principal subject.

form. (1) Either side of a signature. A form usually contains a multiple of eight pages, but may be more or less. (2) Type locked in a chase and ready to be put on a letterpress. Alternative term: *typeform.* (3) In the case of offset, a finished, camera-ready proof may be referred to as a form. See also: *imposition.*

form roller. The device that transfers dampening solution or ink from an oscillating roller to the printing plate. Most lithographic presses typically have one or two dampening form rollers and three to five inking form rollers. Alternative term: *ink form roller.*

format. Size, shape, and design of a printed piece.

formation. The structure and uniformity of a paper's fiber distribution as judged by transmitted light.

former. A smooth, triangular-shaped, metal plate over which a printed web passes prior to entering an in-line folder. The former folds the moving web in half lengthwise. Alternative term: *former board.*

Former

former fold. First fold given paper coming off a web press, often before the paper is cut into sheets. The former fold is made in the direction of web travel, thus parallel to the grain.

forums. Areas on commercial online services where files and message threads are organized by special interest. Similar to BBSs and UseNet News.

forwarding. Backing, rounding, shaping, lining up, and head-banding, among other operations performed before a casebound book is covered.

forwarding mechanism. Conveyor arrangement that carries the sheet from the feeder to the front guide on a sheetfed offset press. Alternative term: *forwarding roller.*

forwarding wheels. Hard, circular casings that advance the press sheet from the feeder to the feedtable on a sheetfed press.

Foss color order system. A printed chart that features an array of colors, tones, and hues combined with black.

foundry type. Hand-set metal type characters.

fountain. A reservoir for the dampening solution or ink that is fed to the plate on a lithographic press. Alternative term: *water pan.*

fountain, enclosed. An ink reservoir sealed from the outside atmosphere by a series of shields that expose only a small area at the impression point. Enclosed fountains inhibit ink evaporation and drying on the surface of the engraved gravure cylinders and reduces explosion hazards when highly volatile inks are used.

fountain blade. On an offset press, the strip of flexible steel or plastic angled against the ink fountain roller. The fountain blade acts as a squeegee against the fountain roller allowing only the amount of ink determined by the setting of the ink keys, to remain on the fountain roller to contact the ductor roller.

Fountain blade and roller

fountain cheeks. The vertical metal pieces connecting the edges of the fountain roller and blade to form an ink-tight trough.

fountain keys. A series of thumb screws or motor-driven screws or cams behind the fountain blade that provide for variable inking across the ink fountain. The keys control the amount of space between the ink fountain blade and the ink pan roller. The amount of space between the blade and pan roller determines the amount of ink feed from an ink key. Alternative term: *ink keys.*

fountain leveler. A sensing device, usually mechanical or ultrasonic, that checks the height of the ink moving over the agitator.

fountain roller. A metal roller that rotates intermittently or continuously in the ink or dampening fountain and carries the ink or dampening solution on its metal surface. The variable speed of the fountain roller will increase or decrease the feed overall to the plate. Alternative terms: *ink pan roller, water pan roller.*

fountain solution. In lithographic printing, a combination of water, gum arabic, and other chemicals used to wet the printing plate and keep the nonimage areas from accepting ink. Some fountain solutions contain alcohol. Alternative term: *dampening solution.*

fountain solution acidity. A measurable pH level from zero to seven that is controlled by the amount of acid added to the fountain solution. The acidic quality of fountain solution cleans and desensitizes the nonimage areas of the plate. Fountain solution acidity is measured with an electric or battery-operated pH meter or with reliable pH strips.

fountain solution concentrate. A mixture of chemicals (compounded acids and gums) that, when combined with water and alcohol or another wetting agent, form fountain solution.

fountain solution conductivity. The property of a fountain solution that allows it to transmit electricity, which provides a measure of its concentration.

fountain solution gum. The molecules of natural or synthetic gelatinous substances that adhere to the nonimage areas of a lithographic plate after it has been cleaned with an acid. Water molecules, which adhere to the gum, wet the nonimage areas of the plate and repel the ink. Applying gum keeps the nonimage areas of the plate from scumming.

fountain splitter. A device that divides the ink fountain so that two or more inks can be used at the same time. Each ink will print on a different section of the press sheet; e.g., red on the left side and blue on the right side.

fountain stops. Adjustable rollers or strips of material placed on the fountain roller of a lithographic dampening or inking system to cut down on the amount of water or ink supplied to the corresponding area of the press plate.

four-color process printing. The photomechanical reproduction of multicolor images achieved by overprinting specified amounts and areas of yellow, magenta, cyan, and black inks.

fourdrinier. A paper machine that forms a continuous web of paper on a horizontal, forward-moving, endless wire belt.

fourth-generation equipment. Phototypesetters that use a laser to expose characters onto photographic film or paper.

foxed. A term used to describe the brown discoloration of old paper, which may appear as spots.

frame. (1) The wood or metal construction that supports the screen fabric in screen printing. (2) A block positioned on a page into which the user can place text or graphics.

frame buffer. Memory used to store an array of image data. Each element of the array corresponds to one or more pixels in a video display or one or more dots on a laser printer or other output device.

frame grabbing. Capturing a single picture element from video or another media so that it can be manipulated and combined with other images for reproduction purposes.

frame relay. An enhanced version of packet switching in which bandwidth is handled more efficiently by breaking data into packets that vary in length for transmission at speeds ranging from 64 Kbps to 1.544 Mbps.

frame-grabber board. An image processing board that samples, digitizes, stores, and processes video signals in a computer.

free sheet. Wood pulp that has been treated with a caustic solution to remove impurities. Paper that is free from groundwood.

freenets Publicly subsidized, volunteer-run Internet gateways frequently based in libraries. Freenets offer limited Internet access to the general public from their regional sites and sometimes via dial-up.

freeware. Software distributed at no cost usually by the original author over the Internet or a commercial online service. See also: *shareware.*

French fold. A press sheet in which all of the pages are printed on one side and folded, first vertically and then horizontally, to produce a four-page signature. The blank side is folded inward before the other folds are made.

French fold
(heads in)

French stitch. A method of binding a prestitched booklet into a saddle-bound magazine.

frequency division multiplex access (FDMA). A method of simultaneously transmitting several communications signals over a transmission medium by dividing its bandwidth into narrower bands, each carrying one signal.

frequency modulation. Method of conveying information on a fixed-amplitude carrier wave by varying the frequency of the carrier. See also: *amplitude modulation.*

frequently asked questions (FAQs). Lists within UseNet News, BBSs, or the information forums on commercial online services that address issues that often come up among new users.

fringe. A small area around a soft halftone dot that does not have enough density to hold back light. Alternative terms: *dot fringe; halo.* See: *dot, soft.*

frisket. A paper mask or stencil placed over certain areas of a photograph during airbrushing.

front guide. See *front stops.*

front matter. The pages preceding the text of a book, including the title and copyright pages, the preface, foreword, table of contents, list of illustrations, and dedication.

front stops. A series of devices that halt the forward movement of a press sheet on the feedboard. The front stops square the sheet in relation to the printing cylinders and determine the print margin. The front stops are part of the three-point register system. Alternative term: *front guides.*

Front stop

Front guide

front-end system. A grouping of interconnected keyboard terminals and related peripherals such as a central processing unit and storage devices that can operate independently of the output device, e.g., phototypesetter, line printer. The front-end system is used to enter, edit, and/or manipulate text and the coding used to drive the phototypesetter. It may operate on- or off-line with the output devices.

frontispiece. An illustration facing the title page of a book; frequently printed on enamel paper and tipped (glued) in.

frontlighting. Light shining on the subject from the direction of the camera.

f-stops. Fixed sizes at which the aperture of the lens can be set. The values of the f-stops are determined by the ratio of the aperture to the focal length of the lens. Alternative term: *f-number*. See also: *effective aperture*.

full binding. A cover made of one piece of material.

full bleed. An image extending to all four edges of the press sheet leaving no visible margins. See also: *bleed; extended color*.

full-scale black. See *black, full-scale*.

fuming ghosting. See *chemical ghosting*.

function code. A computer program that controls those machine operations other than the output of typographic characters.

function keys. Those keys on a computer keyboard that, when used instead of a mouse, instruct the computer to perform specific operations, ranging from executing a program to clearing the screen.

furnish. The mixture of fibrous and nonfibrous materials like fillers, sizing, and colorants in a water suspension from which paper or paperboard is made. Alternative term: *pulp furnish*.

fuser, fuser roll. In electrostatic printing, the component of the toner assembly that is maintained at a high temperature to facilitate toner bonding with the substrate.

f-value. Indicates the ratio of the largest aperture of a lens to its focal length.

G

gallery. A photography studio.

gallery camera. A process camera extending from the darkroom into the area of the photography studio where "roomlight" operations can be performed.

galley. (1) The raw output of a phototypesetter, usually in the form of single columns of type on long sheets of photographic paper, which serve as preliminary proofs. (2) The final typeset (or imageset) copy output to photographic paper, or directly to film. (3) A long, shallow tray used to store and proof handset type.

galvanized. See *mottle.*

gamma. In photography, a measure of the amount of contrast that is characteristic of a particular photographic film, paper, or processing technique. This negative contrast is the result of development and not the contrast of the subject itself.

gamma correction. Compressing or expanding the ranges of dark or light shades in an image.

gamut. The greatest possible range.

gang. (1) A grouping of different or identical forms arranged to print together in one impression. Alternative terms: *gang up; gang run; gang printing.* (2) Multiple photographic images exposed as one unit. Alternative term: *photocombining.* See also: *composite; montage.*

gatefold. A four-page book insert that is larger than some dimension of the page and opens from each side of the center. See also: *foldout.*

Gatefold

gateway. The long-distance link between disparate networks (e.g., TCP/IP and SNA).

gathering. Assembling a set of signatures sequentially. Alternative term: *assembling, collate, insert.*

gear marks. Alternating light and dark marks that appear as bands in halftones and solids parallel to the gripper edge of the sheet. The distance between marks is uniform and equal.

Gathering

gear streaks. Parallel streaks appearing across the printed sheet at the same interval as gear teeth on a cylinder.

gelatin resist. In conventional gravure, a layer of a colloidal material with a pattern of thick and thin areas corresponding to the highlight and shadow areas of a piece of copy. After the carbon tissue is placed on the copper cylinder, the paper backing is removed with hot water and the developed gelatin is dried in preparation for staging and etching. It resists penetration from the etchant in all areas except those representing tone values of copy.

ghosting, gloss. Condition that occurs during sheetfed printing when the vapors from ink printed on one side of a press sheet chemically interact with the dry ink densities overprinted on the reverse side of the same press sheet or on the next sheet in the pile. The faint, dull images that indicate gloss ghosting usually appear in large shadow or solid areas of the press sheet and develop only when inks containing drying oils are used to print the job. Alternative term: *fuming ghosting.* See also: *chemical ghosting.*

ghosting, mechanical. Condition that occurs when the ink film on the press sheet shows abrupt variations in color densities, especially when a narrow solid printed ahead or behind a wider solid consumes much of the ink on the form rollers. Alternative term: *ink starvation ghosting.*

GIF. See *graphics interchange format.*

gigabit (Gb). One billion bits.

gigabyte (GB). One thousand megabytes or one billion bytes.

gild. To apply gold or other metallic leaf to the trim edges of a book.

glassine. A smooth, semi-transparent paper used to print book dust jackets, candy wrappers, etc.

glazed. (1) A term used to describe press rollers or blankets that have become smooth and hard because of surface deterioration (oxidation) and a gradual buildup of dried ink, varnishes, fountain solution gum, etc. (2) Paper with a high gloss or polish that is applied to the surface during or after manufacture by friction, calendering, plating, or drying.

global-area network (GAN). A group of many wide-area networks linked from country to country.

gloss. The relative amount of incident light reflected from a surface. Printing papers are often said to have varying degrees of specular gloss.

gloss ink. An ink containing varnish or other additives. It dries with a minimum of penetration into the stock and yields a high luster.

gloss white. A white pigment used as an ink extender.

glossmeter. An instrument used to measure the specular reflectance from a surface at a given angle.

glue lap. The area of a printed package or container reserved for the adhesive material used to fasten the folded carton.

gluing wheels. Devices that apply a small coating of glue to the binding edge of a sheet. Gluing wheels are sometimes used instead of stitching on small pamphlets.

gluing-off. Applying glue to the spine of a casebound book after sewing and smashing, but before the book is trimmed.

goldenrod. A sheet of paper used to prepare negative film flats. It serves as a base for drawing the layout and attaching the film negatives. When exposure openings are cut through it, the remainder serves as an exposure mask, since its yellowish-orange color does not transmit actinic light.

gopher. A search utility developed at the University of Minnesota that uses menus to locate Telnet and FTP sites and other networked sources of information over the Internet.

gothic type. A plain sans serif typeface with lines of unvarying thickness.

gradation. The gradual change of tones from one to another in originals, negatives, and reproductions.

grade. A means of ranking paper, film, and other printing supplies.

gradient. A rate of increase or decrease.

grain. (1) The distribution, coarseness, and size of silver particles in photographic emulsions and images. (2) The roughened or irregular surface of a printing plate. (3) In papermaking, the machine direction, or the direction in which the fibers lie.

grain, with the. Binding term in which paper is folded parallel to the direction of the paper grain.

grain direction. (1) In papermaking, the alignment of fibers in the direction of web travel. (2) In printing, paper is said to be "grain-long" if the grain direction parallels the long dimension of the sheet. The paper is referred to as "grain-short" if it parallels the short dimension of the sheet. (3) In book binding, the grain direction of all papers used must run parallel to the book backbone.

grain direction, across. Method of printing at right angles to or opposite the paper grain direction.

grain direction, against. Folding or cutting paper at right angles to the paper grain in the direction of the sheet's fibers.

graininess. The sand-like or granular appearance of a negative, print, or slide resulting from irregularly distributed silver grains that clump together during film development. Graininess becomes more pronounced with faster films, increased density in the negative, and degrees of enlargement.

graining machine. A device used to produce the grain on lithographic plates. Wet-brushing, dry-brushing, or electrochemical processes may be used. Grained plates retain water better in the nonimage areas.

grammage. The weight in grams of a single sheet of paper with an area of one square meter.

granite finish. Paper comprised of multicolored fibers that form a mottled surface resembling granite.

graphic arts. The visual reproduction of type and images by any of the several printing processes.

graphic communications. Allied industries, including printing, publishing, advertising, and design, that participate in the production and dissemination of text and images by printed or electronic means.

graphic images. Type characters or illustrative material, such as halftones or line drawings, which are reproduced by one of the printing processes.

graphical user interface (GUI). A visual way to represent computer commands and objects on screen. The user interacts with the computer by selecting icons and menu items from the screen, usually by moving and clicking with a mouse.Netscape Navigator and Microsoft Internet Explorer are GUIs for the World Wide Web, and Windows 3.X is the GUI that made DOS more palatable. Macintosh, Windows 95, and Windows NT are complete GUI operating systems. See also: *desktop; icon.*

graphics. Artwork, photographs, and charts that are reproduced or presented in visual form.

graphics interchange format (GIF). Originally developed by Unisys for use on CompuServe specifically for compressing photographic images online, GIF is the most common method of encoding and storing picture files on the Internet's World Wide Web.

graphics primitives. Mathematical instructions used to create boxes, circles, bar charts, and pie charts.

grater rollers. Textured press cylinders that support a web before drying, reducing smearing and marking.

gravure. An intaglio printing process in which minute depressions, sometimes called cells, that form the image area are engraved or etched below the nonimage area in the surface of the printing cylinder. The cylinder is immersed in ink, and the excess ink is scraped off by a blade. When paper or another substrate come in contact with the printing cylinder, ink is transferred. See also: *rotogravure.*

gravure, conventional. A method of intaglio printing in which the ink-receptive cylinder cells are etched to vary in depth but not in area, thereby transferring different tones to the substrate.

gravure, halftone. See *halftone gravure.*

gravure screen. A film with fine crossline rulings against an opaque background. It is used to establish gravure cell boundaries photographically.

gravurescope. A microscope designed to measure and inspect the depth and width of cells and cell walls on a gravure cylinder.

gray. (1) Any of a series of neutral colors ranging between black and white. The tint or color formed by blending black and white in varying proportions. (2) When a surface reflects a comparative ratio of each light wavelength in the visible spectrum at a relatively low combined intensity the human eye perceives gray.

gray balance. The values for yellow, magenta, and cyan that produce a neutral gray with no dominant hue when printed at a normal density.

gray balance chart. Near-neutral yellow, magenta, and cyan dot values printed in a grid pattern. A halftone black gray scale is used as a reference to find the three-color neutral areas. The dot values that compose these areas represent the gray (color) balance requirements for a set of color separations. The gray balance chart should be produced in-house under normal production conditions using the process inks, paper, plates, and press that will be used for the job.

gray component replacement (GCR). An electronic color scanning capability in which the least dominant process color is replaced with an appropriate value of black in areas where yellow, magenta, and cyan overprint. Color variation on press is less serious when GCR is used. See also: *undercolor addition; undercolor removal.*

gray level. The analog or digital signal that indicates the value of an original image viewed through a color separation filter.

gray scale. A reflection or transmission film strip showing neutral tones in a range of graduated steps. It is exposed alongside originals during photography and used to time development, determine color balance, or to measure density range, tone reproduction, and print contrast. Gray scales can also be used to check focus and resolution. Alternative terms: *gray wedge; neutral gray wedge; step tablet; step wedge.*

gray scale, continuous. A narrow continuous-tone black-and-white image on film in which the density gradually increases from zero (the transparent film base). Alternative term: *gray scale, step tablet; wedge.*

grayness. An attribute calculated from density readings that relates to the degree of three-color contamination in a cyan, magenta, or yellow process color ink. As grayness values increase, an ink exhibits lower saturation or purity.

grayness, percent. See *percent grayness.*

greeking sheet. A sheet of transfer lettering used to create a facsimile of body copy in layouts.

green. See *additive color process; additive primaries.*

grid. (1) A film master of fonts used in phototypesetting. (2) In art and copy preparation, a preprinted, standardized format or template on a sheet of acetate or (in non-reproducible blue) on a pasteup board. The artist uses such grids as guidelines in the pasteup of a specific, and usually repeatable job, such as a magazine, where the format remains the same, but the content changes month after month.

grid coordinate system. A method of specifying locations within an area to be composed. The length between the desired locations is specified as the "x" and y" "distances (coordinates) from a reference point in the center or a specific corner.

grinder. In gravure, the machine that hones the copper cylinder to the proper size and polishes its surface before engraving or etching.

grinding stone. Composition materials used to cut and polish the copper cylinders or cylinder bases that are used as image carriers in the gravure process.

grindometer. An instrument used to indicate the presence of coarse particles or agglomerates in an ink dispersion. The fineness-of-grind is rated at the point on the scale where the oversized particles first appear in substantial concentration. Alternative term: *grind gauge.*

gripper. (1) The metal clamps or fingers located on impression cylinders and transfer cylinders, that grasp and hold a sheet while being transported through the press. (2) The reference edge of a layout, film flat, or print plate that corresponds to the sheet edge held by the grippers on the press.

Gripper (1)

gripper bite. The amount of paper that extends beneath the press gripper.

gripper-bowing device. A part of the infeed on some sheetfed presses that compensates for the effects of fan-out by intentionally distorting the printing sheet.

ground glass. A sheet of glass with a grained, matte (translucent), or frosted surface. It is mounted and hinged into the back of a graphic arts camera so that it can be swung into the focal plane in place of the film holder and used to assist in focusing the image.

groundwood. Pulp produced during papermaking by grinding bark-free logs against a revolving stone in the presence of water. It is used principally in newsprint and lower grades of book paper. Alternative term: *mechanical pulp.*

groundwood free. See *wood free.*

groupware. Software programs designed to promote collaboration among colleagues at diverse locations connected by a computer network. See also: *whiteboard.*

guide edge. The side of a sheet at right angles to the gripper edge that is used to control the lateral (side-to-side) position of the sheet as it travels through the press or folder.

guide marks. Register and trim lines in the margin of a film flat that aid in plate positioning, sheet centering, trimming, and folding.

guide roller. A cylinder on the roll stand between the roll of paper and the dancer roller. It is used to compensate for slight paper variations. Alternative term: *cocking roller.*

guide side. The area on the press that controls the position of the sheet during printing. It is usually the side closest to the press operator.

guillotine cutter. (1) A manual or electronic device with a long, heavy, sloping blade that descends to a table or bed and slices through a stack of paper. (2) In photoengraving and metal platemaking, a heavy steel knife, operated by electricity or foot treadle, that trims sheets of copper, zinc, or magnesium or cuts the excess from electrotype and stereotype casts.

Guillotine cutter (1)

gum. (1) In lithography, a water-soluble colloid, such as gum arabic or cellulose gum, that desensitizes the nonimage areas on a printing plate, making them ink repellent. It is also used to preserve the plate for future use. (2) A general term referring to natural, resinous binders that are used in the formulation of inks and varnishes.

gum blinding. Condition that results when ink fails to adhere to an image wetted with water or gum.

gusseting. Waviness or actual creases that form at the top of the inner pages in a closed-head press signature.

gutter. In typography, the inside margin (white space) between facing pages or columns of type. In bookbinding, the margin at the binding edge. Alternative terms: *gutter margin; back margin.* See also: *alley.*

H

hair cut. A smooth, curved slice in a paper web that usually occurs because a piece of felt from the manufacturing process is embedded in the web and passes through the calender.

hairline register. A standard for accuracy in which the maximum deviation between printing colors is 0.003 in. (0.08 mm).

halation. A photographic term used in platemaking to describe light that spreads beyond the sharp definition of an image. Poor contact between the negative flat and the negative-working plate during platemaking distorts the image by allowing light to expose nonimage areas, causing a blurred effect. Dirt, masking materials, or tape prevents proper contact between the film negative and the plate. In positive platemaking, dot loss occurs. See also: *antihalation backing; flare.*

halftone. A printed reproduction of a continuous-tone image composed of dots that vary in frequency (number per square inch), size, or density, thereby producing tonal gradations. The term is also applied to the process and plates used to produce this image.

halftone cell. A halftone dot created on a laser printer or imagesetter. The cell is created by grouping printer dots into a grid. When more dots are present in the grid, the cell appears larger.

halftone gravure. Intaglio printing process in which the engraved cylinder cells vary both in area and depth.

halftone mottle. The appearance of blotchy patterns instead of smooth tonal values in halftone tints.

halftone screen. A sheet of glass or film that is used as an intermediate between continuous-tone copy and photosensitive material. Continuous-tone images are exposed to the photosensitive material through the screen's regular arrangement of transparent and opaque areas. This produces an image pattern of small, solid dots (or narrow lines) that vary in size (or width) and represent tonal gradations. Halftone screens with higher screen rulings (e.g., 133 lines/in. as opposed to 65 lines/in.) produce higher resolution images. See also: *contact screen; crossline screen.*

halftone step scale. A photographic test image that is used to evaluate printing conditions. Consisting of a series of uniform tints with increasing dot diameters, it is frequently printed on a film flat and in the trim margin of the press sheet. Alternative terms: *step wedge; gray scale; step tablet.*

halftone tint. An area printed with all halftone dots of the same percentage to provide an even tone or color. See also: *screen tint; tint.*

halide. In photography, silver bromide, silver iodide, or silver chloride used in the light-sensitive emulsion.

hand. A quantity of signatures or books, approximately equal to what someone can hold in a single hand.

hand composition. Method of setting type manually from a case with a composing stick.

handshake. An exchange of signals between modems or computer terminals to verify compatibility and establish whether or not transmission can begin.

hanging indent. Typesetting the first line of a paragraph to the full text width, while succeeding lines are spaced in by a constant amount from the left margin.

hanging punctuation. Commas, hyphens, etc., set outside the normal line length on the left- and right-hand sides of the column of type to achieve optical alignment or a certain aesthetic appearance.

hangout. The amount that the book protrudes beneath the clamp on a perfect binder.

hansa yellow. A light-resistant organic pigment.

hard copy. See *copy, hard.*

hardbound book. See *casebound book.*

hardening bath. A solution used to toughen photographic images.

hardware. The electric, electronic, magnetic, and mechanical components of a computer system. See also: *software.*

Hazard Communication Standard. An OSHA regulation that requires chemical manufacturers, suppliers, and importers to assess the hazards of the chemicals that they make, supply, or import, and to inform employers, customers, and workers of these hazards through material safety data sheets (MSDS). See also: *material safety data sheets.*

HDSL. See *high-bit-rate digital subscriber lines.*

head. (1) A line of display type signifying the title of a work or conveying crucial information. A headline. (2) The top of a page, book, or printing form. (3) A compact device that reads, scans, writes, or records data on a surface medium, particularly the fixed or moving electromagnetic elements used for reading and writing data on magnetic tapes, disks, and drums.

head margin. The distance between the top edge of the trimmed page and the top edge of the body of type (text matter) on a page.

head stops. Devices that align the front or gripper edge of the sheet before it is fed into the press. Alternative term: *front stops.*

head trim. The amount of paper that is cut off above the sheet above the head margin; usually about ⅛ in. (3 mm).

headband. (1) An ornamental strip of reinforced cotton or silk attached to the top and bottom of the inner back of a bound book. (2) In typography, a decorative strip printed or engraved at the top of a page or chapter.

headbox. The part of the paper machine that delivers a uniform dispersion of fibers in water at the proper velocity through the slice opening to the paper machine wire.

header. A book's title or a chapter title printed at the top of a page and often with a folio (page number). Alternative term: *running head.* See also: *folio; footer.*

heat sealing. The converting operation in which two or more surfaces are fused together using specific heat, time, and pressure.

heat tunnel. On the shrink-wrap equipment used in materials handling, the warming device through which the product travels as the wrapping is applied. Alternative term: *shrink tunnel.*

heatset ink. See *ink, heatset.*

heat-transfer paper. The substrate used in thermal-transfer printing. The design is first printed on it with inks containing sublimable dispersed dyes. Next, under applied heat and pressure, the first substrate is placed in contact with another substrate to which the design adheres. Alternative term: *sublimation.*

heat-transfer printing. See *thermal-transfer printing.*

heavy bodied. Inks with a high viscosity or stiff consistency.

Helio-Klischograph. An electronic scanning system used to engrave gravure printing cylinders through a modulated signal that reads densities from a positive copy and transmits this information to a diamond head, which cuts the image cells into the cylinder. The Helio-Klischograph has largely replaced chemical etching in the gravure printing process.

helium-neon laser. A red laser light source in which helium-neon gas is stimulated to produce a monochromatic red light. This light is used to expose red-sensitive photographic films or paper, plates, or cylinders. It is also used in some scanners for electronic dot generation.

hemp. A papermaking fiber obtained from rope or from the hemp plant that grows in Central America and the Philippines.

hertz. A unit of measurement of electrical vibrations in cycles per second.

hickey. An imperfection on a printed sheet caused by dirt, hardened ink, or other unwanted particles that cling to the press, blanket, or plate during lithographic printing. Hickeys appear as either a small, solid printed area surrounded by a white halo, or an unprinted spot surrounded by printed ink.

Hickey

hickey-picking roller. A roller that has synthetic fibers embedded in its surface, to help it remove hickeys from the surface of an offset printing plate or to fill in the white ring on the plate surface. This roller replaces one of the ink form rollers.

HiFi color. See *color, HiFi.*

high. A photographic term designating a halftone negative that has been fully exposed and developed so that the printing dot sizes made from it will be slightly smaller than those from a normal reproduction.

high key. A photographic or printed image in which the predominant detail lies in the highlights.

high-bit-rate digital subscriber lines (HDSL). A communications mode being promoted by the cable television and telephone industries for their upcoming cable-based Internet services. HDSL can be used over copper wiring and permits two-way 1.5-Mbps transfer of information in a similar scenario. See also: *asymmetrical digital subscriber lines.*

high-contrast emulsion. A photographic material that changes in developed density markedly with only slight changes in exposure.

high-contrast image. The relationship of highlights to shadows in continuous-tone or halftone photography, i.e., the darker portions of the image are uniformly very dark; the lighter portions are uniformly very light; and the midtone range is non-existent or very small.

highlight. The lightest or whitest area of an original or reproduction, represented by the densest portion of a continuous-tone negative and by the smallest dot formation on a halftone and printing plate.

highlight dots. The very small black dots on a halftone film positive, or the very small clear dots in the film negative of the corresponding areas.

highlight halftone. A reproduction in which the highlights are devoid of dots to accentuate the contrast.

highlight mask. A light negative image that is registered with a normal-density continuous-tone negative to enhance highlight tone contrast.

highlight stop. The lens aperture used in halftone photography to combine high-light dots in the negative and record highlight detail.

high-mesh count. Fine woven screen printing fabrics with a count of 300 or more meshes/inch (120 meshes/centimeter).

high-speed printer. A printer that operates "on-line" at a speed comparable to the speed of a computer or data processor.

histogram. A graphical representation of the pattern of variation that exists in a par-ticular process measure, such as solid ink density. It is usually depicted by vertical bars drawn to indicate the frequency level of data readings collected within specific ranges of measurement, such as the frequency of density readings between 1.20 and 1.41, in increments of 0.03. This representation allows for easy interpretation of the central tendency and dispersion of the data.

Histogram

holdout. The extent to which paper resists or retards the penetration of the freshly printed ink film.

home page. The electronic location of a specific information source on the World Wide Web. Also known as a Web site, it usually provides links to related information sources.

host. A computer that functions as the beginning and end point of data transfers.

hot melt. (1) A molten wax or plastic adhesive material that is applied with a roller or knife or through the casting or extrusion method at elevated temperatures in liquid form. It solidifies upon cooling and imparts high gloss and good barrier properties to paper and board. (2) A bookmaking glue that is solid at room temperature and must be heated to achieve liquidity.

hot-melt ink jet. A form of ink jet printing using hot-melt inks that solidify very quickly on paper and exhibit excellent dot shape, contrast, edge definition, and hold-out characteristics.

hot-metal. Type produced by casting molten metal to form individual characters or slugs. See also: *cold type.*

hue. A visual property determined by the dominant light wavelengths reflected or transmitted.

hue, primary. (1) Any three hues, normally a red, a green, and a blue, so selected from the spectral scale as to enable a person with normal color vision to match any other hue by the additive mixture in varying proportions. Alternative terms: *physical primary hues/colors; physical color primaries.* (2) In the subtractive color process, the primary hues are yellow, magenta, and cyan; those transparent inks/colors that absorb only (or mostly) the additive primaries of blue, green, and red, respectively.

hue error. (1) A measure of the hue deviation from a theoretically perfect subtractive process (primary) color. Hue error is usually expressed as a percentage. (2) In the Preucil Ink Evaluation System, the amount of the largest unwanted absorption of a process ink, expressed as a percentage of the wanted absorption content. In other words, the extent to which the colors reflected by a process ink are not balanced.

humidity, relative. The amount of moisture present in the air, expressed as a percentage of the amount of moisture required to saturate the air at a given temperature.

Hunter L,a,b values. Scales developed by Hunter Associates Laboratory, Inc. that are widely used to define and measure color.

hydrometer. An instrument used for measuring the specific gravity of liquids.

hydrophilic. Water-receptive.

hydrophobic. Water-repellent.

hygro-expansivity. The percentage that a paper shrinks or elongates as a result of a change in its moisture content.

hygrometer. An instrument used to measure the relative humidity of air. See also: *psychrometer.*

hygroscope. An instrument used to measure the moisture content of a pile of paper relative to the humidity of the pressroom. Readings from a hygroscope help the press crew to determine if paper conditioning is necessary.

hygroscopic. The ability of a paper's cellulose fibers to absorb or release moisture and, in so doing, expand or contract. Such moisture changes cause the fibers to distort three times more in the direction of their width than in the direction of their length.

hyperlink. An emphasized word or phrase that connects related documents in a hypertext system.

hypermedia. A method of delivering specific information from a larger body of information stored on a computer. Multiple-pathway search-and-retrieval functions guide the user through the process.

hypertext. The nonlinear format used to create electronic documents with links between related elements.

hypertext markup language (HTML). The hypertext document format used on the Internet's World Wide Web.

hypertext transfer protocol (HTTP). The Internet standard supporting the exchange of information on the World Wide Web.

hyphen, hard. A hyphen required as part of a hyphenated or compound word, as opposed to a hyphen used solely for word division.

hyphenation. The division of a typeset word between syllables at the end of a line.

hyphenless justification. The alignment of lines of type through the use of interword and letter spacing instead of end-of-line word hyphenation.

hypo. Sodium thiosulfate, a chemical used to remove undeveloped silver from photographic emulsions; also a "fixer" component.

hysteresis. The difference in the moisture content of a paper as indicated by its ascending and descending curves for relative humidity. Because of hysteresis, the equilibrium moisture content of a paper (when conditioned to a specified relative humidity) will differ, depending upon its previous moisture history.

I

icon. In a computer system, a picture or drawing, such as a paint brush or trash can, that represents a file or function. Clicking the mouse on the icon activates the procedure or opens the file.

ideogram. A picture or symbol used in a system of writing to represent an idea.

illuminating. (1) Lighting a photographic subject properly. (2) Gilding book pages and manuscripts and decorating them with several colors. A popular practice in medieval times when books were rare and finished by hand.

illustrations. Drawings, sketches, graphics, photographs, etc., used in conjunction with printed matter.

image. (1) Any picture, drawing, subject, or reproduction visible to the human eye that portrays the original in the proper form, color, and perspective. (2) A picture formed by light. The optical counterpart of an original focused or projected in a photographic camera.

image analysis. Use of a television camera connected by a digitizing board to a computer for the study of patterns and other geometric measurements on a sample image. Ragged edges may also be judged with an image analyzer.

image area. On a lithographic printing plate, the area that has been specially treated to receive ink and repel water.

image assembly. See *film image assembly; imposition; stripping.*

image carrier. The device on a printing press that carries an inked image either to an intermediate rubber blanket or directly to the paper or other printing substrate. A direct-printing letterpress form, a lithographic plate, a gravure cylinder, and a screen used in screen printing are examples of image carriers.

image distortion. See *dot gain; misregister; slur.*

image file. The computer entity representing an image. It can be transmitted electronically and stored in memory.

image fit. The agreement in distance between the register marks on each color from the gripper to the tail edge of the press sheet. See also: *misregister; register.*

image orientation. The spatial relationship of the different parts of an image.

image twist. Misregister that occurs when the plate is not mounted parallel to the cylinder axis. The result is a crooked image.

image width. Distortion resulting from a difference in the horizontal distance between marks on the plate and on the printed sheet.

imagesetter. A device used to output fully paginated text and graphic images at a high resolution onto photographic film, paper, or plates. See also: *PostScript™; raster image processor; typesetting, digital; vectors.*

Imagesetter

imaging devices. Equipment, such as a process camera, contact printing frame, or electronic scanner, that casts light images of originals onto photosensitive paper or film under controlled conditions.

imbibition. A method of color printing in which an image is caused to absorb, or "imbibe," a dye, which is transferred to a sheet of specially prepared paper.

impact printer. Any machine that produces characters by striking individually inked letters onto paper. See also: *daisy-wheel printer; strike-on.*

impactless printing. See *nonimpact printer.*

impaling pins. Sharp pieces of metal that maintain web control within a folder. The web is punctured by the pins, just behind the web cutoff point, to control and pull the web around the folder cylinder, releasing it when the fold is started.

imposetter. A device used to output fully imposed signatures at a high resolution onto photographic film, paper, or plates. See also: *imposition.*

imposing camera. See *multi-imaging camera; step-and-repeat.*

imposition. Assembling the various units of a page before printing and placing them on a form so that they will fold correctly. Alternative term: *image assembly.* See also: *film image assembly; stripping.*

imposition, head-to-head. Arranging pages on a form during stripping so that the top of one page butts against the top of the opposite page.

imposition layout. A guide that indicates how images should be assembled on the sheet to meet press, folding, and bindery requirements.

imposition systems. Step-and-repeat imaging cameras or computerized methods of assembling the units of pages into signatures for printing. The latter method is sometimes referred to as electronic imposition. See also: *multi-imaging camera; stripping.*

impression. (1) The printing pressure necessary for ink transfer. (2) A single print.

impression cylinder. The hard metal cylinder that presses the paper against the inked blanket cylinder, transferring the inked image to the substrate. The impression cylinder on most sheetfed presses uses paper grippers to hold the sheet through its rotation. Alternative term: *back cylinder.*

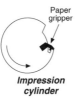

Paper gripper

Impression cylinder

impression cylinder pressure. The force of the impression (or back) cylinder against the blanket cylinder.

imprinting. Reproducing a few lines of type, such as a company's name and address, on previously printed sheets.

incandescent. Energy sources that emit light from a heated wire.

inch. To move the printing press slowly; small degrees of movement.

incident light. Rays of light that travel from a light source to an object.

incline press. A screen printing press in which the screen maintains a position parallel to the printing bed, but recedes diagonally during the feed/take-off cycle.

incunabula. Early printing, specifically that done during the 15th century.

indent. Setting type so that a portion of it aligns at a predetermined distance from the left or right margin of the column.

index. An ordered reference list of key words and subjects along with notations indicating where they can be found within a document or file.

indexing. (1) In bookbinding, gouging the edge of the text and printing or affixing reference tabs marking the major divisions or subjects found within. (2) To prepare an ordered reference list of key words and subjects along with notations indicating where they can be found within a document or file.

india ink. A dense black color used in the preparation of artwork and mechanical drawings

indicator. A dye that changes in color with shifts in pH.

indicia. Permit information for the post office as printed on a "self-mailer" brochure, magazine, or label.

infectious developer. A special chemical used to process line and halftone work. An infectious developer has a slow development rate that gradually increases to a maximum at the end of the development cycle. Alternative terms: *high-contrast developer; lith developer.* See also: *noninfectious developer.*

infeed. (1) The section of a sheetfed press where the sheet is transferred from the registering devices of the feedboard to the first impression cylinder. (2) The set of rollers controlling web tension ahead of the first unit on a web press.

inferior character. A letter and/or number positioned below the baseline of type and set in a smaller face. Alternative term: *subscript.* See also *superior character.*

infrared. The region of the electromagnetic spectrum that includes wavelengths from 780 nanometers to about 3,000 nanometers. Infrared radiation serves as a source of heat.

infrared drying. Using infrared radiation as the source of heat to set the ink on the substrate.

infrared drying unit. The section of a screen-printing web press in which the freshly printed substrate moves along a conveyor belt under infrared lamps and reflectors that set the ink.

inhibitor. A compound (usually organic) that retards or stops a chemical reaction, such as corrosion, oxidation, or polymerization.

initial letter. A large capital or otherwise decorated character that begins a chapter or paragraph.

ink. A printing ink is a dispersion of a colored solid (pigment) in a liquid, specially formulated to reproduce an image on a substrate.

ink, fluid. An ink with a low-viscosity vehicle. Fluid inks are used in flexography and gravure. Alternative term: *liquid ink.* See also: *ink, paste.*

ink, halftone. An ink specially formulated to reproduce fine detail such as halftone dots on coated stock. It has a high tinctorial strength and is finely dispersed.

ink, heatset. An ink used in high-speed web offset printing that dries primarily by evaporation while the job is still on the press. The inked web passes through a high-velocity, hot-air dryer and then over chill rolls that cool and set the ink before the substrate is transferred to the folder.

ink, job. A heavy-bodied ink formulated to print on uncoated stock run on small sheetfed presses.

ink, long. A lithographic ink with high surface tension, as exhibited when a sample is drawn upward with a spatula from a stationary position and a long string of ink develops when a droplet falls from the spatula. This test can also be used to demonstrate flow.

ink, oxidative-drying. Oil-based inks that set as a result of the chemical reaction between oxygen and the cobalt or manganese driers in the inks, which serve as the catalyst in the drying process, causing ink pigments to adhere to the paper. These inks are most commonly used in sheetfed offset presswork.

ink, paste. An ink with a high-viscosity vehicle. Paste inks are used in lithography and letterpress. See also: *ink, fluid.*

ink, quick-setting. Inks that set by a combination of rapid penetration into paper stock and slow hardening by polymerization. Jobs can be "backed up" sooner if quick-setting inks are used.

ink, soy. See *ink, vegetable.*

ink, thermosetting. An ink that polymerizes to a permanently solid and fusible state when heat is applied.

ink, vegetable. Inks considered to be environmentally friendly because they replace some of the hydrocarbons with soy or other vegetable oils.

ink abrasion. The wearing or grinding action of an ink against a plate.

ink absorbency. The extent that an ink penetrates a substrate.

ink agitator. A revolving cone-shaped device that moves from one end of the fountain to the other keeping the ink soft and flowing.

ink coat, clear. A colorless, printable compound of varnish used as a base on decal paper and as a protective layer printed over a color decal design in screen printing.

ink color strength. The ability of an ink to give a color value to paper; the pigment-to-vehicle ratio.

ink driers. Compounds added to inks that dry by oxidation to aid in their hardening.

ink drum. A metal roller in the ink distribution system of a press that moves back and forth sideways to help mix the ink and reduce ghosting. Alternative terms: *oscillator; vibrator.*

ink dry back. An optical loss of density and color strength that may occur while an ink is setting. To achieve the proper dry density, the ink is printed with a wet density slightly higher than the projected dry density.

ink feed. The amount of ink delivered to the ink form rollers.

ink film graininess. A rough or sandpaper-like appearance in what should be a smooth, continuous ink film on the press sheet.

ink film thickness. The depth of a wet ink film in the ink train or on the ink form rollers.

ink form roller. See *form roller.*

ink form roller setting. The correct pressure adjustment of an ink form roller against the oscillator and the plate.

ink fountain. The trough on a printing press that holds the ink supply to be transferred to the inking system. The operator controls ink volume from adjustment screws or keys on the fountain or from a remote console. The ink fountain consists of an ink reservoir, ink keys, and an ink pan or fountain roller.

ink setting. (1) The increase in viscosity or body (resistance to flow) that occurs immediately after the ink is printed. (2) An adjustment the press operator makes to the inking system to control ink volume.

ink strength. The coloring power of an ink.

ink tack. The sticky or adhesive quality of an ink, which is measured by determining the force required to split an ink film between to surfaces. See also: *tack*.

ink transfer. The amount of ink supplied to a substrate, expressed as a percentage of the total ink available.

ink transparency. The degree to which light passes through an ink film without being absorbed or appreciably scattered.

ink trapping. See *trapping*.

ink vehicle. A complex liquid mixture in which pigment particles are dispersed.

ink-dot scum. On aluminum plates, oxidation characterized by scattered pits that print sharp, dense dots, or ink material trapped in the grain.

inker-feed dampening system. An integrated, continuous-flow dampening system that delivers the dampening solution to the first ink form roller.

inking system. The section of a lithographic press that controls the distribution of ink to the plate. Alternative term: *inking mechanism*.

ink-jet printing. A nonimpact printing process in which a stream of electrostatically charged microscopic ink droplets are projected onto a substrate at a high velocity from a pressurized system. The electrically controlled flow of droplets is either intermittent or continuous.

Ink-jet printing

Inkometer. An instrument that measures the tack and length of printing inks in numerical terms.

ink/water balance. In lithography, the appropriate amounts of ink and water required to ink the image areas of the plate and keep the nonimage areas clean.

in-line converting. Converting done directly from the last printing station or drying unit into the converting machinery in one continuous operation.

in-line finishing. Manufacturing operations such as numbering, addressing, sorting, folding, diecutting, and converting that are performed as part of a continuous operation right after the printing section on a press or on a single piece of equipment as part of the binding process. In-line finishing is common in web printing operations.

input. (1) To enter data or program instructions into a computer system. (2) The data or instructions themselves.

input device. Any mechanism capable of providing the necessary electrical impulses or mechanical signals to transmit data to a machine.

insert. (1) In stripping, a section of film carrying printing detail that is spliced into a larger film. (2) In printing, a page that is printed separately and then bound into the main publication. (3) Assembling signatures one inside of another in sequence. See also: *assembling; collate; gathering.*

insert, free-standing (FSI). A four-page, eight-page, etc., self-contained signature typically added to a newspaper.

inside mortise. An opening cut into a mounted letterpress plate so that text or other matter can be inserted.

intaglio. (1) Any form of printing in which the image areas are engraved or etched below the nonimage areas on the printing plate or cylinder to provide ink-retaining reservoirs or wells. Gravure is considered an intaglio printing process. (2) In papermaking, watermarking from countersunk depressions in the dandy roll to provide a whiter or denser design instead of increased transparency.

integral tripack. Photographic film or paper with three main emulsion layers coated on the same base. Each layer is sensitive to one primary color of light. During processing, a subtractive primary color dye image is formed in each layer.

integrated halftone density. The effective density of a halftone area containing several halftone dots and thus some high-density and low-density areas. It is defined as the logarithm of the reciprocal of the average transmittance or reflectance of the area.

integrated services digital network (ISDN). A communication network intended to carry digitized voice and data multiplexed onto the public network. ISDN uses a group of channels to provide for the simultaneous digital transmission of voice, text, images, and multimedia traffic. It is available in three categories: Basic Rate ISDN (BRI), Primary Rate ISDN (PRI), and Broadband ISDN (B-ISDN). Basic Rate ISDN is a baseband network bundle of two 64-Kbps B (bearer) channels for the transfer of voice, graphics, and data, plus one 16-Kbps D (delta) channel that carries data and call setup information. In the U.S., Primary Rate ISDN provides 23 baseband transmission channels (and one channel for call setup) with data transfer rates starting at 1.544 Mbps.

integrating light meter. An instrument that measures the intensity and the length of an exposure according to predetermined setting.

intelligent character recognition (ICR). A sophisticated form of optical character recognition (OCR) in which the computer determines the probable meaning of a character not by looking for an exact match with a character pattern stored in memory but by analyzing the shape of the character. ICR is, therefore, able to interpret a wide range of different typefaces and point sizes, thus differing from OCR, which is restricted to the specific face and point size combinations stored in the memory. See also: *optical character recognition.*

intensification. Increasing the opacity (or density) of developed and fixed photographic negatives by treating the images with chemicals known as intensifiers.

interactive. A computer program, game, presentation, or other product in which the user has some control over its functioning by using a mouse, keyboard, or other device to communicate with the computer. For example, clicking on a button to go to a certain point in an electronic book is an interactive function.

interface. (1) The electronic device that enables one kind of equipment to communicate with or control another. (2) The combination of hardware and software that allows difference electronic devices to share resources.

interimage reflection. Light that passes between layers of ink and the substrate. Interimage reflection can contribute to additivity failure and other print quality characteristics.

interleave. To insert separate sheets of paper between foil, printed paper, or other stacked sheet material to facilitate handling or to prevent blocking or smudging.

interline spacing. See *leading.* Alternative term: *line spacing.*

intermediate. (1) A contact print from an original negative or positive. (2) A print made from the key layout to produce a set of blueline flats for stripping.

intermediate roller. A friction- or gravity-driven roller between the ductor and form rollers that transfers and conditions the ink. A distributor contacts two rollers. A rider contacts a single oscillator. Alternative term: *transfer roller.*

intermittent jet. See *drop-on-demand ink jet.*

internegative. Negative made from a transparency (positive) to generate photographic prints. Prints made from internegatives are of higher quality than prints made directly from transparencies, but lower in quality than those made directly from a first-generation negative.

Internet. The "official" name for an international network of computer networks linked to provide and share information and resources about a seemingly limitless number of topics. The Internet, as we know it today, grew out of an effort formulated by the United States government in the late 1960s to protect the important data stored on its computers and to ensure the continued electronic transport of this data in the event of a nuclear war.

Internet Explorer. Microsoft's graphical World Wide Web browser.

Internet protocol (IP) address. The 32-bit binary number that identifies the exact location of a computer on the Internet or a network running TCP/IP. See also: *domain name service; transmission control protocol/Internet protocol.*

interpolation. A mathematical technique used in some scanning and graphics programs to increase the apparent resolution of an image.

interrupt request (IRQ). On a PC, the hardware lines over which modems and printers indicate to the microprocessor that data is ready for transfer.

inverse video. Displaying characters on a computer screen in a mode opposite to that of a normal presentation (e.g., white letters on black instead of black letters on white). Alternative term: *reverse.* See also: *knockout.*

inverted pyramid cell. The most common engraved cell formation found on the anilox rollers used in flexographic printing. It carries the ink or coating for transfer to the substrate.

iris diaphragm. The adjustable aperture fitted into the barrel of photographic lenses. It consists of a series of thin metal tongues overlapping each other and fastened to a ring on the lens barrel. The operator turns the ring backward or forward to make the aperture smaller or larger.

ISO 9000 (Q90). "Quality Management and Quality Assurance Standards—Guidelines for Selection and Use." (1) This standard explains fundamental quality concepts, defines key terms, and provides guidance on selecting and using the ISO 9001, 9002, and 9003 standards. (2) A series of international standards (ISO 9000, 9001, 9002, 9003, and 9004) developed in 1987 by the ISO Technical Committee (TC) 176 on quality systems. This series, together with the terminology and definitions contained in ISO Standard 8402, provide guidance on the selection of an appropriate quality management system for a supplier's operation. These standards are not particular to any industry, product, or service. In the United States, the ISO 9000 Series has been adopted as the ANSI/ASQC Q90 Series.

ISO 9001 (Q91). "Quality Systems—Model for Quality Assurance in Design/Development, Production, Installation, and Servicing." A comprehensive standard covering all of the elements listed in ISO 9002 and 9003. In addition, it addresses design, development, and servicing capabilities.

ISO 9002 (Q92). "Quality Systems—Model for Quality Assurance in Production and Installation." This standard addresses the prevention, detection, and correction of problems during production and installation. More extensive and more sophisticated than ISO 9003, it is typically the standard under which printers pursue registration.

ISO 9003 (Q93). "Quality Systems—Model for Quality Assurance in Final Inspection and Testing." The least comprehensive of the ISO standards, it addresses the requirements for detecting and controlling problems during the final inspection and testing.

ISO 9004 (Q94). "Quality Management and Quality System Elements—Guidelines." This standard guides suppliers in developing and implementing a quality system and determining the extent to which each quality system element is applicable. It examines each element of the quality system in greater detail and can be used for internal and external auditing purposes.

isopropyl alcohol. A component of lithographic dampening solution that makes it easier to obtain ink/water balance and reduces the water surface tension so that it covers the nonimage areas of the plate more evenly. Less dampening solution is carried to the blanket because isopropyl alcohol evaporates so rapidly.

italic. A slanted version of a typeface with vertical lines that are between 8° and 20° from the perpendicular to the character baseline. In typeset copy, italic type is used to signify periodical titles and other special information. See also: *oblique.*

J

jacket. The wrapper placed around a finished casebound book.

Java™. A programming language that enables developers to write small applications including animation and other advanced features that can be downloaded and run very quickly with most Internet browsers. See also: *applet.*

jaw folder. Three cylinders in the in-line finishing area of a web press that make one or two parallel folds at right angles to the direction of web travel. Alternative terms: *parallel folder; tucker folder.*

jet. (1) The intensity of black or near-black inks or colored surfaces. (2) See *ink-jet printing.*

jet dryer. An in-line finishing section on a screen-printing press in which hot air is projected at a high velocity onto the freshly printed substrate as it moves along a conveyor belt.

job jacket. The work order on which the instructions for each phase of production are written. The job jacket may also contain the original copy, photos, and line art for the job.

job stick. See *composing stick.*

jog. To align flat, stacked sheets or signatures to a common edge, either manually or with a vibrating table or hopper. Some in-line finishing systems are equipped with a jogger-stacker that piles and aligns folded signatures as they are delivered.

joggers. Two movable devices in the delivery of a sheetfed press that work along with the rear sheet guide and a front gate to align and stack printed press sheets.

Joggers

joint. The flexible portion of a casebound book where the cover meets the spine. It functions as a hinge, permitting the cover to be opened and closed without damaging the spine. Alternative term: *hinge.*

Joint Photographic Experts Group (JPEG). The compression scheme based on the discrete cosine transform (DCT) lossy compression algorithm, that is a defacto standard on the Internet. As developed by the Joint Photographic Experts Group in collaboration with the International Standards Organization (ISO) and the

Consultative Committee for International Telegraphy and Telephony (CCITT), JPEG allows the user to control the compression ratio and reproduction quality at the point of compression. It can also incorporate other algorithms, such as one-dimensional modified Huffman compression for lossless compression. See also: *lossless algorithm; lossy algorithm.*

Jones diagram. A graph that represent steps in tone reproduction from the original to the separation negatives and the printed sheet. The relevant information at each stage is linked to the next by plotting the graphs on a quadrant in such a way that the influence of each successive step is displayed.

jordan machine. A conical rotor and housing that refines fiber slurry in papermaking. It shortens the fibers and improves sheet formation.

justification. The process of composing a line of type by spacing between the words and characters to fill an exact measure, thus aligning the type at both margins. Hyphenation is sometimes employed to achieve justification. In other cases, only the spacing between words is adjusted. See also: *alignment; flush right; flush left; ragged; word spacing.*

justification, vertical. (1) The use of variable spacing between lines, or type elements, vertically in order to fill out a desired column or page depth. (2) Modifying point size and intercharacter spacing instead of vertical spaces in order to force a given block of type to fill a desired depth.

jute. Paper fibers obtained from cutting burlap sacks or from the original source, a plant of the same name that grows in India and Pakistan. Jute is used to form exceptionally hard and durable papers.

K

K and N ink absorbency test. A practical method of comparing the ink absorption rate of different papers by applying a thick film of a nondrying ink to overlapped samples of different papers for a specified time, then removing and wiping them clean; with the depth of stain indicating relative ink absorbency.

K film. A chemical wood pulp produced by the sulfate process, or paper or paperboard made from such pulp.

kaolin. A fine, white clay used as a filler or coating pigment in paper manufacture.

kauri-butanol number. A value given to solvents to indicate their dissolving power relative to a standard—natural kauri gum. For example, blanket washes with a high KB number should be avoided because the solvent is more easily absorbed by the rubber and evaporates more slowly.

Kelvin. A unit of temperature equal to 1/273.16 of the Kelvin scale temperature of the triple point of water.

Kelvin temperature scale. A thermometric scale on which the unit of measurement equals the Celsius degree and according to which absolute zero is 0 K, the equivalent of −273.15°C. Acceptable viewing conditions in the graphic arts are measured in Kelvin. Alternative term: *absolute temperature scale.*

kenaf. An Indian plant with a long fiber in its bark that is suitable for papermaking.

kermit. An older asynchronous communications protocols for file transfer and communication with UNIX machines. It is much slower than other modem protocols. See also: *modem; modem transfer protocols; XMODEM; XMODEM-CRC; YMODEM-G; ZMODEM.*

kerning. Manipulating type character widths and white space to achieve aesthetically pleasing results. Alternative term: *mortise.* See also: *spacing; word spacing.*

AV AV

Kerned (left) and unkerned letters

key. (1) The master layout or flat that is used as a positioning guide for preparing color artwork and/or stripping other film flats. The key is usually prepared from the black printer but may include detail from other colors where registration marks do not appear in the black. Alternative term: *key flat.* See also: *keyline.* (2) In photography, the emphasis on lighter or darker tones in a negative or print. High key indicates the prevalence of light tones; low key the prevalence of darker tones.

key, full-range. A black printer that carries a printable dot throughout the full range of the illustration. The positive has normal contrast.

key, selective. An accent key used to create dark outlines in areas specified by the printer or the client.

key, soft. A black printer that carries a printable dot throughout the full range of the illustration, but with a lower contrast. Its darkest tones do not exceed that of a normal middletone.

key negative. The negative in a set of color separations that represents photographically the portions of the copy that will print as black.

key number. A numeral that appears in small print on an insert. It encodes the publication, issue, and edition into which an insert is to be bound.

key plate. In color printing, the standard plate to which the other color plates are registered. The key plate is normally the plate with the most detail, never the yellow plate.

keyline. A tissue overlay prepared by an artist and used to convey instructions; indicate reverses, backgrounds, and different color areas; or denote special effects. See also: *key*.

kiss impression. The minimum pressure at which proper ink transfer is possible.

knife. (1) In folding machines, the three or four blades at different levels and at right angles to each other that force the paper between the folding rollers. The sheet of paper is pushed from one knife folding mechanism to the other until the desired number of folds have been made. Alternative term: *tucker blade*. (2) A sharp steel blade that trims excess from sheets and/or cuts them to a specific size. Automatic trimmers and cutters have knives that can be programmed to make precise cuts.

knife rollers. See *roller, lint*.

knockout. Type that appears as white on a black or dark colored background. Alternative terms: *reverse; dropout*. See also: *inverse video*.

Knockout

kraft. A thick, usually brown paper or cardboard made from unbleached sulfate wood pulp. It is often used as bag and wrapping paper.

L

lacquer. A solution in an organic solvent that is combined with modifying resins and plasticizers and applied to a substrate to impart glossy, decorative features and provide a protective coating.

laid. A paper finish produced with a dandy roll that has closely spaced wires.

laid antique. A paper finish that simulates the finish of original handmade paper. It is made with a dandy roll.

laid line. One of the fine, closely spaced marks on a laid finish paper. The widely spaced, perpendicular marks are chain lines.

laid paper. A substrate that shows the wire and chain marks when light passes through it.

lake. An ink colorant formed when a soluble dye is converted into a pigment in the presence of an inorganic white base such as alumina hydrate or white gloss.

laketine. A colorless reducer (magnesia in linseed oil) used to extend lithographic inks and lessen their color strength.

laminate. A product made by bonding together two or more layers of material, usually with an adhesive.

lampblack. A black pigment with a carbon base that is used to reduce gloss and produce dull or soft finishes.

LAN. See *local-area network*.

lands. A grid of unetched vertical and horizontal lines on a rotogravure cylinder that form the boundaries of the recessed cells and provide support for the doctor blade.

landscape mode. See *orientation*.

lap. (1) The edge where one color overprints another. Alternative term: *bleed; extended color; full bleed*. (2) The extra edge on one side of a signature gripped by binding equipment during the inserting process. Alternative term: *lip*. See also: *lip*.

lap, economy. A single sheet with an extended lap on a signature that is folded off-center to conserve paper. See also: *lap; lip.*

lap lines. Unwanted lines that are visible when two images from adjacent pieces of film are assembled to appear as one image. Exposing these adjacent films onto a single piece of film or plate can yield a lap line where the films touch each other. Alternative term: *butt lines.*

lap register. Overlapping two colors at their junction to improve image fit and lessen image distortion on the press.

large-scale integration (LSI). The use of integrated circuit technology to place up to 100,000 transistors on a single computer chip.

laser. A high-energy, coherent (single-wavelength) light source. The small spot of light produced by the laser makes it possible to expose light-sensitive and photo-conductive materials at high speed and high resolution.

laser modulation. Varying the light intensity from a laser to create an image.

laser printer. A nonimpact output device that fuses toner to paper to create near-typeset quality text and graphics. The basic technology is similar to that of a photocopier.

Laser printer

laser scanner. A device that uses color filters, electronic circuitry, and beams of light to produce tone- and color-corrected separations from color originals mounted on rotating drums.

laser typesetting. A technique whereby the light source directly imprints images onto paper or film.

laserwriting. Output of digital images onto paper, usually at a resolution of 300 dots per inch.

latent charge. In electrostatic printing, the charge remaining in the areas not exposed to light and dissipated.

latent image. The invisible reproduction retained in an exposed photographic emulsion. Development converts the latent image to a visible image.

lateral hard dot. A gravure process in which shadow dots are square (as in conventional gravure) and the sides of the dots are lined up parallel or lateral to each other. These dots get proportionately smaller as in the areas where they represent middletones and highlights.

lateral reversal. The transposition of text and display type or illustrations so that they will appear as a "mirror image." The conversion of right-reading material to wrong-reading material.

latitude. The degree to which a photographic material produces satisfactory results despite some errors in exposure and development.

lay. The arrangement and position of printed forms on a press sheet.

lay sheet. The first of several sheets run through the press to verify lineup, register, type, and nonimage areas.

layback. The nonprintable distance from the edge of the printing plate to beyond the gripper margin.

layout. A guide prepared to show the arrangement and location of all the type, illustrations, and line art that are combined together to compose the film flat.

layout, rough. A drawing developed from a thumbnail sketch, but more detailed and larger.

layout sheet. The imposition form that indicates where to place negatives on a film flat in locations corresponding to the printed page on the press sheet or a folded dummy.

leader. A character consisting of two or more dots set in a row. • • • • • • • • • • • Leaders are inserted between text on the left- and right-hand sides of   *Leader, dot* a line. In lists, directories, tables of contents, etc., the leader guides the eye from the left-hand text to the right-hand text in the line.

leading. The amount of space between the baseline of one line of type and the baseline of the adjacent line. The space is inserted to separate the type characters on the two lines. Alternative terms: *interline spacing; line spacing.*

leading, additional. Space inserted between lines of type to supplement normal interline (between lines) leading. It is used to make the text aesthetically pleasing, more readable, or fit better in a defined area.

leading, negative. Type set with less space from baseline to baseline than the size of the type itself. Alternative term: *minus leading*.

leading, primary. The prevailing leading between the lines of a piece of typeset text, excluding variations used between elements such as subheads or paragraphs.

leading, reverse. The ability of a phototypesetter to move back up a column or page in a specified amount. Reverse leading is often useful for setting multicolumn work, fractions, and inferior and superior characters.

leading, secondary. (1) An alternate leading value used repeatedly between particular elements such as subheads or paragraphs. (2) In some phototypesetting systems, an alternate value that is used to film advance an individual line upon command. (3) An additional value that is added to the film advance (primary leading) for an individual line upon command.

leaf. (1) A separate, usually blank, sheet of paper in a book. (2) A pigmented stamping material used to decorate book edges.

leafing. The phenomena that occurs when metal flakes in metallic inks float to the surface of the ink, giving it a particular luster.

legend. The title or description beneath or adjacent to an illustration.

length. In rheology, a term used to describe the ability of an ink to flow. The ink is referred to as long or short.

lens. An optical device consisting of glass elements mounted in a barrel that collect and distribute light rays to form an image.

lens, coated. A camera lens covered with an ultra-thin bluish-colored film to minimize glare or flare from extraneous lights in the camera room. This lens is not used for color correction.

lens barrel. The outside covering and support for the several glass elements of an optical device.

lens scale. The chart mounted above the glass elements on a process camera. It aids the operator in quickly and accurately setting iris diaphragm apertures, particularly in halftone photography.

lens speed. The largest aperture, or smallest f-number, at which a lens can be set. A "fast" lens transmits more light and has a larger opening than a "slow" lens.

lensboard. The support that holds the lens in alignment with the optical axis of the camera and allows it to move along that axis in connection with the reproduction percentage adjustment. Alternative term: *front case.*

letter. A graphic, which, when used alone or combined with others represents in a written language one or more sound elements of the spoken language. Diacritical marks used alone and punctuation marks are not letters.

letter, primary. A lowercase letter such as "e," "m," "n," "o," or "c" that does not have ascenders or descenders.

letter fold. Creasing a sheet several times in the same direction with two or more creases wrapping around the inner leaf.

letter quality. A computer printout that resembles the characters produced by a traditional typewriter.

letterpress. The method of printing in which the image, or ink-bearing areas, of the printing plate are in relief, i.e., raised above the nonimage areas. See also: *flexography; relief plate; relief printing.*

Letterpress, rotary

letterset. An offset letterpress printing process. The relief image on the letterpress plate is first transferred to a rubber blanket and then to paper. Unlike offset lithography, this process does not require a dampening system. Alternative term: *dry offset.*

letterspace. To add space between the characters of a word or group of words, either for emphasis, or for aesthetic purposes when justifying short lines in a body of composition.

leveling. Cutting off a small amount of the backbone after roughening on a perfect-bound book. This is done to give the book a flat, square appearance.

library binding. A book bound in conformance with the specifications of the American Library Association. The requirements include stitched signatures, sewn-on four-cord thread, strong endpapers, muslin-reinforced endpapers, and flannel backlining extended into the boards.

lift. A group of sheets cut or trimmed together.

lifting. How well one ink color adheres to a previously printed color, or how well ink adheres to the sheet in lithography. Alternative term: *trapping.*

ligature. Two or more characters that are specially modified in design to be cast or exposed together as one unit, frequently with connecting strokes. Some examples include "fi" and "fl."

fi fl
Ligatures

light. Electromagnetic energy with wavelengths (about 380 to 750 nm) that affect vision.

light face. A term used to describe body text, which is usually set in type that is less bold than the Roman typeface in the same family and size.

light fog. The cloudy appearance of an image caused by accidentally exposing light-sensitive photographic material to extraneous illumination.

light integrator. A device that measures the intensity and duration of an illumination source. A combination of a timer and a light meter, it is used to determine and control uniform film or plate exposures.

light meter. A device used to determine the correct exposure for negatives, positives, and color transparencies. It has three scales; one set for the speed of the emulsion used and one set to the meter reading of the illumination source. The correct exposure (in seconds or fractions of a second) is read from the third scale opposite the various apertures (lens openings) that can be used. Alternative term: *exposure meter.* See also: *photometer.*

light pen. The stylus that detects light on a computer display. Like a mouse, it is used to create and move the elements shown on the monitor in page-layout, text-composition, and computer-graphics programs as well as other interactive communications between a computer system and an operator.

light reaction. In a photographic emulsion or coating, the chemical response produced by exposure to illumination.

light sensitive. A material that is chemically altered after it is exposed to light.

light spectrum. The electromagnetic wavelengths, typically measured in nanometers, that are visible to the human eye. Each color in the light spectrum has a different wavelength.

light table. A glass-topped work area illuminated from underneath and used for pasting up layouts, stripping, opaquing, and otherwise viewing images with transmitted light.

light trap. A baffle entrance or staggered passageways or doors arranged so that photographers can enter and exit a darkroom without admitting stray light. Alternative term: *light lock.*

light-emitting diode (LED). A small electronic component used on some alphanumeric display panels.

lightfastness. The ability of a printed substrate to resist deterioration (fading and yellowing, etc.) caused by sunlight or artificial light.

lighting. The illumination falling on a subject, particularly the direction or arrangement of the illumination.

lightness. Property that distinguishes white from gray or black (dark tones).

lightroom. The area immediately outside of a darkroom, in which the copyboard, lensboard, and illumination system of the graphic arts camera are housed.

lightweight paper. Printing paper that falls in the range of 17–40 lb./25×38-in. ream (25–59 g/m^2).

line art. A drawing with no grays or middletones. Traditionally, black lines on white paper. In computer publishing, an object-oriented graphic. While scanned-in line art is bitmapped, line art created (mathematically) in the computer is a vector, or object-oriented, graphic. See also: *bitmap; object-oriented; raster; vectors.*

line conversion technique. Method of changing a continuous-tone image into a line illustration with bold, dark areas on a light background and no intermediate tones. Alternative term: *two-tone posterization.*

line copy. Type matter and drawings that can be reproduced without the use of a halftone screen. Alternative terms: *line art; line work; line drawing.* See also: *line film.*

line engraving. A printing form in which the image area is cut or etched. Tonal effects are achieved by cross-hatching or by varying the line width or spacing. A halftone screen is not used.

line film. In photography, a film negative or positive with detail consisting solely of solid printing elements such as rules, line drawings, and text matter, as distinguished from halftone and continuous-tone negatives. See also: *line copy.*

line gauge. A ruler scaled in picas and points for a typographer's use. Line gauges come in different sizes, materials, and configurations and may include other scales such as inches, agate lines, etc.

line interleaved. Color data that is organized in the computer line by line (i.e., a line of yellow, a line of magenta, a line of cyan, a line of black, etc.).

line length. The width to which a justified line of type is set. Line length is usually expressed in points and picas in the U.S. or in didots and ciceros in Europe. Alternative term: *line measure.*

line printer. A peripheral device that generates computer output line by line.

line spacing. See *leading.*

line speed. The maximum rate at which data signals can be transmitted over a given channel. It is usually expressed as bits per second or baud rate.

line up. (1) In lithographic stripping and platemaking, to square and position all of the printing detail on the negatives or positives so that the elements are properly aligned. (2) Aligning mixed typefaces or point sizes by adjusting the leading so that all characters are positioned to a common baseline.

linearization. Process of controlling image quality and eliminating variables by adjusting all of the output elements of an imaging system.

linecasting machine. A keyboard or tape-controlled hot-metal device that sets complete lines of type.

linen finish. A paper embossed with the pattern of a linen cloth or plated with actual linen cloth.

linen tester. A small magnifying glass mounted at a distance above its base equal to the focal length of the lens. Originally designed for counting threads in linen, modern achromatic linen testers are widely used to examine negatives, plates, and proofs. See also: *loupe; magnifier.*

liner. A thin, flat sheet of corrugated board that is glued on both outer sides of fluted corrugated board.

liner, release. The component of pressure-sensitive stock that functions as a carrier for the face sheet. Alternative term: *backing sheet.*

lines per inch. Designates the resolution of a halftone screen. Screens with a higher number, such as 120 or 133, have a higher resolution than screens with lower numbers, such as 65 lines per inch. Alternative term: *screen ruling.*

lines per minute. A speed rating given to all typesetters. Expressed in terms of the number of lines of 8-point type, 11 picas wide, set in one minute.

lineup table. A work space specially designed for accurately squaring copy, negatives, and printed sheets.

lining. The reinforcing material pasted on the spine of a casebound book before the cover is applied.

lining tool. A graver with a number of cutting points that match the rulings of standard halftone screens. It is used to manually cut between the dots of a halftone plate. Alternative terms: *multiple graver; shooter.*

lint. Loosely bonded paper surface fibers and dust that accumulates on an offset plate or blanket and interferes with print quality. Alternative terms: *linting; fluffing.*

lint roller. See *roller, lint.*

lip. In saddle-stitched binding, the extended edge of one side of a signature that is gripped to open the signature to the center spread to facilitate inserting. Alternative terms: *lap; pickup.* See also: *lap.*

Lip, low-folio

liquid laminate. A plastic coating material for paper.

liquid photopolymer. A clear, slightly yellow, light-sensitive material that is used to produce relief printing plates for flexography. The liquid photopolymer solidifies when exposed to ultraviolet (UV) light during the platemaking process.

liquid-crystal display. A monitor in which images are formed by a liquid crystal material instead of a laser.

lith developer. See *infectious developer.*

lith film. A high-contrast, slow-speed orthochromatic material used for photomechanical work in the graphic arts. Alternative term: *camera film.*

litho crayon. A pencil-shaped stick consisting of soap, tallow, shellac, wax, and lampblack. Fine artists use it to sketch on grained paper and draw directly on litho stones and metal plates. In the past, it also served as a delicate staging medium for creating halftone relief etchings manually.

litho stone. A natural homogeneous limestone originally employed as the chief printing surface in lithography. Some fine artists still create images with litho stones.

lithography. A printing process in which the image carrier is chemically treated so that the nonimage areas are receptive to water (i.e., dampening or fountain solution) and repel ink while the image areas are receptive to ink and repel water. The image carrier is said to be *planographic,* or flat and smooth. See also: *offset printing.*

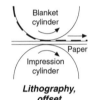

Lithography, offset

lithography, waterless. A planographic printing process that relies on special surface properties of the printing plate, instead of a water-based dampening solution, to prevent ink from adhering to nonimage areas of the plate. The nonimage areas of this "waterless" plate consist of an ink-repellent silicone rubber layer. The process also requires special inks and temperature-controlled inking systems.

live matter. Type that will be printed.

livering. An irreversible increase in the body of an ink often caused by a chemical change during storage.

lobe. A small piece of a film negative that projects beyond its normal trimmed rectangular form to retain positioning marks for registration.

local-area network (LAN). A group of interconnected computers that allow several people at the same business site to access the same set of documents. See also: *network.*

logotype. A ligature, special symbol, trademark, trade name, or any other combination of characters, words, or phrases produced as a single graphic and allocated a given width in a typesetting system.

long-distance network. See *network; wide-area network.*

lookup table. A chart, stored in computer memory, that stores the dot sizes needed to produce given colors. The processed input signals of certain color scanners are used to search the table to find the values that will produce the color represented by the signals.

loose color. Term refers to the film negatives or positives of images that have been color-separated and are returned to the customer as separate negatives instead of as laminated or overlay proofs.

loose line. A line of type in which interword spacing is excessive. A pattern or *river* of white space is often visible in a paragraph with a significant number of loose lines.

loose register. Term used when each color image on a press sheet is relatively independent of all others and slight variations in press register are inconsequential.

loose-leaf binding. A process in which individual sheets can be inserted and removed at will from a section of a larger document often held in a three-ring binder.

lossless algorithm. A mathematical formula for image compression that assumes that the likely value of a pixel can be inferred from the values of surrounding pixels. Because lossless compression algorithms do not discard any of the data, the decompressed image is identical to the original.

lossy algorithm. A mathematical formula for image compression in which the data in an image that is least perceptible to the eye is removed. This improves the speed of data transfer but causes a slight degradation in the decompressed image.

loupe. An adjustable-focus magnifier incorporating a precise measuring scale, with or without a self-contained light source. It is used to inspect fine detail. See also: *linen tester; magnifier.*

low key. A photographic or printed image in which the main interest area lies in the shadow end of the tonal scale.

lowercase. The uncapitalized letters of the alphabet. Originally called lowercase because the lead type version was located in the lower portion of the California Job Case. Alternative term: *minuscules.* See also: *uppercase.*

lug. Metal pins used to hold strips of punched metal or plastic in position against an image carrier or camera back.

lupe. See *loupe.*

lux. A metric unit of illumination.

luxometer. A photoelectric device used to control the duration of camera exposures according to actinicity and fluctuation of camera lamps.

lux-second. A unit of exposure expressed in the metric measure for illumination. A lux-second is equivalent to that produced by the illumination intensity of 1 candela at a distance of 1 meter for 1 second. The English unit of exposure is the footcandle-second.

M

M weight. The heaviness of 1,000 sheets of paper in a specific basic size.

machine code. A computer command in language that the computer or typesetter can understand without translation.

machine dependent. A computer or typesetting function that is limited by the speed or processing characteristics of the equipment with which it is associated.

machine direction. The grain position, or the direction that the sheet moved as it was formed in the papermaking machine. See also: *grain direction.*

machine engraving. Process of cutting designs onto a gravure printing cylinder mechanically with a lathe and special cutting tools.

machine etching. Mechanically or electrically applying etching solution to the metal surface of printing plates.

machine finish. Method of smoothing a paper's surface by passing it through sets of calendering rollers on the papermaking machine.

machine glaze. A highly polished finish that is applied to one side of the paper as it dries against the polished surface of a large-diameter cylinder on a papermaking machine.

machine language. A set of instructions that a computer or typesetter recognizes directly and then interprets to execute a particular process or program.

machine readable. Text encoded and stored in digital format, or, in the case of optical character recognition, translatable to digital form by an appropriate input device.

machine-independent language. Computer programming codes that require compilers to translate from a source program to a machine-coded object program. Some examples include BASIC, COBOL, and FORTRAN.

macro. A predetermined sequence of commands programmed as one command during the assembly of a computer program. Macros enable users to execute a number of commands with a single keystroke.

magazine. In hot-metal typography, the storage compartments in the circulation system of the character matrices.

magenta. The subtractive transparent primary color that should reflect blue and red and absorb green light. It is one of the four process-color inks used in the printing process. Alternative term: *process red.*

magenta printer. (1) The plate that prints magenta ink. (2) The color separation film that will be used to produce the magenta printing plate.

magnetic brush developer. (1) The brush that transfers toner particles to charged areas of a photoconductor in dry toner systems and some magnetographic printing systems. (2) A method of transferring toner to develop an electrostatic image in which iron filings are included in the toner.

magnetic ink. Ink pigments that are treated so that optical character recognition equipment can recognize and read the printed characters later. The account numbers and transfer information on bank checks are printed with magnetic inks.

magnetic ink character recognition. (1) Specially designed machine-readable characters used extensively in check printing. (2) Using a special machine to identify characters printed with magnetic ink.

magnetic media. Any form of computer storage with a magnetic surface that retains data.

magnetic printing. Printing method in which a magnetic printhead transfers its image to a magnetized drum that picks up toner with the opposite magnetic polarity and transfers it to the substrate to form the printed image when the drum is demagnetized. Alternative term: *magnetographic printing.*

magnetic storage. Any disk, film, tape, drum, or core that is used to house electronic information.

magnetic tape. A medium for storing large amounts of binary electronic data bits, especially color separation and correction information in the graphic arts.

magnifier. A convex lens system used to enlarge the appearance of objects and to examine photographic and printing detail. See also: *linen tester; loupe.*

mailing lists. Discussion groups or information forums in which users participate via electronic mail. Some mailing lists are "echoed," or posted, to the UseNet News network. See also: *UseNet News.*

main exposure. The primary camera exposure made through a halftone screen to produce a halftone negative. Additional secondary (bump and flash) exposures may be made to improve detail.

main frame. The central processing unit (CPU) of a computer. This term usually refers to large computers that process considerable amounts of data, such as payroll.

major filter. See *filter, major.*

major-minor filter. See *filter, major-minor.*

makeovers. (1) In lithography, producing screened positive separations in several different sizes from a single set of continuous-tone negative separations. (2) Any printing plate or film that has to be remade because it is defective.

makeready. All of the operations necessary to get the press ready to print a job.

makeready book. A pile of clean, unprinted sheets interspersed with waste sheets and used during makeready.

makeready tissue. A thin paper, usually 0.001 or 0.002 in. thick, used to compensate for variables in packing during offset and letterpress printing. See also: *packing.*

makeup. Assembling text, illustrations, graphs, charts, rules, tabular material, and running heads or feet into a completed page. Stripping, pasteup, and electronic pagination are all forms of makeup. Alternative term: *page layout.*

Malcolm Baldrige National Quality Award. An award established by Congress in 1987 to raise awareness of quality management and to recognize those U.S. companies that have implemented successful quality management systems.

MAN. See *metropolitan-area network.*

manifest system. See *cradle-to-grave system.*

manifold paper. A very thin paper, frequently used as carbon-copy paper in multipart forms.

manila. A fiber used to manufacture strong, tough papers. It is obtained from cordage or rope or directly from the hemp plants that grow in the Philippines and Central and South America.

manuscript. The original text copy submitted to the typesetter electronically, on a computer disk, or in typewritten form.

mapping. Converting encoded data from one format to another, particularly in database management.

margin. The white space extending from the edge of the printed image to a page's trim edge.

marks. The lines on films, flats, printing plates, and press sheets that serve as guides for positioning, registering, printing, and binding a job.

markup. Indicating the typographic specifications for a job, including type style and size, format and spacing, and sometimes machine codes, directly on the manuscript, to guide the typesetter.

mask. (1) A photographic negative or positive of a subject. It is placed over a color transparency or individual separation to selectively increase total density. Masks are used to reduce the tonal scale, improve highlight or shadow detail, and correct color excesses or deficiencies. The process itself is referred to as *masking.* (2) A sheet placed over or around printing detail on a transparency to prevent the passage of actinic light during exposure. (3) A pasteup overlay that indicates the placement of art requiring special handling. (4) A thin sheet used to secure the white margins on a photograph.

masking, two-stage. A color correction process in which a full-range positive premask is made from one separation negative. It is combined with another separation negative to make a final mask that, when returned to the first negative, will correct for some of the unwanted ink absorptions without lowering contrast. A total of three premasks and three final masks are produced in this process.

masking film, peelable. See *Rubylith.*

masstone. The color of an ink in bulk, such as in a can, or of a thick ink film. It is the color of light reflected by the pigment and often differs from the printed color of the ink.

master. (1) The original from which subsequent copies are made. (2) The final copy (paginated film or paper) upon which all changes have been made and approved before printing.

master page. The page in a computer pagination program on which all headers, rules, and other elements that will repeat on all of the pages of a document are set.

masthead. Information identifying the title, ownership, management, subscription rates, and other pertinent information concerning a newspaper or periodical. Alternative term: *flag*.

material safety data sheet (MSDS). A product specification form used to record information about the hazardous chemicals and other health and physical hazards employees face in an industrial workplace, along with guidelines covering exposure limits and other precautions. Employers are required to compile and maintain files of this information under the OSHA Hazard Communication Standard set forth by the U.S. federal government. See also: *Hazard Communication Standard*.

math coprocessor. The secondary microprocessor that performs complex calculations thereby increasing the speed of the central processing unit.

matrix. (1) An arrangement of typesetting characters in a case or font grid. (2) In hot-metal typesetting, the molds from which relief metal type characters are formed by pouring or pressing hot metal. (3) In flexographic platemaking, the mold cast from a metal engraving into thermosetting materials from which a rubber flexo plate is shaped.

matte. A flat, dull, slightly roughened surface that scatters the specular component of light and causes any underlying tones to appear lighter. A matte surface lacks gloss or luster.

matte finish. (1) A dull, nonreflecting photographic surface. It is usually less suitable for reproduction than a photograph with a glossy finish. (2) Paper with a dull surface.

maximum latency time. The longest duration for a memory unit to move to a new location on a disk.

Maxwell triangle. Equilateral color polygon that shows the composition of the ranges of colors produced by additive mixtures of red, green, and blue light.

measure. The length of a typeset line, expressed in picas.

measurement area. The effective area of a target "seen" by the densitometer.

mechanical. The assembly of all page elements, including text and line art, properly proportioned and positioned, in camera-ready form. Alternative term: *pasteup.*

mechanical binding. See *binding, mechanical.*

mechanical pulp. See *groundwood.*

mega. One million.

megabit. One million bits.

megabyte. One million bytes.

megahertz (MHz). One million hertz.

memory. The area in an electronic device where binary-coded information is stored.

menu. The display of the computer control program that appears on the monitor. This list of operations a computer can perform presents options or choices for the user.

menu-driven. The computer program that allows the user to direct operations by selecting from a series of hierarchical choices displayed on the monitor.

mercury vapor lamp. An enclosed light source that produces radiation by passing an electrical current through gaseous mercury. At one time, mercury vapor lamps were the primary means of exposing sensitized printing plates. This is no longer true.

mesh. The open space between the threads of a woven screen printing fabric; also, the threads collectively on the fabric itself.

mesh aperture. The space between the woven threads of screen printing fabric, through which the ink passes during printing.

mesh marks. (1) A fine, cross-hatch pattern left by the mesh of the screen printing fabric, after an ink film without sufficient flowout has dried. (2) A condition occurring when certain areas of the screen do not properly separate from the substrate, because of poor fabric tensioning or insufficient off-contact distance.

mesh opening. In screen printing, a measure of the distance across the space between two parallel threads, expressed in microns.

metallic ink. An ink with fine aluminum, bronze, or copper powders in its pigment.

metameric. A color that changes hue under different illumination sources.

metamerism. The process in which a change in an illumination source will cause visual shift in the hue of a color.

metering nip. The line of contact between two rollers in the dampening system of a lithographic press.

metering roller. (1) In lithography, a roller that transfers dampening solution either to the oscillator from the pan roller or directly from the water pan to the transfer roller. (2) A transfer roller that supplies a thin, even layer of coating to a substrate.

metering unit. A series of two or more rollers on a web press paper roll stand. The metering unit smooths the web and maintains constant web tension throughout the printing unit. Alternative term: *infeed rollers.*

metropolitan-area network (MAN). Groups of computers linked over a limited regional area.

mezzograph. (1) A halftone screen with a grain formation instead of ruled lines. (2) A printing plate in which the details and tones have been transferred through a halftone screen with a grain formation. Alternative term: *metzograph.*

mezzotint. An engraving produced on a roughened copper plate. The highlight and midtone areas are hand-scraped to reduce ink retention; while shadow areas are burnished to strengthen ink retention.

microlines. Resolution elements used in the graphic arts to ensure the optimum exposure of photomechanical materials. The width of the parallel lines on the target and the distance between the lines is measured in microns.

micrometer. A calibrated instrument used to measure the thickness of paper and plate and blanket packing.

micrometer, dead-weight. A device that uses the unrelieved weight of an anvil to obtain repeatable measurements from plates, blankets, and packing. See also: *blanket thickness gauge; Cady gauge.*

microprocessor. The silicon chip housing the thousands of transistors and other components at the base of a personal computer's central processing unit. See also: *central processing unit.*

microwave communications. A transmission method that utilizes a range of frequencies within the electromagnetic spectrum above 1 gigahertz (GHz). Large line-of-sight antennas or dishes are used to transmit the microwave signals for at least 25 miles before the signal must be amplified or repeated.

MIDI. See *musical instrument digital instrument.*

midtone dot. A point in a middle-gray area of a halftone. Its area equals or approaches the average of the nearby background areas. Together all midtone dots have a checkerboard-like appearance.

midtones. The range of tonal values between halftone highlight and shadow areas. Alternative term: *middletones.* See also: *quartertone.*

mileage. The surface area covered by a given quantity of ink or coating material.

milking. A coating buildup on the nonimage areas of the offset blanket that usually occurs when the coating softens because it does not adequately resist water.

mill broke, dry. Trimmings, clippings, and other paper mill waste, such as that from small unusable butt rolls or obsolete inventories.

mill broke, wet. The fibers that drain off and the damp paper that breaks away during the slurry phase of papermaking. See also: *slurry.*

milling head. The device on a perfect binder that chops off the folded spines of the signatures to expose the individual sheets to the glue.

MIME. See *multipurpose Internet mail extensions.*

minor-minor filter. See *filter, minor-minor.*

minuscules. See *lowercase.*

misregister. Printed images that are incorrectly positioned, either in reference to each other or to the sheet's edges. See also: *register.*

misting. Flying ink that forms fine droplets or filaments that become diffused throughout the pressroom.

mnemonic. Something that is easy to remember, such as a mnemonic code used in typesetting to denote a typeface (TR for Times Roman) or the size of a headline or text.

modem (modulator/demodulator). The interface, or communications link, between one computer workstation and another, or a network of computers. A modem converts digital information into analog signals suitable for transfer over (analog) telephone lines. It also converts the analog signal from phone lines into digital information. See also: *interface.*

modem transfer protocols. The set of standard rules that computers use to communicate and exchange files with one another when connected via modem. See also: *kermit; XMODEM, XMODEM-CRC, YMODEM, YMODEM-G, ZMODEM.*

moiré. An undesirable, unintended interference pattern caused by the out-of-register overlap of two or more regular patterns such as dots or lines. In process-color printing, screen angles are selected to minimize this pattern. If the angles are not correct, an objectionable effect may be produced.

molleton. A thick cotton fabric similar to flannel. It has a long nap and is used to cover form rollers in conventional lithographic dampening.

monitor screen. A cathode-ray tube or liquid crystal display device on which image information is displayed in conjunction with a workstation. See also: *display device.*

Monitor screen and keyboard of workstation

monochromatic. A single color or shades of a single color.

monochrome. An original or reproduction in one color. See also: *monotone.*

monospace. A term used to refer to type characters that are assigned equal width values.

monotone. A reproduction in one color, particularly in gravure photography. See also: *monochrome.*

montage. (1) A group of related subjects that have been combined together to form a single, or composite, illustration. Alternative term: *photocombining*. See also: *composite*. (2) Mounting several color separation films that will print in the same color in register for subsequent transfer to the printing form. See also: *gang*.

mortise. See *kerning*.

mortising. (1) In stripping, to cut out incorrect text and replace it with the correct text on film cut to fit the space without overlapping. (2) In typesetting, kerning characters for aesthetic reasons.

Mosaic (NCSA). The first graphical World Wide Web browser as developed by the University of Illinois' National Center for Supercomputing Applications (NCSA) in 1993. By supporting the display of photographic images and the ability to access sound and video, it has fueled the expansion of Internet connectivity in the business and consumer sectors and, in turn, commercial applications for the WWW. Several other licensed versions of Mosaic are available, and Marc Andersson, the student who created Mosaic went on to develop the commercial browser Netscape Navigator. See also: *Netscape Navigator*.

mottle. A blotchy, cloudy, or galvanized appearance instead of a smooth, continuous ink film on the press sheet. Mottle patterns are random rather than symmetrical and occur when the substrate does not absorb the ink evenly.

mount. (1) To secure the page elements to a layout board. (2) To fasten the plate or blanket to an offset press. (3) The wood or metal base on which a letterpress printing plate is permanently fastened for use on a press.

mouse. A small, hand-held device used to position the cursor on the computer screen. When the mouse is rolled across its pad or another flat surface, the cursor moves a corresponding distance across the display monitor.

Mouse

movable type. The individual metal or wooden type characters that are taken from the typecase, arranged to form words and sentences, and then returned to the case for reuse later.

Mullen tester. A machine that measures the bursting strength of paper.

multicolor. Two or more colors.

multicolor press. Two or more connected printing units (each with its own inking and dampening system), a feeder, a sheet transfer system, and a delivery. Two or more colors can be printed on one side of a sheet during a single pass through the press.

Multicolor press

multi-imaging camera. A device that produces an imposed signature on one piece of film from several single-page transmission or reflection originals. Alternative term: *imposing camera.* See also: *step-and-repeat.*

multimedia. Combining more than one means of providing information—text, audio, animation, and full-motion video—for use as a teaching tool, in a presentation, or for entertainment purposes. CD-ROMs are often used to store the enormous amount of data necessary to create and run a multimedia product.

multiple printing. Reproducing two or more images, by separate exposures, onto a single piece of film. If the images are to any extent superimposed, the process is called *surprinting.*

multiple-sheet proof. See *overlay proof.*

multiplexing. Transmitting multiple messages simultaneously over one communications channel.

multipurpose Internet mail extensions (MIME). The Internet standard that defines how graphics and other multimedia files are transferred via email and through web browsers.

multitasking. The ability of a computer to run more than one application at a time.

Munsell color system. A method of classifying surface color in a solid. The vertical dimension is called value, the circumferential dimension is called hue, and the radial dimension is called chroma. The colors in the collection are spaced at subjectively equal visual distances.

Murray-Davies equation. In the graphic arts, a relationship used to calculate the relative apparent dot area in a halftone tint by comparing the light absorbing power of the tint to that of a solid. See also: *Yule-Nielsen equation.*

musical instrument digital interface (MIDI). The communications protocol for the exchange of information between computers and synthesizers.

Mylar. DuPont's registered tradename for its clear polyester film, which is used in stripping operations.

N

nailhead. A paper-covered book that is thickest at the spine. A book that has an end profile resembling a nail.

nanometer. A unit of measuring wavelengths of electromagnetic radiation. One nanometer is one-billionth of a meter. Visible light wavelengths range from 400–700 nanometers.

narrow band. Data transmission facilities operating at speeds up to 200 bits per second.

narrow-band filters. Translucent devices that permit a relatively limited range of light wavelengths to pass through.

National Ambient Air Quality Standards. Maximum allowable level for a certain pollutant in outdoor air.

NCR (No-carbon-required) paper. See *carbonless paper.*

near-letter quality. A term describing type produced by a dot-matrix printer with additional print head wires that create a more solid-looking character, or an ordinary number of print heads that strike each character a second time to increase dot density.

negative. A photographic film or plate that is exposed and processed to provide a reversed image of the tones found on the original—highlights and shadows or color values (i.e., white as black). See also: *positive.*

Negative (left) and original image

negative paper. A specially coated photographic material used to produce paper negatives.

negative sheet. See *diffusion transfer.*

negative varnish. A protective film applied to the face of photographic negatives.

negative-working plate. A printing plate that is exposed through a film negative. The plate areas exposed to light become the image areas.

Netscape Navigator. The first commercial graphical World Wide Web browser as developed by Marc Andersson who had created the Mosaic graphical browser while a student at the University of Illinois. See also: *Mosaic (NCSA)*.

network. A computer system that allows several users at remote terminals to exchange data electronically through a common central computer or with a modem over conventional telephone lines. See also: *local-area network; long-distance network*.

Network,
bus topology

network interface card (NIC). The device that links one workstation to another in a network.

Neugebauer equations. A set of linear equations used to calculate the tristimulus values of halftone color mixtures and combinations when the dot areas of the contributing colors are known.

neutral. Any color that has no hue, such as white, gray, or black.

neutral density filter. A translucent device that uniformly reduces all colors of light.

neutral pH paper. Acid-free paper that is neither acidic nor alkaline.

neutral wedge. See *gray scale*.

news inks. Printing inks specially designed to run on newsprint. Consisting basically of carbon black or colored pigments dispersed in mineral oil vehicles, news inks dry by absorption. Emulsification, oxidation, and heatset systems are also employed.

newsgroup An individual information forum about a specific topic on UseNet News. See also: *UseNet News*.

newspaper lines. A setting speed used for newspaper phototypesetters, usually in terms of the number of lines of 8-point type, 11 picas wide, set in one minute.

newsprint. A paper manufactured mostly from groundwood or mechanical pulp specifically for the printing of newspapers. It has a basis weight of about 25 to 32 pounds.

Newton's rings. A pattern of minute, colored, concentric, annular shapes that form between closely spaced polished surfaces (such as between the back of the film and the vacuum-frame glass). These colored patterns result from an interference between the transmitted exposure light and its reflected beam from the closely adjacent surface. They sometimes reproduce as unwanted mottling of halftones or tint areas.

nib. The head of an electrically actuated small wire or stylus through which charges can be deposited on printing material, or heat can be applied locally to an inking ribbon.

nip. (1) The line of contact between two press cylinders. (2) A crease line at the joint of a case-bound book. It gives books uniform bulk and reduces the swelling caused by the sewing thread. See also: *smash.*

nippers. In bookbinding, the flat irons on a "building-in" machine or casing-in line. When heated, the nippers clamp the book joint, joining the case and the book at the base.

nipping. In binding, squeezing and clamping books or signatures after sewing or stitching to remove excess air and reduce the swell caused by stitching. Hard papers are nipped and soft papers are smashed. See also: *smash.*

no-carbon-required paper. See *carbonless paper.*

nodal points. Two areas on the axis of a lens positioned so that a ray of light entering the lens in the direction of one of the points leaves the lens as if it had originated in the other point, parallel to the actual original direction.

node. Any workstation on a computer network.

nominal weight. The basis weight for ordering and specifying paper. The actual basis weight to which it is made, allowing for manufacturing tolerances.

nonactinic. Photographic term for light rays that do not affect certain sensitized surfaces within a reasonable length of time. Nonactinic light rays do not influence an exposure or cause any other sort of photographic change.

nonbearer-contact press. A press designed with a slight gap or clearance between the bearers on the plate and blanket cylinders to keep them from running in contact with each other.

noncontact printing. See *nonimpact printer.*

nongear streaks. Marks that appear in the printing and run parallel to the cylinder axis; however, they bear no relation to the distance between the gear teeth.

nonimage area. The portion of a lithographic printing plate that is treated to accept water and repel ink when the plate is on press. Only the ink-receptive areas will print an image.

nonimpact printer. A printing device that creates letters or images on a substrate without striking it. Large, high-speed and ordinary office photocopiers, as well as laser and ink-jet printers are just some examples.

noninfectious developer. Solution used to process continuous-tone photographs. See also: *infectious developer.*

nonpareil. (1) A unit of type equivalent to one-half of a pica or approximately one-twelfth of an inch. (2) In bookbinding, a pattern of variegated colors in a small incomplete oval design on marbled endpapers.

nonprocess printing. Color printing in which the desired color is achieved by using an ink of that color (such as a PMS color) instead of yellow, magenta, and cyan (the process colors).

nonread color. Any highly reflective color that cannot be detected by a scanner or OCR device. Nonread colors are used as visual guides and do not interfere with data readings. Alternative term: *nonscan ink.* See also: *read color.*

nonread ink. The ink vehicle used to create a nonread color. See also: *dropout ink; read color.*

nonreflective ink. Most often a black ink used to form the optical characters that are read by OCR devices. This nonreflective ink contrasts greatly with the paper, and enables the scanner to form a recognition pattern to identify the characters.

nonrepro blue. A color that a photographic film does not differentiate from the white areas of the pasteup. Because this color will not print, special nonrepro blue pens and markers are used to indicate crop marks, instructions, and corrections on the actual pasteup board.

nonreproducible colors. Colors in an original scene or photograph that are impossible to duplicate with a given set of colorants (process inks or PMS colors), because they are outside of the color gamut.

nonscan ink. See *nonread ink.*

normal-key copy. Photographic copy in which the main interest area is in the middletone range of the tone scale or distributed throughout the entire tonal scale.

no-screen exposure. See *bump exposure.*

notch. Small serrations along one edge of a film negative that are used to identify and position it.

notch binding. Small serrations cut in the spine of a perfect-bound book and filled with glue. This method eliminates the need to mill material off the spine of the book.

nozzle. The orifice through which jets of ink are ejected to form an image in the ink-jet printing process.

numbering. Printing figures by hand or machine in a consecutive order.

O

object linking and embedding (OLE). A Microsoft standard for creating dynamic links between documents that can be updated automatically. OLE is also used to embed a document created in one application within another application. It is incorporated into both Windows and Macintosh system software.

object-oriented. Graphic images created with mathematical descriptions, in terms of x-y coordinates instead of the pixels found in a bitmap. Object-oriented graphics can usually be displayed or printed at the full resolution of the monitor or output device, offering more precision than bitmapped images. See also: *bitmap; line art; raster; vectors.*

oblique. A simulated italic character produced electronically from standard Roman fonts.

obliquing. Electronically slanting characters by distorting an upright typeface so that each character is properly seated on the horizontal baseline while its upright axis deviates somewhat from the vertical in a forward or backward direction.

Occupational Safety and Health Act. A federal law enacted in 1970 to protect workers from industrial hazards. Occupational Safety and Health Administration (OSHA) inspectors may appear unannounced or at the request of an employee to examine any plant for violations of the safety and health standards set forth by the act.

ochre. Naturally occurring yellow iron oxide pigment.

octavo. A sheet folded to form 8 leaves or 16 pages, or a book prepared from sheets so folded. The page size varies with the sheet dimensions, but this binding term is sometimes used to designate a page that is approximately 8×5 in. Alternative terms: *8vo or 8°.*

off bearers. In lithography, the cylinder arrangement in which the plate and blanket cylinder bearers do not contact each other while running on impression.

off square. A paper or cardboard sheet that has been cut or trimmed in such a way that two or more corners deviate from an exact 90° angle.

off-color. Print lacking the correct or standard color.

off-contact printing. Screen printing with the screen lowered to a point slightly above the substrate. The squeegee is drawn across the screen with downward pressure, pressing the stencil in contact with the substrate.

offline. (1) System components that are not interconnected and cannot communicate directly. (2) A mode of computer operation in which there is no physical link between peripheral equipment or devices and the central processing unit. Sometimes one auxiliary program or peripheral unit at a time can be connected, or put "on-line," but only if other units and programs are temporarily disabled. See also: *online.*

offline converting. Coating, cutting, folding, embossing, stamping, or otherwise altering newly printed sheets or rolls of material to form the final printed piece or product on a machine separate from the printing press. Printing plants may have dedicated converting equipment or they may send the work to companies that specialize in converting. See also: *in-line finishing; in-line converting.*

off-machine coating. Applying coating to paper in an operation separate from papermaking. See also: *on-machine coating.*

off-press proofing. A simulation of the printed piece created photochemically for the purpose of checking color, position, and register prior to making printing plates. See also: *prepress proofing.*

offset. The transfer of unwanted wet ink from a freshly printed press sheet to the back of the next sheet that is deposited against it in the delivery pile. See also: *setoff.*

offset gravure. A printing process in which the gravure image carrier (usually a cylinder) transfers ink to a rubber blanket that deposits the ink on the surface to be printed. Offset gravure is used to achieve special printed effects on metal surfaces and, in combination with flexography, to print on flexible packages.

offset printing. An indirect printing method in which the inked image on a press plate is first transferred to a rubber blanket, that in turn "offsets" the inked impression to a press sheet. In offset lithography, the printing plate has been photochemically treated to produce image areas and nonimage areas receptive to ink and water respectively. See also: *dry offset; lithography.*

Offset lithography

OK sheet. A press sheet that closely matches the prepress proof and has been approved by the customer and/or production personnel. It is used as a guide to judge the quality of the rest of the production run.

OK with corrections. A proof marked to indicate that, except for a few minor corrections, it is approved and satisfactory.

oldstyle type. Roman typefaces that are based on earlier hand-drawn characters and distinguished in design from modern typefaces by their clear, strong features; the comparative uniform thickness of all strokes; the absence of hairlines; the irregularities among individual letters; and the diagonal serifs, curves, and cross-strokes.

oleophilic. Oil-receptive, as in the image areas of a lithographic printing plate.

oleophobic. Oil-repellent, as in the dampened nonimage areas of a lithographic printing plate.

on-contact printing. Screen printing with the underside of the screen in full contact with the substrate.

on-demand printing. See *demand printing.*

one-piece film. See *composite.*

one-side combination layout. A layout that combines several different forms on the same plate. Alternative term: *gang-run layout.*

one-side multiple layout. A layout with two or more duplicates of the same image on one plate. Alternative term: *step-and-repeat layout.*

one-up. Printing a single image once on a press sheet. See also: *simplex; two-up.*

onionskin. A lightweight, air-dried, cockle-finish bond paper.

online. The state of a computer being connected to and communicating with another electronic device for the purpose of distributing or retrieving information. See also: *electronic mail; offline.*

on-machine coating. Applying coating to the paper in-line as it is made on the paper machine. See also: *off-machine coating.*

opacimeter. An instrument used to measure the opacity of paper.

opacity. The degree to which light will not pass through a substrate or ink. See also: *contrast ratio; covering power.*

opaque. (1) Any material that will not permit the passage of light. (2) In photography, a nontransparent pigment (usually red or black) applied to pinholes or other areas of film negatives to prevent light from passing through during platemaking.

open. (1) Slightly underexposing and developing a halftone negative so that the printed illustration will be fuller and darker than the original because the halftone dots formed are somewhat larger than would normally be obtained. (2) A word used to characterize the visual appearance of typographic matter that is widely spaced or surrounded by large amounts of white space. This effect is used to avoid the dense, block-like appearance of solid masses of type.

open prepress interface (OPI). A set of standardized protocols that allows desktop equipment to be linked with color electronic prepress systems (CEPS).

open system interconnection (OSI). The ISO protocol standard for cross-system communications. It divides the communications process into physical, data-link, network, transport, session, presentation, and applications layers and defines what protocols should be implemented at each layer. OSI has also incorporated the IEEE's physical network standards for Ethernet, token-ring passing bus, and Token Ring into its specifications. See also: *Ethernet; token-passing bus; Token Ring.*

open unit. A printing unit configuration that consists of a plate cylinder, blanket cylinder, and impression cylinder. The plate cylinder is located in line, usually above the blanket cylinder while the impression cylinder is at a near right angle to the blanket cylinder. This configuration prints one color on one side of the substrate. A typical multicolor sheetfed press utilizes multiple open-unit printing units connected by transfer cylinders.

operating system. The master program that a computer needs to start up and perform basic tasks. It allows the computer to control itself and perform other functions, such as managing memory allocation for application software and data files.

operation, real-time. A computer system that processes data as other portions of the system transmit it.

opponent-process model. A theory of color vision that assumes the existence of long-, medium-, and short-wavelength cone receivers linked to cells that process stimuli in an opponent. Refined by Leo M. Hurvich and Dorothea Jameson, it contains elements of the Young-Helmholtz and Hering theories.

optical axis. The photographic term for an imaginary line drawn directly through the focus and the center of the lens.

optical bar recognition (OBR). See *optical mark recognition.*

optical brightener. A colorless dye that absorbs ultraviolet radiation and emits it as visible radiation. The visual brightness of paper is increased by using an optical brightener.

optical centering. Positioning type or art slightly above true center to make it appear centered with respect to the top and bottom of the page.

optical character readers (OCR). Equipment that scans, interprets, and converts any copy or graphic elements to a machine-readable format. See also: *optical mark readers.*

optical character recognition (OCR). A technique in which any printed, typed, or handwritten copy or graphic images are scanned by an electronic reader that converts the information into a form that can be read, interpreted, and displayed by computers. See also: *intelligent character recognition.*

optical character recognition (OCR) inks. Inks composed of low-reflectance pigments, such as carbon black, which can be read by OCR devices. See also: *optical mark recognition inks.*

optical character recognition (OCR) paper. Paper made for the specific needs of optical character recognition equipment.

optical density. See *density.*

optical disk. A form of data storage in which a laser records data on a disk that can be read with a lower-power laser pickup.

optical dot gain. See *dot gain.*

optical mark readers (OMR). Electronic equipment that scans, interprets, and converts barcoded information into a machine-readable form. Optical mark readers detect the presence of clearly positioned, accurately spaced bar marks rather than data characters. Print quality is less important than it is during optical character recognition. OMRs are used in inventory control systems, libraries, and grocery stores. Alternative term: *optical bar readers.* See also: *optical character readers.*

optical mark recognition. A technique by which electronic readers scan, interpret, and translate bar marks, rather than data characters, into a machine-readable form.

optical mark recognition (OMR) inks. Inks composed of low-reflectance pigments similar to OCR inks, which can be read by OMR devices. Alternative term: *optical bar recognition inks*. See also: *optical character recognition inks*.

optical reversal. Using mirrors or prisms to laterally reverse camera images.

optical scanning. Using OCR devices to "read" specific, programmed patterns, which, when identified, are stored in computer memory.

optical sensitizing. Rendering photographic emulsions color sensitive by adding sensitizing dyes.

optimum color reproduction. A duplication that represents the best compromise within the capabilities of a given printing system.

organic pigments. General classification of pigments manufactured from coal tar and its derivatives. Organic pigments are generally stronger and brighter than inorganic pigments.

orientation. The direction in which a page is printed, i.e., the portrait (vertical) or landscape (horizontal) mode.

original. Any artwork, mechanical, photograph, object, or drawing that is submitted to be reproduced in the photomechanical process.

original equipment manufacturer. A producer who sells goods to another company for use as components in their own equipment or for resale to end-users. An OEM may sell only to companies for resale or may also compete in the end-user marketplace.

orphan. The first line of a paragraph that is also the last line on a page or column, generally considered poor typography. Sometimes, the last line of a paragraph which is also the first line on a page is referred to as an orphan. See also: *widow*.

orthochromatic. Photographic plates and films sensitive to all portions of the visible spectrum (electromagnetic radiation with wavelengths between 375 and 560 nanometers), except red light. See also: *color sensitive; panchromatic*.

orthographic. Photographic materials sensitive to green, blue, and ultraviolet light.

oscillating form roller. A special roller on an offset lithographic press used to reduce mechanical ghosting.

oscillator. A gear-driven roller that not only rotates, but moves from side to side, distributing and smoothing out the ink film and eliminating image patterns from the form roller. This side-to-side movement reduces mechanical ghosting. Alternative terms: *oscillating drum; vibrator rollers.*

Ostwald system. A method of color notation based on a central gray scale surrounded by solid colors in horizontal and vertical rows.

out of register. See *misregister.*

outfeed and rewind section. The area at the end of a flexo press that moves the substrate (either sheets or rolls) out of the press and, in the case of rolls, rewinds the web.

outline. (1) To opaque out the background around the margins of an object in a halftone negative. (2) To box in an illustration with a line border. (3) A silhouetted reproduction. (4) Open characters as opposed to those that are solid color. (5) On a computer screen, those characters shown in rough form to simulate final output while saving the memory required to create fully formed characters. (6) The act of creating open characters from solid originals, usually done by photographic means.

GATF

Outline (4)

outline halftone. A halftone in which all or part of the background has been eliminated. See *halftone.*

output. (1) Data that has been processed. (2) The hard copy that has been generated from electronic equipment. (3) Transferring data from internal storage or memory to an external storage device, such as magnetic tape or a floppy disk.

output device. The machine that translates the electrical impulses representing data as processed by a computer into permanent results. A laser printer, imagesetter, or phototypesetter are some examples.

overcorrection. Removing too much of a contaminating color when correcting color separations for the hue error present in the printing inks. The result is a loss of important detail in the final reproduction.

overdevelop. To subject exposed photographic material to a developing solution for excessive time or at excessive temperature, agitation, or concentration.

overexposure. A condition in which too much actinic light reaches the film, producing a dense negative or a washed-out print or slide.

overfeed system. A sheetfed offset press infeed system in which the front guides position the sheet on the feedboard and cams then buckle the front edge of the sheet to force it into the impression cylinder grippers and against the stops that register the sheet.

Overfeed system

overhang cover. A book cover that is larger than the size of the enclosed book pages.

overhead. The portion of an image file that carries format, character size, font, loading, and similar information other than the actual representation of the image elements themselves.

overlay. A sheet of translucent or transparent tissue, acetate, or Mylar attached over the face of the primary artwork (pasteup) and used to indicate surprints, knockouts, overlapping or butting flat colors, placement of alternate or additional copy, or previously separated color art.

overlay proof. Thin, transparent pigmented or dyed sheets of plastic film that are registered to each other in a specific order and taped or pin-registered to a base sheet. Each film carries the printed image for a different process color, which, when combined, creates a composite simulating the final printed piece.

overleaf. The other side of a page.

overmatter. Surplus copy or art at the end of a job, page, or article. Overmatter is saved for future use or killed, and the portion of the text affected is edited accordingly.

overpacking. Packing the plate or blanket to a level that is excessively above the level of the cylinder bearer.

overprint. (1) A color made by printing any two of the process inks (yellow, magenta, and cyan) on top of one another to form red, green, and blue secondary colors. See also: *surprint.* (2) In lithographic platemaking, exposing a second negative onto an area of the plate previously exposed to a different negative. This is a method of combining line and halftone images on the plate. Alternative terms: *double printing; multiple burns.* (3) Solid or tint quality control image elements that are printed over or on the top of previously printed colors. Overprint patches are used to measure trapping, saturation, and overprint color densities. Like other quality control elements, overprints may be measured from a color bar in the trim of a press sheet or from the printed image itself.

overrun. The quantity of printed copies exceeding the number ordered to be printed. Trade custom allows a certain tolerance for overruns and underruns.

overset. (1) Typeset characters exceeding the individual line length desired, usually unintentional. (2) Typeset material that exceeds the space allotted but is billed to the client because there was no mistake on the part of the typesetter.

oversewing. See *binding, cleat-laced.*

overstrike. Superimposing one type character over another to correct copy. This method may be used instead of the insert and delete functions.

overtrapping. In process color printing, the transfer of an excessive amount of one color over another.

oxidation. (1) Combining oxygen with the drying oil in a printing ink to promote a slow chemical reaction that produces a dry ink film. (2) In photography, a developer that lessens in effectiveness after contact with the air.

P

packet switching. Wide-area network architecture in which messages are divided into small manageable groups called packets for data transfer. Each packet carries the address of the destination computer.

packing. (1) The procedure for producing the pressure between the plate and blanket cylinders. (2) The paper or other material that is placed between the plate or blanket and its cylinder to raise the surface to printing height or to adjust cylinder diameter to obtain color register in multicolor printing. See also: *makeready tissue.*

packing caliper. The amount of packing necessary to achieve proper plate or blanket height in relation to its cylinder bearers. Alternative term: *packing thickness.*

packing density. The number of useful storage cells by each unit of dimensions, i.e., the number of bits per inch stored on a magnetic tape or drum track.

packing gauge. A device used to measure the height of the plate or blanket cylinder in relation to its cylinder bearers.

packing thickness. See *packing caliper.*

padding. (1) The act of filling out the remainder of an electronic field, record, or block with null codes or meaningless characters, sometimes spaces in place of alphabetic characters and zeros in place of numeric characters. (2) Applying a flexible adhesive to one edge of a stack of clamped loose sheets to create a "pad" of sheets when the glue dries.

page. One side of a sheet or leaf of paper.

page description language (PDL). In an electronic publishing system, the format by which all of the elements to be placed on the page, their x-y coordinates (respective position on the page), and the page's position within the larger document are identified in a manner that the output device can understand. Alternative terms: *page descriptor; document descriptor.* See also: *imagesetter; PostScript™; raster image processor; vectors.*

page flex. The stretching and strain that the pages of a bound book can withstand before coming loose from the binding. See also: *page-pull test.*

page layout. A dummy indicating page size; trimmed job size; top, outside, and foot trims; untrimmed page size; and head, foot, outside, and bind margins.

page makeup. (1) A computer program that allows the user to position type and other elements automatically so that fully paginated electronic output can be generated. (2) Manual placement of art, type, photos, etc. into page positions by adhering each element to a "board" ready for camera work. See also: *pagination.*

page printer. A printer capable of producing hard copy one character at a time to a full page format; as opposed to a line printer that prints one line of characters at a time.

page proof. A sample of type elements assembled into page form.

page reader. See *optical character readers; optical character recognition.*

page-pull test. A test that measures the force required to pull a page from the backbone of an adhesive-bound book. See also: *page flex.*

pagination. (1) The process of page makeup. (2) Numbering pages with associated running heads and feet, sometimes including trim marks. (3) Breaking down an electronic file or printed galley into individual pages. See also: *page makeup.*

paint mill. A mixing unit used to combine ink vehicle with pigment, by passing the mixture through a succession of rollers. See also: *ball mill.*

paint program. Graphics-oriented computer programs that create smooth curves and subtle tonal variations in bit-mapped areas. Electronic airbrushing and pixel-level editing are other features of paint programs.

palette. The finite set of distinct colors that can be displayed by a video, printing, or computer system. In computerized systems that create color, the palette of available colors is frequently displayed as an on-screen menu from which specific colors can be selected. See also: *color gamut.*

palette knife. A small, flexible blade used to mix small batches of ink on a slab.

pallet. (1) A low, sturdy platform on which materials may be placed for handling in quantity. (2) A fixture on a T-shirt (screen) printing device that supports the item to be printed.

Pallet (1)

pan film. See *panchromatic.*

panchromatic. Photographic plates and films sensitive to all colors visible in the spectrum, including red and blue. See also: *color sensitive; orthochromatic.*

panel pictures. A group of same-size photos, pasted up adjacent to one another, to be shot as a single halftone.

panel printing. A solid block of color, ink or foil, which is used as a background for other printed or stamped material and sometimes surrounded by a decorative border.

Pantone Matching System (PMS). The most commonly used ink-mixing and color-reference formula.

paper. Matted fibers, usually made from wood, applied to a fine screen from a water suspension to form thin sheets.

paper, air-dried. A web removed from a paper machine and dried without tension or restraint in an enclosed area filled with circulating hot air.

paper, baggy. A web that unwinds with nonuniform draws and has a width that does not uniformly support web tension.

paper, coated. Wood pulp or rag-based printing paper with a layer of white clay or pigments and a suitable binder applied to its surface. This coating improves surface uniformity, light reflectance, and ink holdout. Generally, coated paper is most often used in high-quality, four-color printing.

paper, flatness. A surface measurement. The degree of levelness of a given sheet.

paper, fuzz/fluff. Loosely bonded surface fibers.

paper, high-bulk. A thick stock with a coarse surface.

paper, latex-treated. Impregnating the fibrous network of a substrate with a plastic material that enhances durability, tear resistance, and wet strength. With its flexible, leatherlike properties, latex-treated paper may also be coated to improve printability and resistance to oils, grease, and water.

paper, low-bulk. A thin sheet with a smooth surface.

paper, NCR. See *carbonless paper.*

paper, recycled. See *recycled paper.*

paper, uncoated. Paper that has not been treated or processed with a surface coating during manufacture. The rougher surface absorbs inks more readily.

paper, water receptivity of. In lithography, the ability of a paper to absorb some water from the blanket, preventing water buildup on the plate.

paper, wild formation of. An irregular fiber alignment that could cause the image on the printed sheet to be mottled.

paper abrasion resistance. The ability of the paper surface to resist being abraded, or rubbed away, during the printing process.

paper absorbency. The ability of paper to absorb fluids or the ink vehicle.

paper acidity. A pH value (below 7) of a specific stock or its surface coating. Paper can also be neutral or slightly alkaline.

paper basis weight. In the United States, the weight in pounds per ream of paper cut to its basic size. The size varies with different grades and varieties of paper. It also varies from country to country.

paper conditioning. Bringing the paper's temperature to equilibrium with the temperature or atmosphere of the pressroom without removing its wrapping or exposing it to atmospheric and humidity changes.

paper formation. The uniformity of paper fiber distribution in a sheet. It is usually measured by the uniformity of the light transmitted through the paper.

paper grain direction. See *grain direction.*

paper grain direction, across. See *grain direction, across.*

paper grain direction, against. See *grain direction, against.*

paper humidity conditioning. The process that allows a paper's moisture content to reach equilibrium with the surrounding atmosphere.

paper moisture resistance. The ability of a stock to withstand the effects of dampness.

paper picking. A disturbance of the paper's surface that occurs during ink transfer when the force (ink tack) required to split an ink film is greater than that required to break away portions of the paper's surface.

paper sizes, international. The common paper sizes used in Europe and Japan. They are: A3 (11.7×16.5 in.); A4 (8.3×11.7 in.); A5 (5.8×8.3 in.); B4 (10.1×14.3 in.); B5 (7.2×10.1 in.); and B6 (5.1×7.2 in.). See also: *basis weight.*

paper smoothness. The evenness of a paper's microscopic surface contour.

paper tape. An input device that receives a series of punched holes representing letters and numbers. The tape is placed on a reader that senses the holes and converts them to machine-readable electrical pulses.

paperback. A book with a flexible paper binding. Alternative term: *softcover.* See also: *paperbound.*

paperboard. A paper product with a greater basis weight, thickness, and rigidity than paper. With a few exceptions, paperboard has a thickness of 12 points (0.3 mm) or more. Alternative term: *cardboard.*

paperbound. An adhesive-bound book with a paper cover. Alternative term: *softcover.* See also: *paperback.*

papeterie. A heavily filled, uncoated paper with a smooth, vellum, or embossed finish.

papyrus. A tall plant native to the Nile region, the pith of which was sliced and pressed into matted sheets by the early Egyptians to produce the first writing material with many of the properties of paper. The word "paper" originated from papyrus.

parallax. The apparent shift in alignment or register between two photographic images or superimposed films or flats when the viewing angle changes.

parallel fold. Any sequence of folds most often equally spaced (parallel) to the first fold.

parallelism. The exact alignment of the copyboard, lensboard, halftone screen holder, and focal plane in a process camera.

parameter. A definable characteristic or property of a machine, or a changeable characteristic that is unvarying during an operator-specified task.

parchment. A fine, translucent paper made from the tanned hide of a sheep or goat.

parchment, artificial. A somewhat translucent paper that is produced from a wildly formed fibrous structure.

Pareto diagram. A special variation of the vertical bar graph used to rank the causes of problems from the most to least significant, such as the frequency of specific adjustments made during press makeready. Helpful in prioritizing problem-solving efforts, it is based on the 80/20 rule which suggests that 80% of the effects of a particular situation come from 20% of all possible causes.

Pareto diagram

Pareto principle. First defined in 1950, it suggests that 80% of most problems come from 20% of the possible causes.

parity bit. An additional data bit that is used to check the correctness of the associated group of data bits. The parity bit is included, or omitted, from the data bits to produce the necessary odd or even total number of bits. Alternative term: *parity check.*

passive matrix display. A monitor that uses a single transistor to control an entire column or row of electrodes. These displays are cheaper than active matrix displays, but provide lower contrast and resolution. See also: *active matrix display.*

paste drier. A highly viscous drier prepared by grinding the inorganic salts of manganese or other metals in linseed oil varnishes.

pastel drawing. An illustration made with chalk, clay, charcoal, and/or pigments in a wax base.

pastels. Soft or light colors usually in the highlight to midtone range.

paster. (1) A device used to apply a fine line of paste on either or both sides of the web to produce finished booklets directly from the folder without saddle stitching. The paste is applied from a stationary nozzle as the web passes underneath it. (2) An eight-, twelve-, or sixteen-page booklet that is pasted instead of saddle-stitched together. (3) An automatic web splicer on a press. (4) The rejected web with a splice in it.

pasteup. The camera-ready assembly of type and line art (drawings), e.g., line copy prepared manually or electronically for photographic reproduction. Alternative terms: *mechanical; photomechanical.*

patent base. Sectional metal blocks used as supports to hold letterpress printing plates in position on the press or to hold metal type in position on the chase. Alternative term: *patent block.*

patrices. Metal dies of raised characters used to produce the character molds, which are then used to make metal type.

PDF. See *Adobe Acrobat; portable document format.*

peaking. Electronic edge enhancement produced by exaggerating the density differences at tonal boundaries to create the visual effect of increased image sharpness. See also: *unsharp masking.*

pebbling. Embossing paper after it has been printed to give it a rippled effect.

peel, automatic. A spring or cam device on larger automatic screen-printing presses that lifts the screen behind the moving squeegee.

peer-to-peer environment. A LAN in which network administration is shared by many computers instead of handled by a centralized file server. See also: local-area network.

PEL. Another term for picture element. (1) In computer graphics, the smallest element of a display surface that can be independently assigned color and intensity. (2) The area of finest detail that can be reproduced effectively on a recording medium. See also: *pixel.* (3) See *permissible exposure limit.*

pen plotter. A printing device using liquid ink dispensed from individual color cartridges, usually to form line and text images.

percent grayness. Densitometric relative measure of achromatic density in a color as compared to the major filter density. See also: *grayness.*

perf. See *perforating.*

perf strip. A band that is bound into saddle-stitched publications so that single-leaf inserts can be tipped in. If perf strips were not used, publications could only accept four-page inserts. Alternative term: *hangers.*

perfect binding. The use of glue to hold the pages of a book or magazine together. Alternative term: *adhesive binding.*

perfecting. Printing both sides of a sheet in the same pass through the press. In xerography, perfecting is called duplexing.

perfecting press. A printing press that prints both sides of a sheet in a single pass through the press. Alternative term: *perfector.*

perfector, convertible. A sheetfed press with a special transfer cylinder in the gripper system that allows the sheet to tumble end for end between printing units so that the other side of the sheet is printed by the second unit. On a two-unit convertible perfector, two colors can be printed on one side of the sheet, or one color can be printed on each side in a single pass through the press.

Transfer cylinder

Perfector, convertible

perforating. Punching a row of small holes or incisions into or through a sheet of paper to permit part of it to be detached; to guide in folding; to allow air to escape from signatures; or to prevent wrinkling when folding heavy papers. A perforation may be indicated by a series of printed lines, or it may be *blind;* in other words, without a printed indication on the cutline. Alternative term: *perf.*

peripheral equipment. The various input and output devices, storage units, and other hardware that form a computerized system, other than the computer itself. Any auxiliary equipment.

perl. See *practical extraction and report language.*

permanence. The ability of a paper to resist change in one or more of its properties during storage and with aging.

permissible exposure limit (PEL). A regulation established by OSHA that states the maximum amount of time employees can be exposed to airborne contaminants.

pH. The degree of acidity or alkalinity of a substance or solution measured on a scale of 0 to 14, with 7 as the neutral point. Numerous instruments are available for measuring pH value.

Photo CD™. A format developed by Kodak for storing compressed still photographic images on CD-ROM disks. The digital photographs can be viewed on home players or can be retrieved with computer-based systems. See also: *CD-ROM.*

photocell. A device that converts the energy in a light ray into electrical energy.

photocombining. See *composite; gang; montage.*

photocomposing machine. See *multi-imaging camera; step-and-repeat.*

photocomposition. See *phototypesetting.*

photoconductive. A material that carries electricity in the light and serves as an electrical insulator in the dark..

photoconductor. (1) A medium for transferring images to paper. (2) An insulator that conducts electricity when it is illuminated with electromagnetic radiation with wavelengths shorter than a critical value.

photocopy. A reproduction of an original formed by fused toner particles in a non-impact process such as xerography.

photodiode. A small solid-state device capable of detecting the presence or absence of light. It is the principal component of light detection and measuring instruments.

photoelectric. Process of converting light energy into electrical energy.

photoelectric cell. Any light-detecting or measuring element that produces an electrical signal relative to the light stimulus striking the element. Alternative term: *photocell.*

photoengraving. The process of making printing plates by exposing line and halftone negatives onto a sensitized metal, converting the image into an acid resist, and etching the image areas in relief as required for letterpress printing.

photographic proofs. Blue, brown, or silver prints made from negatives or positives and used to check layout and imposition before plates are produced.

photography. The use of actinic light to produce a latent or permanent image on sensitized materials.

photography, digital. See *camera, digital.*

photogravure. Using photographic methods in the production of plates or cylinders for gravure, or intaglio, printing.

photoimposition. Exposing a single image in a succession of specific positions on a plate or film, either by manually moving the pin-registered image or by using a step-and-repeat (photocomposing) machine.

photoinitiator. A substance that, by absorbing light, becomes energized.

photolettering. Setting type photographically by manually exposing one character at a time through a special machine.

photomechanical. All processes in which printing surfaces are produced with the aid of photography.

Photomechanical Transfer (PMT). Trademark of 3M. See *diffusion transfer.*

photometer. An instrument for measuring the intensity of a light source and comparing the relative intensities of light emitted from different sources of illumination. See also: *light meter.*

photomicrographs. Photographs of microscopic objects used in research.

photomicrography. Producing greatly enlarged pictures of very small objects by photographing them through a microscope.

photomontage. Combining or blending several photographic images into a single print to present a variety of subjects as an integral illustration.

photomount. Heavy cardboard used as a backing paper for photographs.

photomultiplier. A highly sensitive photocell that transforms variations in light into electric currents. Photomultipliers create the input signals to the computing circuits in electronic color scanners.

photopolymer. A plastic designed so that it changes upon exposure to light. Photopolymer films and plates are used in the printing process.

photopolymer plate. A relief printing plate made of light-sensitive flexible plastic and most often used in flexography.

photoresist. A light-sensitive coating that is applied to a metal surface, selectively dissolved after exposure, and washed from the unexposed portions. Photoresists protect the metal against etchants and other chemicals used in platemaking.

photoresponse, total nonuniformity. The difference in the responsive levels between the most and least sensitive elements under uniform illumination.

phototypesetter. (1) A machine that exposes and outputs photosensitive paper or film according to the signals it receives from a computerized typesetting system. (2) A person who sets type using phototypesetting equipment. See also: *typesetter.*

phototypesetter, first-generation. Photocomposing machines that were patterned after hot-metal concepts. A photo image in the matrix or grid was used to expose a character on photographic material, instead of to cast a metal character. See also: *hot-metal.*

phototypesetter, fourth-generation. See *imagesetter.*

phototypesetter, second-generation. Those phototypesetting machines with font masters that are comprised of photographic images on a film strip, a font disk, or a font grid matrix, which is mechanically positioned in the optical path, with a flash lamp behind the character master. Moving and fixed lenses and mirrors in front of the character master size, focus, and position the characters on the image-receiving photographic emulsion.

phototypesetter, third-generation. See *typesetting, digital.*

phototypesetting. The act of composing type and reproducing it on photographic film or paper. Alternative term: *photocomposition.* See also: *composition; typesetting.*

photounit. The housing for the optics, energy source, and photographic materials on which a typographic image is produced in phototypesetting. The keyboard, computer, and other peripherals are usually separate units.

physical standards. The specifications for network hardware, communications, and cabling that determine how the system will be accessed and controlled.

pi characters. Miscellaneous type characters, e.g., bullet, star, box, rule, arrow, etc, that are used occasionally to compose a particular job. See also: *sort.*

pi font. A collection of miscellaneous type characters, mathematical symbols, accent marks, and technical symbols that are not part of a normal type font.

pica. A printer's unit of linear measure, equal to approximately one-sixth of an inch. There are twelve points in a pica and approximately six picas in an inch.

pick resistance. How well a paper surface resists force before splitting or rupturing.

pick tester. An instrument that measures a paper's resistance to splitting or rupturing through the application of inks with varying degrees of standardized tack.

picking. The delamination, splitting, or tearing of paper surface fibers that occurs when the tack of the ink exceeds the surface strength of the paper.

pick-up. Film, photos, or type from a previously printed job that is earmarked for reuse in an upcoming job.

piece accents. Special phototypesetting characters that can be double-exposed in conjunction with a regular character to produce an accented character. Using a piece accent can reduce the number of characters required in a complete font.

piece fractions. Typesetting typically uncommon fractions by assembling separate elements for the numerator and denominator to the left and right of a fraction mark, or above and below a horizontal fraction rule. A piece fraction might be created by setting the numerator in superior figures, then a fraction mark (/), then setting the denominator in inferior figures.

pigment. Fine, solid particles derived from natural or synthetic sources and used to impart colors to inks. They have varying degrees of resistance to water, alcohol, and other chemicals and are generally insoluble in the ink vehicle.

pile board. A raisable platform on which the paper to be printed is loaded. Alternative term: *pile table.*

Pile board

pile feeder. An automatic sheet feeding mechanism on a printing press or sheet folder.

pile height. The maximum height of the paper pile in the feeder of a sheetfed offset press. The pile height is usually ³⁄₁₆ in. (5 mm) below the forwarding flaps at the front of the pile.

pile height regulator. A device that senses the height of a pile and controls its position. On a sheetfed press, it is usually a pressure-foot control.

piling. A buildup of paper, ink, or coating on the offset blanket, plate, or rollers in such a quantity that it interferes with print quality. Alternative term: *caking.*

piling ghosting. A latent image that appears on the reverse side of coated paper printed on a blanket-to-blanket web offset press, usually as a result of uneven pressure caused by piling on the blanket adjacent to the image.

pin register. The use of standardized register pins and holes to ensure accurate register of copy, film, and plates during pre-press; especially for process-color printing. See also: *register; register punch.*

Pin register

pinhole. A small, unwanted, transparent area in the developed emulsion of a negative or positive. It is usually caused by dust or other defects on the copy, copyboard glass, or the film.

pit. The physical cavity representing one bit on an optical disk surface, created in the "on" mode of a digital signal.

pitch. (1) The number of characters per inch to be printed. The larger the number, the smaller the size of the print. (2) A unit of width of type, based on the number of characters that can be placed in a linear inch; for example, 10-pitch type has ten characters per inch.

pixel. Picture element. The smallest tonal element in a digital imaging or display system. See also: *PEL.*

pixel interleave. System of organizing color data within a computer pixel-by-pixel (i.e., a pixel of yellow, a pixel of magenta, a pixel of cyan, a pixel of black, etc.). See also: *pixel.*

pixel swopping. See *cloning.*

pixelization. A technique used to represent areas of complex detail as relatively large square or rectangular blocks of discrete, uniform colors or tones.

plain paper. (1) Paper lacking a thermally receptive, photoreceptive, or dielectric coating. (2) Paper made from one grade of stock, such as plain chipboard and plain strawboard.

planimeter. A device used to visually and mathematically evaluate a dot area. The equipment includes a microscope, a television camera and receiver, and a small computer.

planographic. A term used to describe a flat image carrier, such as a lithographic printing plate, which has no relief images and has image and nonimage areas on the same level (or plane).

plastic binding. A form of mechanical binding using plastic strips, combs, or coils in place of stitching. The binding edge is punched with slots or holes through which the formed plastic material is inserted.

plasticizer. (1) An ink additive that promotes flexibility, so the ink film will adhere to a creased or crinkled substrate. (2) An agent added in the manufacture of certain papers, such as glassine, or employed in papermaking compositions of protective coatings, such as nitrocellulose lacquers, to impart softness and flexibility. Plasticizers also make the rubber compound in rollers and blankets softer.

plastometer. See *durometer.*

plate. A thin metal, plastic, or paper sheet that serves as the image carrier in many printing processes.

plate, rubber. In flexography, printing plates made by molding and curing rubber in a matrix produced from a relief printing form, i.e., a form with image areas raised above the nonimage areas.

plate and packing height. The total thickness of the plate and its packing.

plate bender. See *bender.*

plate blinding. See *blind image.*

plate clamp. A device that grips the lead and tail edges of a printing plate and pulls it tight against the cylinder body. The position of the clamps is relevant to the image position or register of the image in relation to the other printing plates and the image's squareness on the sheet.

plate cylinder. In lithography, the cylinder that holds the printing plate tightly and in register on press. It places the plate in contact with the dampening rollers that wet the nonimage area and the inking rollers that ink the image area, then transfers the inked image to the blanket, which is held on its own cylinder.

Plate cylinder

plate finish. A smooth, hard paper surface produced by supercalendering.

plate scanner. A device that measures all of the various densities in a plate's image area at selected increments across the plate before it is mounted on the press. The press operators then set the ink fountain keys to match the ink densities indicated by the plate scanner's measurements before they begin printing the job.

plate-feed dampening. A continuous-flow dampening system that has separate dampening and inking form rollers.

platemaking. Preparing a printing plate or other image carrier from a film or flat, including sensitizing the surface if the plate was not presensitized by the manufacturer, exposing it through the flat, and developing or processing and finishing it so that it is ready for the press.

platen. In letterpress, a movable flat surface that is pressed firmly against paper and inked type to produce a printed image.

platen press. A printing press with a flat printing surface and a flat impression surface.

plate-to-blanket squeeze. See *squeeze.*

plating range. The density range over which a satisfactory electroplate can be deposited on a gravure image carrier.

"pleasing" color. Printed color subjective in nature (e.g., flesh tones, sky, etc.). Alternative terms: *reference color; memory color.*

plotter. An output device for recording an image in raster fashion on a photographic emulsion or a printing image carrier such as a plate or cylinder.

plug-and-play. The ability of a computer to detect and configure a new piece of hardware automatically, without the user having to reconfigure the hardware elements.

plug-in. A software utility developed to operate through another application, performing a specific task.

ply. (1) A designation of thickness for blanks and other paperboards. (2) The number of individual sheets of paper that make up a set of business forms.

ply thickness. The number of layers that make up a sheet of cardboard.

pockets. The hoppers on a binder that are loaded with the signatures to be bound into a book.

point. (1) The smallest American unit of typographic linear measurement, equal to 0.0138 in. Type height is measured in points. (2) Units of measure that indicate the caliper of paper in thousandths of an inch. (3) An alternative term for the punctuation mark called a "period."

point light source. A small, tubular aperture designed to produce a narrow-width travel path for light.

point size. Specifying the height of the body of a typeface in units of linear measure equal to 0.0138 in. Alternative term: *type size.*

point source. Stationary location or facility from which pollutants are discharged or emitted.

point system. The system of measuring by points and picas in typographic composition. It has been in use since 1878.

point-and-click access. Use of graphical-user-interface (GUI) software and a mouse to execute computer commands.

point-to-point protocol (PPP). See *serial-line Internet protocol (SLIP).*

polarization. The action or process of affecting radiation and especially light so that the vibrations of the wave assume a definite form.

polarize. To cause light waves to vibrate in a definite pattern.

polarizing filter. A device that causes light waves to vibrate in a definite pattern.

polishing. Method of obtaining the final finish on a copper gravure cylinder.

polymerization. A chemical reaction—usually carried out with a catalyst, heat, or water, and often under high pressure—in which a large number of relatively simple molecules combine to form a chain-like macro-molecule. Some printing inks dry by polymerization (a chemical reaction between the binder and solvent leaves a tough and hard ink deposit on the substrate).

polymetal plate. See *bimetal plate.*

pop-ups. A sheet that is diecut, creased, and folded in two directions. It is flattened for delivery and, when opened, expands to form a three-dimensional image.

porosity. The property of a paper sheet that allows the permeation of air and ink.

port. The connecting point between an electronic device and the equipment that transfers data to the rest of the system.

portable document format (PDF). A computer file format that preserves a printed or electronic document's original layout, type fonts, and graphics as one unit for electronic transfer and viewing. The recipient uses compatible "reader" software to access and even print the PDF file. See also: *Adobe Acrobat.*

portrait mode. See *orientation.*

position marks. See *register marks.*

position proof. A color proof in which text, graphics, and pictures are combined and checked for location and registration before printing.

positive. A photographic reproduction with the same tonal values as those in the original scene. The image areas on the film or plates are represented by opaque dot values. See also: *negative.*

positive-working plate. An image carrier that is exposed through a film positive. Plate areas exposed to light become the nonimage areas because they are soluble in the presence of developing agents.

post binder. A looseleaf binding method in which straight rods are used instead of rings to hold the pages together. The binder can be expanded as the bulk of the contents increases. The front and back covers are separate pieces.

Post binder

poster board. A specific weight of cardboard beginning with a caliper of 24 points. Standard sheet sizes are 22×28 in. (559×711 mm) and 28×44 in. (711×1118 mm).

posterization. A special effects photographic technique that renders continuous-tone copy into an image represented by a few broad, flat, dark middletones and shadow areas. All highlight and light middletone areas are eliminated.

PostScript™. Adobe Systems, Inc. tradename for a page description language that enables imagesetters developed by different companies to interpret electronic files from any number of personal computers ("front ends") and off-the-shelf software programs. See also: *imagesetter; page description language; raster; raster image processor; vectors.*

PostScript™, encapsulated. A file format used to transfer PostScript™ image information from one program to another.

powderless etching. A copper etching process in which the etchant contains a filming agent that protects the sides of the dots or cells during etching.

practical extraction and report language (perl). A UNIX language widely used to create common gateway interface (CGI) scripts for World Wide Web forms interaction. See also: *common gateway interface.*

precedence code. A unique character in a stream of input data, which is used to denote a change in mode. A dollar symbol enclosed in a bracket, for example, might be used to indicate a change in command or format.

preflighting. An orderly procedure using a checklist to verify that all components of an electronic file are present and correct prior to submitting the document for high-resolution output.

pre-gather. Binding just a single section or part of a larger book.

preloaded pressure. The amount of force required to hold the plate and blanket cylinders in firm contact when the cylinders are overpacked to create the recommended squeeze pressure.

premask. A film positive contact-printed from a separation negative and used in combination with another separation negative to make the final or principal mask.

premelter. A device that warms and melts adhesive before it is placed in a glue pot on a perfect binder.

prepress. All printing operations prior to presswork, including design and layout, typesetting, graphic arts photography, image assembly, and platemaking.

prepress proof. See *proof.*

prepress proofing. Producing a simulation of the final printed piece by photochemical methods (such as an overlay of dye or pigment images on transparent film base) instead of photomechanical methods (ink on paper). Alternative term: *offpress proofing.*

preproof. A computer typesetting term used to distinguish output from a dot-matrix or laser printer from a proof of actual phototypeset copy. Preproofs are used to correct, revise, and mark-up the copy to be typeset.

preproofing, ink. In gravure, running a set of positives on a flat copperplate or a set of test cylinders to generate proofs for client approval before starting the production run.

preproofing, photocontact. Obtaining full-color proofs from final negatives or positives by using dyes or pigments transferred to a white base material, or by using dyed or pigmented transparent films that, as an overlay, provide a colored transparency of the copy.

prepunched film. Photographic film in which holes have been cut in advance to fit a specific lugging or pin-register system.

prescan analysis. Examining a color original before mounting it on the scanner to permit the operator to make scanner programming decisions off-line instead of on the scanner.

prescreen. A halftone positive print that is pasted down with line copy, to avoid the need to strip a halftone negative into a line negative.

prescreened film. High-contrast, orthochromatic, conventional-emulsion film that has been pretreated to produce a halftone negative by camera exposure to continuous-tone copy without the use of a halftone screen.

presensitized plate. A sheet of metal or paper supplied to the user with the light-sensitive material already coated on the surface and ready for exposure to a negative or positive.

press. The machine that creates the final printed image.

press gain. Mechanical dot gain. See *dot gain.*

press proof. See *proof.*

press section. In a papermaking machine, the area where water is removed from the web by suction and applied pressure.

press sheet. A single sheet of paper selected for the job to be printed on the press.

pressrun. (1) The total of acceptable copies from a single printing. (2) Operating the press during an actual job.

presswork. All operations performed on or by a printing press that lead to the transfer of inked images from the image carrier to the paper or other substrate. Presswork includes makeready and any in-line finishing operations specific to the press (folding, perforating, embossing, etc.).

Preucil apparent trap. The quantity—density of the overprint minus the density of the first-down ink—divided by the density of the second-down ink; where all densities are taken through the complementary color (primary filter) of the second-down ink.

Preucil ink evaluation system. A color evaluation system in which a reflection densitometer is used to measure a printed ink film through Wratten #25, #58, and #47 filters relative to the substrate. These measurements are converted into hue error and grayness parameters for plotting on color diagrams.

preventive maintenance. A scheduled routine designed to prevent breakdowns and/or unscheduled downtime.

preview screen. A video display unit that allows the operator to examine type, art, or color separations in a "what-you-see-is-what-you-get" (WYSIWYG) mode before generating hard-copy output.

primaries. Colors that can be used to generate secondary colors. In the additive system, these colors are red, green, and blue. In the subtractive system these colors are yellow, magenta, and cyan. The printing process employs the subtractive color system.

print. (1) In photography, an image made by reproducing a negative (or positive) on a sensitized opaque support of paper, metal, or other materials. (2) The line or halftone image on metal plates used in photomechanical printing processes. (3) An impression from a plate, engraving, etc.

print contrast. The ratio of the difference in the density of a 75% (three-quarter) tone and a solid print to the density of the saturated solids on the press sheet.

print engine. The engineering name given to internal components, such as those in copiers, that produce electrostatic proofs or images.

print quality. The degree to which the appearance and other properties of a print approach the desired result.

printability. The combination of print quality characteristics that enhance the reproduction of an original in any printing process.

printer. (1) Any computer device that produces results in readable form on paper. (2) Color-separated halftone films that will transfer the characteristics of each specific process color in a given job to the corresponding printing plate prior to presswork. (3) The person or company that operates printing presses.

printer, impact. Any device that uses pressure from a typebar, type head, or matrix pin and inked ribbon to strike a direct impression on a substrate.

printer, line. A computer output device that simultaneously prints all of the characters in a line of type.

printer, nonimpact. Any device that reproduces an image without striking the substrate. Some examples include xerography or laser printing in which the image is created by fused toner particles, or ink jet printing in which a stream of ink propelled from the printer forms the image.

printhead. (1) The mechanical or electrical part of a printer that generates the type characters, usually a component of a nonimpact printer like an ink-jet or thermal printer. (2) The screen carriage, squeegee/ flood bar assembly, and mechanical controls and fixtures on a screen printing press.

printing. The art and methods by which an original is reproduced in quantity. In the photomechanical process, this is generally accomplished by applying an inked image carrier to the substrate as it travels through a high-speed press.

printing box. A light-tight housing used in some forms of contact printing to position the negative against the photographic paper in front of the internal light source where it is exposed. It includes an adjustable mask (or frame) to create the white border on prints.

printing couple. The portion of a printing press that applies a printed image to one side of a press sheet. The inking and dampening systems and plate, blanket, and impression cylinders on an offset press are considered parts of the printing couple.

printing cylinder. See *cylinder.*

printing frame. See *contact printing frame.*

printing pressure. The force, in pounds per square inch, required to transfer the printed image to the substrate. In lithography, this includes the pressure between the plate and blanket, the blanket and the impression cylinder, and the impression cylinder and the substrate.

printing process. The method used to reproduce written and pictorial matter in quantity. The major conventional printing processes are lithography, letterpress, gravure, flexography, and screen printing. The major nonimpact printing processes are ink jet, electrophotography, ionography, magnetography, and thermal transfer printing.

printing screen. The frame, fabric, and stencil assembly used in screen printing.

printing stroke. Moving the squeegee across the printing screen to force the ink through the stencil and screen, forming the imprint.

printing unit. The sections on printing presses that house the components for reproducing an image on the substrate. In lithography, a printing unit includes the inking and dampening systems and the plate, blanket, and impression cylinders.

printout. The hard-copy text output of any computer printer.

prism. A triangular piece of glass with silver on one side. When it is attached to the lens of a process camera this optical instrument produces a lateral inversion of the image projected by the lens. See also: *spectrum; spectrum, visible; white light.*

process camera. See *camera, process.*

process capability. A statistical measure of the natural variation of a given characteristic, such as glue film thickness, relative to customer specifications for that characteristic. The capability can only be determined after a process has been brought into a state of statistical control. A process is capable if its natural variation is less than the range of specifications limits and the process is approximately centered between the limits.

process color efficiency. A relative measure of how effective a process color is at absorbing its additive primary and transmitting the other primaries, i.e., how effective it is as a subtractive primary.

process colors. The three subtractive primary colors used in photomechanical printing (cyan, magenta, and yellow, plus black).

process control. A system using feedback to monitor and manage a certain procedure. Input and output data are tabulated according to specific formulas and compared with certain standards and limits. The process is then adjusted as necessary. Alternative term: *statistical process control (SPC)*. See also: *quality control.*

process direction. The path of the printed medium through an electronic publishing system. See also: *slow-scan direction.*

process ink gamut (PIG) chart. A color diagram used to compare the range of colors that can be produced from any given ink set and substrate combination.

process inks. The yellow, cyan, magenta, and black colorants that, when combined in a photomechanical printing process, reproduce four-color images.

process photography. (1) Creating line and halftone images for photomechanical reproduction. Alternative term: *graphic arts photography.* (2) The equipment, materials, and methods used in preparing color-separated printing forms for color reproduction.

processing. Chemically treating photographic papers, films, and plates after exposure.

processing, real-time. Formulating text matter or developing photographic materials in a sufficiently rapid manner so that the results are available in time to influence the final output.

processing tray. An open container that holds one of the solutions used to hand-process photographic materials.

processor. An automatic device that feeds exposed photosensitive paper (such as typeset galleys) or film over rollers through baths to develop and dry them before they reach the delivery area.

processor, computer. In hardware, the arithmetic unit that interprets instructions and manipulates the data accordingly. Alternative term: *central processing unit (CPU).*

program. A systematic series of software instructions designed to direct a computer to perform a specific task.

programming language. A set of syntactical rules or commands used to write instructions for a particular computer or operating system. The instructions are input to a compiler or assembler program that translates the programming language to machine language, enabling the computer to execute specific tasks.

projection printing. A system of lenses and lamps used to cast an image onto a sensitized plate. The image formed may be larger or smaller than the projected negative or positive.

prompt. The visual or written "hint" that appears on a computer screen to remind the user of a choice to be made.

proof. A prototype of the printed job made photomechanically from plates (a press proof), photochemically from film and dyes, or digitally from electronic data (prepress proofs). Prepress proofs serve as samples for the customer and guides for the press operators. Press proofs are approved by the customer and/or plant supervisor before the actual pressrun.

proof, progressive. A set of press proofs from the separate plates used in process color work, showing the printing sequence and the result after each additional color has been applied. (Press proofs of each individual process color and black; each combination of two process colors; each combination of three process colors; and all four process inks combined.) Alternative term: *progs.*

proof, soft. An intangible, unstable image, such as that on a video screen. See also: *copy, soft.*

proof press. A printing machine used to produce photomechanical proofs. It has most of the elements of a true production machine but is not meant for long pressruns.

proofing. Producing simulated versions of the final reproduction from films and dyes or digitized data (prepress proofing) or producing trial images directly from the plate (press proofing).

proofreader. A person who checks copy for errors and marks them for correction prior to printing.

proofreaders' marks. A series of symbols and abbreviations used by a proofreader to mark errors on copy and the corrections to be made.

proofreading. Checking galleys, proofs, and bluelines for errors and marking where corrections should be made.

proportion scale. In reproduction photography and platemaking, a circular slide rule used to establish enlargement and reduction percentages and the ratio of the reproduction size to the original size. Alternative terms: *proportion rule; proportion wheel.*

proportional spacing. See *spacing, proportional; spacing, true proportional.*

proportionality failure. The change in the hue of an ink as dot size, or thickness, varies. Proportionality failure occurs when the ratio of red-green-blue light reflectance in the halftone tints is not the same as that in continuous ink solids.

proprietary systems. Computer workstations that are custom-designed for one specific task such as color correction, dot etching, or page layout. Proprietary systems rely on specific hardware and software components, and they are often not easily linked to modular systems that use off-the-shelf software and hardware components from several different manufacturers.

protocol. A set of rules that governs the transfer of data in telecommunications.

protractor. An instrument used for measuring angles.

psychrometer. A wet and dry bulb hygrometer that is used to accurately determine relative humidity. See also: *hygrometer.*

publisher. The owner and/or primary producer of a periodical or line of books.

pull down. See *drawdown.*

pull sheets. A group of sheets removed from the delivery of the press for inspection.

pull test. A measure of the sturdiness of a perfect-bound book.

pulp. The substance produced mechanically or chemically from fibrous cellulose raw materials for use in papermaking.

pulp substitutes. An intermediate grade between pulp and wastepaper that does not require deinking.

pulpwood. Logs, chips, sawdust, shavings, slabs, and edgings that have been ground or shredded in preparation for papermaking.

pulsed-xenon lamp. The primary light source in graphic arts photography. It provides a very constant output with a spectral composition resembling sunlight.

punch. A die used in finishing operations to perforate holes or slots in paper or board for looseleaf or mechanical binding or other applications, such as mounting.

purity. A synonym for saturation.

pushout. See *creep; shingling.*

Q

quad. A blank piece of metal used in handset type to create the space between words. The term is also used to refer to spacing and alignment in phototypesetting.

quad center. To set copy in the middle of a line, with all excess space equally placed at each end of the line.

quad left. A command code in a phototypesetter that instructs the machine to position all text to the left end of the line. A minimum of interword spacing and letterspacing is used in the portion of the line containing characters, and the right portion contains only space. Alternative term: *flush left; unjustified text*. See also: *quad right; tabular material*.

quad middle. A command code in a phototypesetter that instructs the machine to insert all justifying space at the point in the line where the quad code appears, pushing text material equally toward the right and left ends of the line. A minimum of interword spacing and letterspacing is used in the text portion of the line.

quad right. A command code in a phototypesetter that instructs the machine to position all text to the right end of the line. A minimum of interword spacing and letter-spacing is used in the portion of the line containing characters, and the left portion contains only space. Alternative term: *flush right*. See also: *quad left; tabular material*.

quadracolor. A function of some color scanners in which a set of four separations is produced on one film.

quality. The totality of features and characteristics of a product or service that bear on its ability to satisfy stated or implied needs in conformance to customer expectations.

quality assurance. All those planned and systematic actions necessary to provide adequate confidence to both company management and customers that a product or service will satisfy given requirements for quality.

quality audit. A systematic and independent examination to determine whether quality activities and related results comply with planned arrangements and whether these arrangements are implemented effectively and are suitable to achieve objectives.

quality control. The day-to-day operational techniques and activities that are used to fulfill requirements for quality, such as intermediate and final product inspections, testing incoming materials, and calibrating instruments used to verify product quality. See also: *process control.*

quality management. That aspect of the overall management function that determines and implements the quality policy. This includes strategic planning, allocation of resources, and other systematic activities for quality, such as quality planning, operations, and evaluations.

quality policy. The overall quality intentions and direction of an organization as formally expressed by top management.

quality system. The organizational structure, responsibilities, procedures, processes, and resources that printers use to control the many printing variables in order to generate products of consistent quality that meet defined specifications.

quality systems auditor. The certified individual who evaluates a printer's quality system. See also: *ISO 9000.*

quality systems registrar. An organization that provides certified quality auditors who evaluate a printer's quality system. See also: *ISO 9000.*

quality system registration. The process of periodically accessing or auditing a printer's quality system. This audit is performed by a certified auditor (individual) from a quality system registrar (company) who compares the printer's system to the registrar's interpretation of an ISO 9000 standard. Interpretations may vary from registrar to registrar. See also: *ISO 9000.*

quarter binding. A method of casebinding in which two different materials are used for the front and back covers and the spine of a book, e.g., cloth or leather for the spine, and paper for the front and back covers.

quartertone. Picture tonal values in range of a 25% dot. See also: *midtones.*

quarto. (1) A sheet folded into four leaves or eight pages. (2) A booklet, or the pages of a book, formed by folding the sheets into four leaves, with a final size usually measuring about 12×9½ in. Alternative terms: *4to, 4°.*

quartz-iodine lamp. An incandescent lamp with a tungsten filament surrounded by iodine and inert gases and enclosed in a quartz bulb. Alternative term: *tungsten-halogen lamp.*

query. A marginal note from editor to author, proofreader to editor or typesetter, or typesetter to editor on the original or proofs to call attention to some matter in question.

quick printing. Printers who provide a fast turnaround of short-run (10,000–15,000 impressions) monochrome jobs no larger than 11×17 in. (279×432 mm) produced on high-speed photoduplicators and photocopiers or presses that are 14×20 in. (366×508 mm) or smaller. These printers, many of whom own franchises of larger quick printing concerns, produce some color work, but seldom accept four-color process jobs.

quire. One-twentieth of a ream of paper. In fine papers the quire is twenty-five sheets, and in coarse papers it is twenty-four sheets.

quoins. In hot-metal or handset typography, the pairs of clamping wedges used to lock up a printing form within a chase.

qwerty. The standard keyboard layout found on computers, phototypesetters, and typewriters used to compose in the English language. Qwerty is the order of the letters on the left-hand upper row of alphabet keys.

Qwerty

R

rag content. The percentage of cotton fiber in paper.

rag pulp. Paper pulp made by disintegrating new or old cotton or linen rags, and cleaning and bleaching the fibers. Rag pulp is used principally for making premium bond, ledger, writing papers, and other papers requiring permanence.

ragged. Type composition set with lines centered in the column, instead of justified, producing raggedness at both sides. See also: *justification.*

ragged left. See *flush right.*

ragged right. See *flush left.*

random access. A system of data file management in which a record is accessible independent of its file location or the location of the previous record accessed. In other words, records need not be accessed sequentially.

random-access memory (RAM). A solid-state computer memory in which the time required to access data is independent of the data location. Random access memory is the main memory of a microcomputer. See also: *read-only memory.*

random proof. See *scatter proof.*

range. All of the values that a function may have; the difference between the highest and lowest permissible values.

rangefinder. A device included on many cameras as an aid in focusing.

rapid-access film. A blue- or green-sensitive film with a high-density continuous-tone emulsion providing the fastest means of producing film intermediates.

rapid-access processing. A method of processing exposed photographic film or paper in developer with an elevated temperature and a shallow bath to produce dry products in under two minutes.

raster. An image composed of a set of horizontal scan lines that are formed sequentially by writing each line following the previous line, particularly on a television screen or computer monitor. See also: *bitmap; line art; object-oriented; vectors.*

raster count. (1) The number of addressable coordinate points on a video screen. (2) In computer graphics, the number of lines in one dimension within a display space.

raster file. An electronic file in which the pixels are scanned and input in rows.

raster image processor (RIP). The device that interprets all of the page layout information for the marking engine of the imagesetter. PostScript™, or another page description language, serves as an interface between the page layout workstation and the RIP. See also: *array processor; imagesetter; page description language; Post-Script™; vectors.*

rasterization. The process of converting mathematical and digital information into a series of dots by an imagesetter for the production of negative or positive film.

RCRA. See *Resource Conservation and Recovery Act of 1976.*

read color. Any markings created in an ink to which an OCR device is sensitive. See also: *nonread color; nonread ink.*

reader's spread. See *breakacross; spread.*

read-only memory (ROM). Nonerasable, permanently programmed computer memory. It can be accessed and "read" by the user but it cannot be edited. See also: *random-access memory.*

read-write head. An electromagnetic device that rotates against a magnetized surface in a disk drive and then writes information to or reads or erases information from the magnetic tape, disks, or drums.

real time. A mode of processing in which a computer performs calculations at the same time the information is passing through its processing units.

ream. Five hundred sheets of paper.

rebind. To reassemble a book in its original form with its original case. Alternative term: *recase.*

receiver sheet. In the diffusion transfer process, the piece of the two-part material that is not sensitive to light. Sensitive to chemicals instead, it accepts the images from "donor" materials during processing.

reciprocity failure. The failure of the effect of exposure to be the same for a given value of the product of illumination intensity and time (when the factors making up the product are varied), which may happen if one of these factors is extremely small.

reciprocity law. A photographic rule stating that exposure is a function of the product of both exposure time and light intensity, but not of either variable alone.

reclaiming. Gathering and reworking used materials. See also: *recovery*.

recording density. The number of bits of data recorded per linear inch on magnetic media, as affected by the speed of the moving surface on which the data are recorded and the rate of data transfer.

recovery. Acquiring an energy value from the incineration or chemical conversion of a product. See also: *reclaiming*.

recto. The right-hand page of an open book, usually an odd-numbered page; sometimes the first or cover page. See also: *verso*.

recyclable paper. Wastepaper or stock separated from other solid waste and designated for reuse as a raw material. Papers that are heavily contaminated (with color or coating) may not be recyclable. See also: *stock; wastepaper*.

recycle. Minimizing waste generation by recovering and reprocessing usable products that might otherwise become waste.

recycled fibers. Fibers recovered from wastepaper, printing and converting waste, and forest and lumber mill residues to be used for the manufacture of paper or paperboard. Alternative terms: *recovered fibers; secondary fibers*.

recycled paper. Paper manufactured from deinked used paper and bleached pulp or from printing and converting waste.

red. See *additive color process; additive primaries*.

red lake C. A warm, bright red pigment used in printing inks.

reducer. (1) An additive that softens printing ink and reduces its tack. (2) A chemical that reduces the density of a photographic image by removing silver.

reelroom. At a web printer, newspaper printers in particular, the separate area where roll stands are housed.

reference colors. Those colors to which the eye most readily responds including flesh tones, green grass, and blue sky. Alternative term: *memory colors.*

reference edge. The area on a data medium used to establish specifications or measurements in or on the data carrier. Alternative term: *guide edge.*

refiner mechanical pulp. Papermaking pulp produced by passing wood chips through a disk refiner instead of pressing the wood against an abrasive grinding stone.

refining. The action of processing fibers mechanically in preparation for papermaking.

reflectance. The ratio between the amount of light reflected from a given tone area and the amount of light reflected from a white area.

reflection. An optical term for the direction change of a ray of light when it falls on a surface and is thrown back into the medium from which it approached.

reflection, diffuse. Optical condition that occurs when parallel incident rays are reflected at various angles from a rough surface.

reflection, specular. Optical condition that occurs when a smooth surface reflects parallel incident rays at a constant angle and these rays remain parallel in the reflected light.

reflection copy. A photographic print, painting, or other opaque copy used as original art for reproduction. Such copy is viewed by the light reflected from its surface and can only be photoreproduced with front illumination (as from a graphic arts camera) as opposed to the backlighting used to view and reproduce transmission copy (i.e., slides and transparencies). See also: *transmission copy.*

reflection densitometer. See *densitometer.*

reflection proofs. Off-press proofs made by applying color images to a single base material one at a time in a certain sequence to produce a composite proof.

reflex copy. A copy made by placing a special photosensitive material, emulsion side down, against the original and exposing the original through the back of the photosensitive material. More light is reflected from the highlights of the original than from the shadows.

reflex paper. A light-sensitive material used for contacting same-size reproductions.

reforestation. Process engaged in by paper companies, among others, in which trees are reintroduced into a region from which they have been harvested.

refraction. The deviation of a light ray from a straight path when passing obliquely from one medium to another, or in traversing a medium of uneven density.

refractive. The ability of a material to bend a light ray from a straight course.

refractive index. A measure of the ability of a material to bend a light ray from a straight course. The result is expressed as the ratio of the speed of light in one medium to the speed of light in another medium (usually air or a vacuum).

refresh rate. The amount of time, measured in hertz, that it takes to rewrite an image on a computer screen.

register. (1) The overall agreement in the position of printing detail on a press sheet, especially the alignment of two or more overprinted colors in multicolor press-work. Register may be observed by agreement of overprinted register marks on a press sheet. In stripping, film flats are usually punched and held together with pins to ensure register. The punched holes on the film flat match those on the plate and press speci-fied for the job. Alternative term: *registration.* See also: *image fit; misregister; pin register; register punch.* (2) Any location in a computer where information has been transferred for processing.

register, commercial. In process-color reproduction, the degree of acceptable misregister, usually no more than one-half of a row of dots. Ultimately, the customer determines what constitutes acceptable misregister.

register bond. A common lightweight writing paper designed for single and multi-copy business forms. The grade is usually made from chemical wood pulps. Important product qualities include printability; good tensile and tearing strength; and good per-forating, folding, and manifolding qualities.

register marks. Small reference patterns, guides, or crosses placed on originals before reproduction to aid in color separation and positioning negatives for stripping. Register marks are also placed

Register marks

along the margins of negative film flats to aid in color registration and correct alignment of overprinted colors on press sheets.

register plate. A device that stops the lateral (sideways) movement of the sheet on the feedboard of a lithographic press. Alternative term: *register block.*

register punch. The device used to cut holes into film flats and plates during prepress to maintain proper image alignment. Register pins are inserted into the holes so that the flats and plates remain in position. The holes and register pins used in prepress must be standardized to suit the particular press on which the job will be printed to ensure accurate alignment throughout the run. See also: *pin register; register.*

registration. See *register.*

relative humidity. See *humidity, relative.*

relief plate. A metal, rubber, or photopolymer printing plate on which the image areas are raised above the nonimage areas. See also: *flexography; letterpress.*

relief printing. A printing process using an image carrier on which the image areas are raised above the nonimage areas. See also: *flexography; letterpress.*

remoisturizer. A device that uses a series of rollers to physically apply liquid to the surface of the web after it is chilled. This replenishes the moisture lost in the dryer of a web offset press.

repeaters. Devices that regenerate electrical signals (data packets) for transmission further down the cable.

replenisher. Chemical solutions that maintain the activity of the developer and fixer solutions used in photography, platemaking, and proofing materials.

reproduction. Duplicating an original by any photographic or photomechanical process.

reproduction percentage. The linear size of a photographic reproduction expressed as a percentage of the linear size of the original copy. Alternative term: *reproduction ratio; reproduction size.*

reproduction proof. An exact and carefully pulled proof of type composition or other printing matter that is suitable for photographic reproduction.

reprographics. Methods of copying as used primarily by architects and engineers to create blueprints, for example.

reprography. Copying and photoduplicating type and images by any one of several processes, including xerography, in quantities below the commercial printing level.

rescreened halftone. A halftone negative or positive made from a printed halftone usually with a diffusion filter placed in front of the camera lens to eliminate moiré patterns.

resilience. The ability of a blanket to regain its thickness after pressure on its surface has been removed.

resin. The solid or semi-solid organic material in a printing ink that binds the pigment to the substrate. Resins can also impart gloss, hardness, heat and chemical resistance, and other important properties to the ink as well as surface hardness to offset plates.

resinated pigment. A pigment surface treated with a resin that makes it more easily dispersible.

resin-coated paper. A high-contrast photographic paper that is coated on both sides with a water-impermeable resin that carries an emulsion on one side. RC papers have good dimensional stability and dry faster than conventional photographic papers.

resist. A plate coating that hardens over the nonimage areas after exposure to light. Mixed with bichromated gum or other coating solutions, the resist keeps the plate developer from contacting the nonimage areas of the metal plate, while etching it slightly.

resolution. The precision with which an optical, photographic, or photomechanical system can render visual image detail. Resolution is a measure of image sharpness or the performance of an optical system. It is expressed in lines per inch or millimeter.

resolution target. Any test image that measures the resolving power of a printing system.

resolving power. The relative ability of a lens or emulsion to reproduce fine detail, as expressed in lines per millimeter.

Resource Conservation and Recovery Act of 1976 (RCRA). U.S. federal hazardous waste, solid waste, and waste reduction program that involves remedial investigations, feasibility studies, and implementing corrective measures.

restrainer. The ingredient in a photographic developer that prevents the image from developing too rapidly and inhibits the appearance of chemical fog.

reticulation. A photographic emulsion that cracks or distorts during processing, usually as a result of wide temperature or chemical-activity differences between the various development solutions.

retouching. Altering continuous-tone prints and halftone negatives or positives to eliminate defects, emphasize detail, and perform minor color corrections. Pencils or dyes are used to retouch actual prints, negatives, and positives manually. Today, images may also be scanned into special prepress systems and retouched electronically.

retrofit. Adding or removing a piece of equipment, or adjusting, connecting, or disconnecting an existing piece of equipment to comply with government regulations and/or changes instituted by manufacturer or industry.

reversal. Converting a negative to a positive image by chemical means.

reversal paper. A light-sensitive material used to produce negative images from positives.

reversal processing. A method of processing photographic materials, whereby the final copy is a tonal facsimile of the original; i.e., black is reproduced as black, and white as white.

reverse (type). See *knockout.*

reverse image. A print on film in which the tone values are the opposite of the original film image after contacting.

reverse-reading. Photographic negative or positive that reads from right to left when viewed from the emulsion side. Alternative term: *wrong-reading.* See also: *right-reading.*

rewind. Rerolling a web onto a new core after printing.

rhodamine. A bluish red pigment used to produce magenta process inks. See also: *rubine.*

rider roller. A rigid, friction-driven roller in the press inking system that helps to break down, distribute, and transfer the ink while remaining in contact with one or more resilient rollers.

right-reading. A photographic negative, positive, or printing plate that reads from left to right (top to bottom) when viewed from the emulsion side. See *reverse-reading*.

ring topology. The embodiment of IBM's Token Ring physical network standard that uses a single wire to connect all network terminals in a continuous loop. Data packets travel around the loop in one unchanging direction with the token indicating which workstation will send or receive a transmission.

risk assessment. Process of gathering facts to estimate the potential harmful effects of a particular product or activity on humans or the environment.

river. The undesirable alignment of interword spaces in successive lines of type, which forms a pattern of white space that flows throughout the typeset material. See also: *underset*.

rods. The light receptors in the eye by which shape and brightness can be distinguished.

roll. Paper or cardboard produced in a continuous strip and wound uniformly around a central shaft or hollow core.

roll coating. Applying a premetered coating film to a paper web with rollers.

roll set curl. Paper curl that occurs because the web has been stored in roll form long enough to cause its curved condition to become permanent. Alternative term: *wrap curl*.

roll sheeter. A device that cuts a roll or web of paper into sheets and sends them to the feeder on a sheetfed press. See also: *roll-to-sheet; sheeter*.

roll stand. The mechanism that supports the roll of paper as it unwinds and feeds into the press.

roll stand, auxiliary. An extra roll stand mounted on top of another roll stand. This reduces downtime by permitting one stand to be reloaded while the other is still unwinding. The auxiliary roll stand cannot be used to feed two webs at the same time unless it is converted to a dual roll stand.

roll stand, dual. A support for two rolls of paper, one stacked above the other, to feed two webs at the same time, or to reduce reloading time if a single web is used.

roller. (1) On printing presses, a cylindrical drum on an axle. Composed of metal or rubber, it distributes and applies ink to the printed form. (2) The cylinders used to convey the paper web through the press or papermaking machine. See also: *rollers, idle.*

roller, idle. Any free-turning cylinder used to support a paper web in its travel through a press to the folder or through a converting machine. Alternative term: *web-lead rollers.*

roller, intermediate. A cylinder driven by friction that transfers and conditions the ink on press. Located between the ductor and form rollers, an intermediate roller is referred to as a distributor if it contacts two other rollers and as a rider if it contacts a single oscillating drum.

roller, lint. A hard roller, small in diameter, that helps to keep the ink system clean by picking up ink skin particles, lint, etc.

roller cover. The absorbent cloth or paper placed over press dampening rollers to enhance the flow and retention of dampening solution.

roller stripping. The failure of ink to adhere to the inking rollers.

roller-setting gauge. A device that shows the amount of pressure exerted when the press operator pulls a paper or metal feeler strip between the two rollers being set.

Roller-setting gauge

roller-stripe gauge. A device that is marked with stripes of specified widths and used to visually determine the width of an ink stripe on a roller or plate.

roll-fed. A printing press or converting machine that receives paper as continuous webs from rolls, instead of as sheets. See also: *web press.*

rolling up. In lithography, inking up the finished plate manually without taking a proof or impression.

roll-to-roll printing. Printing webs of substrates and then rewinding them directly onto another roll core after printing.

roll-to-sheet. The system that feeds sheets cut from rolls into a sheetfed press. See also: *roll sheeter; sheeter.*

rollup. Covering the surface of a gravure image carrier, especially the cell wall tops, with an etch-resistant ink before applying the "bite." See also: *bite.*

rollup process. In letterpress, a method of etching halftone plates by applying an etching ink to a heated plate after the flat etch has been applied. The heat of the plate causes the ink to melt and run down the sides of the dots.

roman type. A term used to describe a regular serif or sans serif face that is neither italic nor bold. Roman typefaces are typically used in books.

roomlight films. Silver-based photographic films that can be handled under yellow safelights or tungsten and fluorescent lights.

rosettes. The patterns formed when halftone color images are printed in register at the correct angles.

rosin sizing. A chemically dispersed material commonly added to a papermaking furnish to impart water resistance to paper and paperboard. See also: *sizing.*

rotary drum. An infeed system on a sheetfed press in which the front guides stop the sheet and move out of the way at the proper time. Grippers on a rotating drum clasp each sheet and transfer it to the impression-cylinder grippers.

rotary press. A printing press in which the printing plate or surface is cylindrical and rotates and prints continuously, usually at high speed, on both web and sheetfed stocks.

rotary screen press. A screen printing press with a fine-wire cylindrical screen that contains a squeegee-like blade which rotates over a continuous roll of paper.

rotogravure. A printing process that uses a cylinder as an image carrier. Image areas are etched below nonimage areas in the form of tiny sunken cells. The cylinder is immersed in ink, and the excess ink is scraped off by a blade. When the substrate contacts the printing cylinder, ink transfers, forming the image. See also: *gravure.*

rough. A crude or basic sketch of a layout, design, drawing, etc.

rounding and backing. Shaping a book to fit its cover. Rounding gives the book a convex spine and a concave fore-edge. Backing makes the spine wider than the thickness of the rest of the book to provide a shoulder against which the cardboard front and back covers rest. It also provides the hinge crease for the joints of the book.

**Rounding (left)
and backing**

routers. Devices that connect separate networks that use the same physical network standard.

routine. A set of instructions that directs the computer to perform a certain function; often a subset of a larger program.

rub-down type. See *alphabet sheets.*

rubine. An organic reddish pigment that is somewhat darker than most magenta inks. It has a greater hue error than bluish rhodamine magenta process inks. See also: *rhodamine.*

rub-off. The degree to which a dry printed ink transfers to adjacent printed material with normal handling.

Rubylith. The Ulano Company's trademark name for a thin red or amber plastic film used by graphic artists, designers, and strippers to indicate placement and size of illustrations. Mounted to a pasteup board or acetate base, one layer of the Rubylith is peeled away, leaving the remaining layer to form a "window" for the illustration. This window appears as a black "mask" on orthochromatic photographic materials. Alternative term: *masking film, peelable.* See also: *window method.*

rule. (1) A printed line, usually specified by its arrangement and thickness or "weight," such as hairline, 2-point, 6-point, or parallel. (2) A stamping die used in bookbinding to form borders, panels, etc.

ruling pen. A mechanical pen used for inking lines.

run. (1) The complete execution of one computer program, one routine, or several routines linked to form an automatic operation. Alternative term: *machine run.* (2) See *pressrun.*

run back. A proofreading term meaning to transport particular text as marked from the beginning of the line back up to the end of the preceding line.

run chart. See *trend chart.*

run down. A proofreading term meaning to break or end a line as noted, forcing the remainder down to the next line.

run of press. Usually describes the "standard" ink colors for a given pressrun.

runaround. Setting text in a form to fit around an illustration or figure when the illustration is less than the column or page width.

run-in head. A subject title that is a part of the first line of text to which it refers.

run-length encoding. A system of encoding digital data to reduce the amount of storage needed to hold the data without any loss of information. Each coded item consists of a data value and the number of adjacent pixels with the data value. This is a very efficient way of encoding large areas of flat color as used in linework and text.

runnability. The mechanical strength of paper. How well it resists tearing during the pressrun.

running foot. See *footer; folio, drop.*

running head. See *header; folio.*

running text. Columnar composition as in newspaper text set without regard for preferred line endings.

runoff. Precipitation, snow melt, etc. that runs off the land and into waterways. It may contain pollutants from the air or land that may have originated at an industrial site.

runoff, urban. Stormwater that may carry pollutants into sewer systems or other waterways.

S

saddle stitch. Binding multiple sheets by opening the signatures in the center and gathering and stitching them with a wire through the fold line. The folded sheets rest on supports called saddles as they are transported through the stitcher. Booklets, brochures, and pamphlets are most often bound this way. Alternative terms: *saddle wire; wire stitch.*

Saddle-stitched booklet

saddle-sewn. Binding multiple sheets on a saddle stitcher with a thread instead of a wire.

safelight. A darkroom light with a limited spectral composition that inhibits it from exposing or fogging specific light-sensitive materials.

safety paper. Paper produced with special chemicals and mechanical properties that make it easier to expose forgery or any alterations of checks and other negotiable, legal documents.

sample pages. Finished pages produced by the typographer or printer to illustrate the quality of an anticipated product, solutions to particular problems, or ability to follow specifications.

sample size. The actual dimensions of the electronic information scanned when a pixel is captured.

sampling rate. The amount, as expressed in inches or millimeters, of electronic information sampled in both scan directions.

sans serif. Typeface designs, such as Helvetica, that lack the small extensions on the ascenders and descenders referred to as serifs. See also: *serif.*

satellite. Transmission device operating in geosynchronous or geostationary orbit 22,300 miles above the Earth. The major components of a geosynchronous (GEO) satellite system include the orbiting unit, an Earth segment composed of transmitters and receivers (dishes), and switching and distribution facilities. Some satellites use microwave relays.

saturation. (1) The degree to which a chromatic color differs from a gray of the same brightness. In other words, how a color varies from pastel (low saturation) to pure (high saturation). In the Munsell system, this is called *chroma*. (2) The quality of visual perception that permits a judgment of different purities of any one dominant wavelength.

saturation exposure. The minimum exposure level that will produce a saturated output signal.

sawtooth. A notched effect where the lines in a design cross the fabric mesh of the screen printing screen diagonally, distorting the design contours.

scalar processor architecture (SPARC). The Sun Microsystems microprocessor that underlies many UNIX operating systems. It handles serial functions and values and mathematical computations in a form of reduced instruction set computing (RISC) and is therefore popular on high-level workstations and servers.

scale. A range of values. See *gray scale*.

scaling. Process of determining the correct final size for an image that must be enlarged or reduced. See also: *sizing*.

scan. The sequential examination or exposure of a character or pictorial image with a moving light beam.

scan rate. The number of lines per inch or centimeter that a scanner reads across a drum.

scanner. (1) An electronic device that uses a light beam to examine color transparencies and isolate each process color on an individual piece of film, or photographic separation, to be used in the reproduction process. (2) Flatbed electronic devices are used in conjunction with desktop publishing systems to scan line art, logos, photographs, and, with optical character recognition (OCR) capabilities, typewritten or printed text supplied by the client. After the artwork, photographs, and text have

Scanner, flatbed

been scanned into the system and stored on disk, they are called up on the computer screen and manipulated and assembled in page form using software and then output as a single unit (on paper or film) from the imagesetter. See also: *drum scanner*.

scanner, plate. See *plate scanner*.

scanner lamp. The source that illuminates an original during electronic scanning.

scatter diagram. A graphical technique used to analyze the cause-and-effect relationship between two variables. Two sets of data are plotted on a graph with the y axis used for the variable to be predicted and the x axis used to indicate the variable that causes the prediction, such as dot gain caused by press speed.

Scatter diagram

scatter proof. A single press proof containing many unrelated images "ganged" (i.e., gathered or placed) randomly on the substrate. Alternative term: *random proof.*

score. To compress or crease cardboard, pasteboard, or heavy paper along the fiber line to facilitate folding or tearing.

scraper. (1) A thin steel disk used to smooth book edges before gilding. (2) In finishing and converting, a mechanism used to regulate the flow of glue in an automatic gluing machine.

screen. (1) Those areas of a plate or press sheet in which tonal gradations are reproduced. See *halftone screen.* (2) The porous mesh, synthetic, or silk material used as an image carrier in the screen printing process.

screen, coated. Applying a direct emulsion to the screen-printing fabric to prepare it for exposure.

screen, conventional gravure. A halftone screen formation in which the dots are positioned laterally instead of diagonally.

screen, electroformed. A screen printing screen produced by plating a developed photosensitive nickel sheet, removing the plating, and cementing it to a frame.

screen, indirect. A screen printing screen made by exposing a coated, photosensitive emulsion onto a plastic support sheet through a positive.

screen angle. The position of the rows of dots on halftone screens in relation to a reference grid with horizontal and vertical lines. The most dominant color screened is positioned at a 45° angle to the reference grid.

screen compensator. The glass positioned in front of a process camera lens when the operator is producing combination line and halftone negatives with two exposures. When the glass crossline halftone screen is removed, the compensator is positioned to allow for the difference in refracted light.

screen curves. See *tone reproduction curve.*

screen distance. With crossline halftone screens, the separation or space between the surface of a halftone screen and that of the plate or film during halftone photography. This distance varies with the screen ruling.

screen fabric. See *fabrics, stencil.*

screen frequency. The number of lines or dots per inch on a halftone screen.

screen gauge. A device that determines the screen ruling used in a printed halftone reproduction, on negative or positive film.

screen holders. See *fabric holder, adjustable.*

screen indicator. A ruled or lined device used to determine the ruling of any screen used in halftone reproduction.

screen marks. See *mesh marks.*

screen negative. A photographic reproduction of a continuous-tone illustration created through a halftone screen. See also: *halftone screen.*

screen opener. A chemical, usually in aerosol spray form, used to clear dried-in areas of a screen printing stencil.

screen positive. The reverse image of a screened negative reproduced by exposing light-sensitive material to a screened negative in contact in a vacuum printing frame.

screen printing. A printing process in which a squeegee forces ink through a porous mesh, synthetic, or silk image carrier, or screen, covered by a stencil that blocks the nonimage areas. The ink pressed through the open image areas of the screen forms the image on the substrate.

screen printing, pressurized. A printing method or device that forces ink through a stencil image with air pressure, instead of a squeegee.

screen range. The breadth of densities (from minimum to maximum) that a halftone screen can produce without a supplemental flash exposure.

screen ratio. In a gravure screen, the relationship of the area occupied by lines to area of white space in a screen. Typically the cylinder cell is two or three times the width of the screen wall.

screen reclamation. In screen printing, the process of stripping the stencil from the screen so that a new stencil can be applied.

screen ruling. The number of ruled grid lines per inch on a halftone screen.

screen speed. The exposure time required to produce a given dot size on a negative with one screen relative to the time required to produce the same dot size with another screen.

screen tint. A halftone film with a uniform dot size throughout. It is rated by its approximate printing dot size value, such as 20%, 50%, etc. Alternative term: *screen tone*. See also: *flat color; halftone tint; tint.*

screen value. The number of lines per square inch on any halftone, tint, or four-color separation.

screen wall. The part of the gravure cylinder cell that serves as a bearer on which the doctor blade rides as the cylinder rotates in the trough of ink.

screened paper print. A halftone illustration on photographic paper. It can be mounted with line copy on a page layout so that the entire page can be photographed at once as line copy for reproduction.

screened photo print. A print reproduced through a halftone screen, i.e., a printed halftone. Screened prints can then be photographed as line copy.

screening. (1) The process of converting a continuous-tone photograph to a matrix of dots in sizes proportional to the highlights and shadows of the continuous-tone image. Screening is usually accomplished photographically by imposing a halftone screen directly in front of the photographic emulsion that will receive the screened image. (2) In gravure printing, the objectionable screen pattern that appears in the solids if cylinder or plate cell walls are excessively shallow or wide.

screening in continuous tones. Screen printing with several colors of ink, or inks of several hues, which have been mechanically combined on the printing screen so that each blends smoothly without creating a demarcation line.

screen-printing machine, automatic. A device that completes part or all of its mechanical cycles without manual effort. Alternative term: *automatic screen-printing press.*

scribe machine. A device used in gravure to mark copper plates or cylinders to obtain correct register.

scriber. A small, sharp hand tool used to draw lines and rules on the emulsion of an exposed photographic negative, or to impart fine printing detail to the negative. Scribers are also used to make corrections to aluminum plates or to cut guide marks into plates.

script. A typeface that resembles cursive handwriting.

scripting language. A simple programming language used to automate basic computer processes.

scrolling. The process of moving lines of data vertically through the face of a computer monitor. The text shifts up and down and out of the operator's viewing area; however, the operator can stop scrolling anywhere for a closer view of the text.

SCSI. See *small computer systems interface.*

scuffing. See *abrasion.*

scum. Condition that occurs in lithography when the plate has become sensitized in the nonimage areas and these areas begin to take ink.

search and replace. The automatic process of locating specific data within a file and replacing it with other data. Systems vary in the ability to simultaneously process more than one condition per pass, in the length of character strings, and in amount, if any, of manual intervention required.

search engine. A program in a database or on the World Wide Web that seeks out information via key words.

secondary colors. Colors that are produced by overprinting pairs of the primary subtractive colors. The subtractive secondary colors are red, green, and blue. Alternative term: *overprint colors.*

secondary fibers. See *recycled fibers.*

second-generation, color-corrected originals. The hard-copy continuous-tone color output of a CEPS. Used as originals, this output includes color corrections applied during input scanning and those accomplished electronically by the CEPS and imaged to continuous-tone photopaper or transparency material.

self-cover. A book binding composed of the same paper used for the inside text pages.

self-extracting file. A compressed file that includes an executable program that causes it to decompress, usually by double-clicking. A self-extracting archive (SEA) is a group of self-extracting files.

semi-concealed cover. In mechanical binding, a single piece of material that is scored and slotted or punched and combined with the actual binding device to form a closed backbone on bound units.

sensitivity guide. A small, calibrated, continuous-tone quality control device used for establishing and maintaining proper plate exposure and processing conditions.

sensitize. (1) To make the image areas of a printing plate more ink receptive. (2) To apply a diazo coating, to an aluminum (wipe-on) plate. See also: *diazo process.*

sensitizer. A term for any of the solutions used to make the photographic surface of a printing plate sensitive to light.

sensitometer. A device used to determine how light-receptive photographic materials are.

separation. See *color separation.*

separation filters. The red, green, and blue filters used during color separation. Each filter transmits about one-third of the spectrum.

sepia. A photographic print with a brownish tint.

serial. To process or transmit data sequentially, or consecutively in time sequence, instead of in simultaneous, parallel (real-time) operations.

serial-line Internet protocol (SLIP). A method of establishing a direct connection between a personal computer and the Internet without first going through an Internet service provider's UNIX network. Point-to-point protocol (PPP) is another such method of access and is considered by some to be more stable. SLIP or PPP accounts are required for individual computers to access the graphical aspect of the World Wide Web.

serif. The short, usually perpendicular line found at the end of the unconnected or finishing stroke of a character. Serifs may vary in weight, length, and shape, and contribute greatly to the style of the typeface. See also: *sans serif.*

serif, square. Typeface in which the serifs are the same weight or heavier than the main strokes.

serigraphy. A fine art screen-printed reproduction of an original artwork.

server. A device on a computer network that allows networked users (clients) access to a specific service on the network. An example is a file server, which allows the users to share data files and application software.

service bureau. A business that specializes in color separation and/or in outputting film, paper, or plates from imagesetters.

service provider. A business that specializes in Internet and LAN/WAN network connectivity.

set solid. Typeset matter with no added space between lines, as measured from one baseline to the next, other than that visibly provided by the shoulder of the type itself.

set width. In composition, the normal space allowed across the body of each character along a line of set type. Alternative term: *set size.*

setback. The distance from the front edge of a printing plate to the beginning of the image area with a space allotment for the gripper margin and for fastening the plate to the cylinder. This distance varies with different press makes and sizes.

setoff. Condition that results when wet ink on the surface of the press sheets transfers or sticks to the backs of other sheets in the delivery pile. Sometimes inaccurately referred to as "offset."

sewing. In bookbinding, fastening printed signatures together with needle and thread or cord.

shade. (1) In ink manufacture, a common synonym for hue. (2) In some color reproduction systems, the gradations of color resulting from the addition of a small amount of black or a complementary color.

shading sheets. Photomechanical drawing materials with a visible or latent pattern of lines or dots on an acetate base. The sheet is positioned over selected areas of line originals to prepare them for tint or tone effects. If a shading sheet contains a latent image, it must be developed to provide the proper pattern.

shadow. The darker or denser areas of an original, film positive, or halftone reproduction.

shadow mask. A light positive image that is registered with a normal-density continuous-tone positive for the purpose of enhancing shadow tone contrast.

shadow stop. With glass crossline screens, the small lens aperture used for the flash exposure in halftone photography.

shareware. Software marketed directly by its author at a cost that is usually much lower than name-brand software. See also: *freeware.*

sheet. A piece of paper of a certain size usually used in presswork.

sheet caliper. The vertical distance between a paper's two sides as measured with a micrometer under specified conditions and expressed in thousandths of an inch or millimeter. Sheet caliper, which refers to the thickness of a sheet, is used to determine back (impression) cylinder pressure settings on a sheetfed offset press.

sheet cleaner. A device that removes loose paper, lint, and dust from the surface and edges of a paper web before it reaches the first printing unit. It usually consists of a brush that rides on the web and a nozzle that vacuums the web clean.

sheet decurler. A device that is designed to take troublesome curl out of press sheets.

Sheet decurler

sheet detector, double. A sensor on the feedboard of a stream-fed press that stops the press if three or more overlapping sheets pass under it. Alternative term: *sheet detector, extra.*

sheet detector, early and late. A device that senses the arrival time of a press sheet at the front stops of a sheetfed offset press.

sheet feeder, successive. A type of feeder where only one sheet of paper, traveling at press speed, is on the feedboard at any given moment. Most common on small presses that use a direct infeed and bearerless printing cylinders.

sheet guide rods. Bars positioned to hold down the back corners of the press sheet as it enters the feedboard.

sheet photopolymer. A flexible, light-sensitive, precast (not liquid) plastic sheet that is used to make relief flexographic printing plates through exposure to ultraviolet (UV) light.

sheet steadiers. Weights positioned at the outside quarters of the feeder pile on a printing press.

sheet transfer cylinder. The cylinder that transports the press sheet between the impression cylinders on a multicolor sheetfed press.

sheeter. (1) A device on a printing press that converts continuous forms into smaller sheets. (2) A specific web press delivery unit that cuts the printed web into individual sheets. (3) A separate device used in screen printing to cut cloth or other substrates into sheets. See also: *roll sheeter; roll-to-sheet.*

sheetfed press. A printing press that feeds and prints on individual sheets of paper (or another substrate). Some sheetfed presses employ a rollfed system in which rolls of paper are cut into sheets before they enter the feeder; however most sheetfed presses forward individual sheets directly to the feeder. See also: *web press.*

sheet-separation unit. A device that uses air and a vacuum to separate the top press sheet from the feeder pile on a sheetfed press. See also: *feeder.*

sheetwise imposition. A printing layout in which separate plates (and film flats) are used to print the front and the back of a single press sheet. Completely different pages appear on each side of the sheet.

Sheffield smoothness tester. An apparatus used to measure the surface smoothness of paper and paperboard by allowing air to flow at a constant pressure between the sample and two concentric annular bands.

shell account. An inexpensive text-based method of dial-up Internet access.

shift (unshift). A code or key on a computer terminal allowing alternate characters to be accessed from the same keystroke.

shingle. During image assembly, stripping center pages nearer to the gutter than the trim marks indicate to allow for bulk at the spine and alleviate pushout of center pages in thick (96 pages or more) saddle-stitched publications.

shingling. Condition that results when the outside edges of the pages in a saddle-stitched book project out, nearer to the center. Alternative terms: *thrust; pushout.* See also: *creep; wraparound.*

Shingling

shore hardness. See *durometer; durometer gauge.*

shoulder. (1) The upper, convex end of the characteristic curve of a photographic emulsion where an equal log exposure increase shows decreasing density differences as the curve's slope gradually diminishes to zero. (2) The portion of the backbone of a book that projects both front and back to the thickness of the covers. (3) In hot-metal typography, the nonprinting top area of the type body that surrounds the character. (4) In photoengraving, the undesirable ledge of metal that surrounds the printing detail as a result of faulty etching.

showthrough. A term used to describe the visibility of printed material from the opposite side of the sheet. This characteristic is proportional to transparency of the substrate and the oiliness of the ink.

shredder head. The device on a perfect binder that cuts off the spines of folded signatures to expose individual sheets for gluing.

shrink wrap. Using heat to affix a thin plastic material around printed and bound products to prepare them for shipment.

shutter. (1) The mechanically accurate blades, curtain, plate, or other cover over a photographic lens or in the back of a camera (at the focal plane) that automatically controls the duration of camera exposures (the amount of light that reaches the film). (2) The movable opaque shield placed behind the lens of a process camera to protect the lens from light while the operator handles photographic materials and develops images in the darkroom.

side gluing. The process of applying an adhesive to the outside of the outermost signature on a perfect-bound book to secure the cover around it.

side guide. A device that serves as the third point of a three-point register system (including the front guides) on the feedboard. Side guides move the sheet sideways to facilitate register.

Side guide

side head. A heading set outside the primary left and right margins of a text column.

side-sewing. A book binding method in which the entire book is sewn as a single unit, instead of as individual sections. Side-sewn books will not lie flat when open.

side-stitch. A method of binding in which the folded signature or cut sheets are stitched along and through the side close to the gutter margin. The pages cannot be fully opened to lie flat. Alternative term: *sidewire.*

Side-stitched book

signature. One or more printed sheets folded to form a multiple page section of a book or pamphlet. Signatures are most commonly grouped as four, eight, sixteen, or thirty-two pages. Various combinations of multiple page signatures create the full complement of pages needed in the printed piece.

silhouette. (1) An outline of the shape of a subject, which is usually printed as a solid or as a uniform tint. (2) To outline a principal subject by using an overlay of Rubylith or opaquing out the background around the subject on a halftone or continuous-tone negative.

silicone applicator. A device that applies a thick layer of silicone to both sides of the printed web to prevent marking and improve signature delivery.

silk screen. See *screen printing.*

silver halide. A silver salt such as silver chloride, silver bromide, and silver iodide suspended in gelatin to prepare the emulsion of photographic film.

silver nitrate. The most important silver compound in photography. Light-sensitive, it forms the base of all other silver compounds used as photographic sensitizers.

silverprint. A brown-colored photographic print made on paper sensitized with silver chloride. The exposed print is simply washed to completely process the image. See also: *brownprint; Van dyke.*

simplex. Using a photocopier or high-speed duplicator to print an image on one side of a page, or just using one side of a sheet of paper during printing. See also: *duplex; perfecting.*

size. Any material, such as starch, alginate, and glue, that is added or applied to paper to reduce its ink or water absorbency.

size, basic. Sheet size, in inches, used to define basis weight for a particular paper. See also: *basis weight.*

sizing. (1) Treating paper with chemicals or other materials to impart resistance to water, oils, and other fluids; seal down its surface fibers; and improve its surface strength. (2) An adhesive used to apply gold leaf or another color to book covers. (3) Sizing a photograph for reproduction. See *scaling.*

skeleton black. A black printer that enhances detail and contrast in the midtones and shadows of a four-color reproduction. Alternative terms: *halfscale black; ghost key.* See also: *black, full-scale.*

skeleton wheels. The series of movable disks that are mounted on a shaft of the delivery cylinder and positioned in the nonprinting areas of the press sheet.

sketch. A rough drawing of proposed artwork, or a rough outline of the layout of a job.

skid. (1) A platform on which paper is packed for delivery to or from the pressroom. (2) Any quantity of paper packed on a skid. Standard skids usually contain in excess of 3,000 pounds of paper.

Skid

slabbing. The practice of removing several layers of paper from the outside of a new roll prior to inspection. Alternative term: *stripping.*

slave. Any device, such as a typesetter, that is primarily driven or controlled by the logic of another system, such as a front-end system. Most modern output devices are operated in the slave mode.

slide. A photographic transparency, usually color, mounted for projection.

SLIP. See *serial-line Internet protocol.*

slip case. A decorative box into which a finished book is inserted with the spine remaining visible.

slip sheet. (1) A sheet of paper placed between two freshly printed sheets to prevent setoff or blocking. (2) A protective covering for sensitized plate surfaces.

slitter. A sharp rotary blade used to separate a single moving sheet or web into narrow strips, frequently during folding.

slitter dust. Small particles of fiber, coating, or both that are chipped off during slitting and may adhere to the edge of the sheet. Slitter dust may interfere with subsequent converting operations.

slow-scan direction. The raster direction along which successive lines of pixels are arrayed, perpendicular to the fast-scan direction. See also: *process direction*.

slug. (1) A complete line of type cast in a single piece of metal. (2) The single tag line that refers a newspaper reader to a story that is continued on another page. (3) In gravure, the term used to describe cylinder cells that are printing blurred or unclear.

slur. A printing defect appearing as a blurred elongation of a printed dot.

slurry. (1) A water suspension of fibers or the suspension of pigment and adhesive used to coat papers. See also: *mill broke, wet.* (2) A water-based abrasive suspension used in the manufacture of printing plates.

small computer systems interface (SCSI). A computer port used to link the machine with external peripherals.

smash. (1) The undesirable compression of a portion of a printing blanket's surface. (2) The heavy pressure used to compress a book so that it will have less bulk. See also: *nip; nipping.*

smash-resistance. The ability of a printing blanket to recover from being momentarily subjected to excessively high pressure.

smoothness. In paper, the degree to which its surface is free of irregularities.

Smyth sewing. Bookbinding by sewing thread through the backfold of a signature and from signature to signature. This links the signatures together, while permitting the opened book to lay flat.

Smyth sewing

snail mail. Postal delivery.

SNAP. See *Specifications for Nonheatset Advertising Printing.*

snowflaking. The tiny, white, unprinted specks that appear in type and solids in offset printing if the ink is excessively emulsified.

socket. An Internet address that combines an Internet protocol address with a port number identifying the application accessed (World Wide Web, FTP, etc.) See also: *Internet protocol address.*

soft copy. See *copy, soft.*

softcover. See *paperback; paperbound.*

software. The stored instructions (programs) that initiate the various functions of a computer (the hardware). Instructions may be written in machine language or in another programming language, then compiled, interpreted, or assembled into machine language. Word processing, page layout, and drawing programs are a few of the software programs used in the graphic arts. There are also other more specialized software programs that control high-end color electronic prepress systems and even some presswork applications. See also: *hardware.*

solarization. An effect whereby subtle changes of colors are replaced by continuous tones or even different colors altogether. In electronic systems, solarization is achieved by reducing the number of available colors from typically 16 million down to between 10 to 100 in discrete steps.

solid. A printed area uniformly and completely covered with ink.

solid image element. An image element with no breaks or divisions in the sample to be measured. It can be either a single color or an overprint of two or more colors. Solid images are measured on quality control elements in the trim of the press sheet or on the printed image itself.

solvent. (1) A material, usually a liquid, capable of dissolving another substance, usually a solid, to form a solution. (2) A component of the vehicle in printing inks that disperses the pigment and keeps the solid binder liquid enough for use in the printing process.

SONET. See *synchronous optical network.*

sort. (1) In electronic publishing, a program that arranges data in sequence following a specified pattern (i.e., a program that alphabetizes). (2) In traditional publishing, a pi character, i.e., one that is not part of the regular font used for a given job. See also: *pi characters.*

source document. (1) The original text and graphics used for a reproduction. (2) A machine-readable collection of lines of text or images that is input into a computer program.

spacing. (1) In typography, justifying a line of type by inserting extra spacing between words. Letterspacing is adjusted to reduce the effects of excess justification. See also: *kerning; word spacing.* (2) In hot-metal typesetting, inserting leads or slugs to open up lines of composition.

spacing, proportional. A typesetting procedure in which additional spaces are placed between words so that a line of text can be fully justified.

spacing, true proportional. A typesetting procedure in which character spacing is adjusted according to character width. For example, the letter "m" requires more width than the letter "i."

SPARC. See *scalar processor architecture.*

spatial resolution. The smallest feature of an image that can be detected as a fraction of the total image.

specifications. A detailed description of the requirements for a job, the typography in particular. Alternative term: *"speccing."* See also: *type "speccing."*

Specifications for Nonheatset Advertising Printing (SNAP). A set of standards for color separations and proofing developed for those printing with uncoated paper and newsprint stock in the United States.

Specifications for Web Offset Publications (SWOP). A set of standards for color separation films and color proofing developed for those involved in publications printing. The SWOP standards help magazine printers achieve accuracy when color separations from many different sources are printed on one sheet.

specimen book. (1) A catalog illustrating the variety and range of typefaces available from a particular company, including fonts, point sizes, sorts, rules, ornaments, etc.

(2) Printed samples of standard ink colors provided by the ink manufacturer, usually as solid color blocks and sometimes with percentage tints or halftone illustrations.

spectral response. The manner in which the eye responds to visible radiation. Often used to describe how the light-sensitive component (photomultiplier or film) in a color separation system responds to visible and invisible radiation.

spectral response range. The spectral band in which the response per unit of radiant power is more than 10% of the peak response.

spectrogram. A diagram showing the relative sensitivity of a photographic material to different colors of light.

spectrophotometer. An instrument used to measure the relative intensity of radiation throughout the spectrum as reflected or transmitted by a sample.

spectrophotometry. The science of measuring color by analyzing the reflection or transmission of samples at specified points across the electromagnetic spectrum. The spectrophotometric curve is the most precise means for specifying colors since metameric pairs can be distinguished.

spectrum. The series of color bands formed when a ray of light is dispersed by refraction; the rainbow-like band of colors resulting when a ray of white light is passed through a prism. See also: *prism; white light.*

spectrum, electromagnetic. The entire range of wavelengths or frequencies of electromagnetic radiation extending from gamma rays to the longest radio waves, including visible light.

spectrum, visible. The range of wavelengths of the electromagnetic spectrum—from about 400–700 nanometers—that cause the sensation of vision. See also: *prism; white light.*

specular highlight. In a photoreproduction, the lightest highlight area that does not carry any detail. Normally, these areas are reproduced as unprinted white paper.

specular reflection. The reflection of light rays at an angle equal to the angle of incidence, as from a mirror.

Specular reflection

spherical aberration. The failure of a photographic lens to bring central and marginal (lens-edge) rays to exactly the same focus.

spine. The back, or bound, edge of a book.

spiral binding. A mechanical binding method in which a continuous wire coil is run through a series of closely spaced holes near the gutter margin of loose sheets. See also: *binding, mechanical.*

Spiral binding

spiral raceway. The section on a gathering machine in which the book is stood on its spine before it is fed into the perfect binder.

splice. The area where two paper rolls are joined to form a continuous roll.

spline. In an image file, the digital representation of a line or curve in terms of coordinates or other symbols, instead of a raster representation. The spline designation is equivalent to vector. See also: *vectors.*

split fountain. A divided ink fountain, or the use of dividers, to provide separate sections capable of holding two or more colors of ink, to permit the printing of two more colors, side by side, in one pass through the press.

spot color printing. The selective addition of a nonprocess color ink to a printing job.

spot glue. An adhesive material used with gatefolds to make sure the folds do not fall open during the binding process. The spots of glue are trimmed off at the end of the bindery line so that the gatefold opens when the customer reads the publication.

spot plating. The process of applying copper or other metals electrolytically over a limited area of a copper-plated gravure cylinder to cover damaged spots that may not print properly.

spray bar dampening. A variation of the inker-feed continuous-flow dampening system that applies a very fine mist of dampening solution directly to the inking system rollers.

spray coater. A machine used to apply a thin layer of a light-sensitive resist to the surface of a gravure cylinder.

spray powder. See *antisetoff spray.*

spread. (1) A line image with edges that have been moved slightly outward to allow a color or tint to intentionally overlap. Alternative term: *"fatty."* See also: *choke* *(skinny); trapping.* (2) An image that extends across two facing pages in a book or magazine, crossing over the binding. Alternative terms: *crossover; reader's spread.* See also: *breakacross.*

Spread

squeegee. (1) A rubber or plastic blade used to force ink through the open areas of a screen-printing stencil and mesh to form an image on the substrate. (2) A blade used to sweep solution from printing plates during manual processing.

squeegee, one-arm. A rubber or plastic blade mounted on a counter-balanced carrying device. In screen printing, it serves the same function as any other squeegee, only, in this case, it is easier to operate very large squeegees.

squeegee angle. See *angle of attack.*

squeegee carriage. A system that holds the squeegee at the proper angle for screen printing. This is especially useful with very large screens.

squeeze. Printing pressure between the plate and blanket cylinders. It is expressed as the combined height of the plate and blanket over their respective bearers on a bearer-contact press and as the combined height of the plate and blanket over their respective bearers minus the distance between the bearers on a nonbearer-contact press.

stabilization. A photographic process in which developing agents are incorporated in the photographic paper to enable rapid-access machine processing.

stabilization paper. A photographic paper with a developing agent embedded in the emulsion. It is used in rapid-access processing.

stack press. A flexo press that has all of its individual color stations vertically stacked one over another.

Stack press, flexographic

stacker. A device attached to the delivery conveyor of a web press that collects, compresses, and bundles printed signatures.

stacker, compensating/counter. A machine that alternates the layering of a stack of printed products by turning them 180° to offset the uneven thickness between face and spine.

staging. In conventional gravure, applying an acid-resistant material to the nonprinting areas of a cylinder or plate prior to etching to protect those areas from the etchant.

stamping. Using a die and often colored foil or gold leaf to press a design into a book cover, a sheet of paper, or another substrate. The die may be used alone (in blank stamping) if no color or other ornamentation is necessary. Special presses fitted with heating devices can stamp designs into book covers.

Stamping

stamping die. Deeply etched or engraved brass or zinc relief plates used to impress designs on book covers. Brass plates are used when the stamping process requires heat.

standalone system. The ability of a computer workstation or other electronic device to operate independently without an online (or continuous) connection to the other units in a system.

standard reference material. A physical sample that has been calibrated to an accepted primary standard or set of standards. A tile or ink spot that has been measured with instruments traceable to primary standards and has attributes that are computed by specified procedures or algorithms may serve as a physical standard at the application level. Standard reference materials may be used as working standards or as a reference to generate daily working standards. Alternative term: *standard color reference.*

standard viewing conditions. See *viewing conditions.*

standing matter. Typeset material or stored data waiting for revisions, updates, or reuse.

stapling. Binding a book or loose sheets of paper with one or more wire staples.

star topology. A LAN configuration in which every terminal is wired directly to the central processor. All data must pass through this processor before it reaches its destination.

start-of-print line. The set of trim marks nearest to the gripper edge of the plate.

static eliminator. A printing press attachment that attempts to reduce the amount of static developing on a press because of low relative humidity and the movement of paper over metal surfaces. It can also be helpful in eliminating ink setoff or paper feeding problems. Alternative terms: *static neutralizer; antistatic device.*

statistical process control (SPC). Method of understanding and managing production processes by collecting numerical data about each step in the process and all materials used in the production sequence, including output. This data is then ana-lyzed to locate causes of variations. See also: *process control; quality control.*

Status "T." A card of carefully calibrated white, black, and color patches used to check the spectral (color) response of wide-band reflection densitometers.

stem. The primary vertical stroke of a type character.

stencil. In screen printing a material that, when adhered to the screen, blocks the mesh to keep ink from reaching the nonimage areas of the substrate.

stencil, direct. A light-sensitive liquid emulsion that is squeegeed into a screen printing fabric, dried, exposed in contact to a positive, and developed to form an out-line (stencil) image after processing. Alternative term: *direct printing screen.* See also: *stencil, indirect.*

stencil, indirect. A photosensitive screen-printing stencil made from a light-sensitive gelatin emulsion coated onto a polyester carrier or backing sheet, which is then exposed to a film positive and chemically processed. After adhesion, the support or backing sheet is removed from the stencil, opening the image areas.

stencil duplicating. A reproduction process in which ink passes through perfo-rations in a stencil master to form an image on copy paper.

stencil knife. A tool for cutting screen printing stencil film. It has a round handle and a blade about ⅛ in. (3 mm) wide, sharpened to a bevel to form a cutting point.

stencil knife, swivel. A stencil knife blade on a freely rotating shaft or point. It can cut curves in the stencil film without rotating the knife handle.

stencil medium. Any film, emulsion, or sheet material from which a screen print-ing stencil can be made.

stencil sheet. Fine paper backed with heavier material on which a typewriter or stylus can cut an impression. When the stencil is mounted on a duplicator cylinder, fast-drying ink penetrates the cut impression and the ink is transferred to the paper to form an image. This stencil method was commonly employed in the mimeographing process.

step tablet. See *gray scale, continuous.*

step-and-repeat. Exposing multiple images onto a single film or a single printing plate from a single negative or positive flat. Special step-and-repeat contact frames, projection platemaker, and multi-imaging cameras are used to automate this process. See also: *multi-imaging camera.*

stereotype. A duplicate relief printing plate made by casting a lead alloy into a paper mold of the original plate.

stet. A proofreader's term for "Let it stand." It indicates that marked-out material should instead be retained as is.

stick. See *composing stick.*

stitch. Binding printed matter by piercing the pages and securing them together with wire or thread.

stitching, loop. A method of saddle stitching whereby the stitch is formed into a semi-circular loop that extends beyond the spine of the publication. These loops slip over the rings of a three-ring binder, serving as an alternative to hole punching.

stochastic screening. A halftoning method that creates the illusion of tones by varying the number (frequency) of micro-sized dots (spots) in a small area. Unlike conventional halftoning, the spots are not positioned in a grid-like pattern. Instead, the placement of each spot is determined as a result of a complex algorithm that statistically evaluates and distributes spots under a fixed set of parameters. With first-order stochastic screening, only the number of dots in an area varies, but with second-order stochastic screening, both the number and size vary. Alternative terms: *FM dots; FM screening.*

stock. The paper or other substrate to be printed.

stone lithography. The original form of lithography in which an image is drawn on limestone with wax or grease. The surface of the limestone has been treated so that the nonimage areas accept water and repel the wax or grease.

stop. The aperture or diaphragm of a camera lens.

stop bath. An acetic acid rinse used as a second step in developing black-and-white images on film or photographic paper. It stops development and makes the hypo last longer.

storage. Any device in which data can be stored and accessed or retrieved at a later time, including computer memory, diskettes and floppy disks, and magnetic tape or disks.

straight matter. (1) Continuous text with no changes in specifications whatsoever except for the choice of an occasional italic or boldface font. (2) Simple, running text with very minimal changes in fonts, measures, point sizes, leadings, indents, etc. (3) Material that is relatively easy to set because it lacks mathematical data, columns, and other more difficult material.

stream feeder. A press feeder that forwards several overlapping sheets of paper across the feedboard, toward the front stops.

strike-in. A term commonly used in printing to refer to how well a substrate absorbs an ink vehicle. For example, inks used in newspaper printing "dry" by strike-in absorption.

strike-on. Impact or direct impression typesetters such as the early VariTyper. Today, daisy-wheel printers are the best known strike-on devices. See also: *daisy-wheel printer; impact printer.*

strip rewind. A partial web break in which the missing portion of the web becomes wrapped up on one of the blankets.

stripping. (1) The act of combining and positioning all of the copy elements from all of the film negatives or positives together as a negative for platemaking. Alternative term: *image assembly.* See also: *film image assembly; imposition.* (2) A condition in which ink is distributed unevenly because it fails to adhere to the metal rollers on the press. (3) Removing several layers of paper from the outside of a new roll prior to inspection. See also: *slabbing.*

stroke. (1) Any part of a character that can be drawn with one movement. (2) The act of cutting in changes or corrections to the original, standing film or paper.

stylus. (1) In computer graphics, the conducting point that places the electrolytic charge on the printing medium. (2) A pointer that is operated by placing it in a display space or on a tablet. See *light pen.* (3) A precision-made, penlike instrument once used for drawing, tracing, lettering, shading, ruling, and writing on stencil sheets in mimeographing.

subhead. A secondary title or heading that is usually set in smaller type, making it less prominent than a main heading.

subsample. The process of recording and saving regular, nonconsecutive bits of data.

subscript. See *inferior character.*

substrate. Any base material with a surface that can be printed or coated.

subtractive color process. A means of producing a color reproduction or image with combinations of yellow, magenta, and cyan colorants on a white substrate.

subtractive plate. A printing plate in which the light-sensitive coating also contains an image-reinforcing material.

subtractive primaries. The colors cyan, yellow, and magenta. Each is formed when one third of the spectrum is subtracted from white light. See also: *additive primaries.*

supercalendering. A method of producing a very high gloss surface on paper stock by passing the sheet between a series of heated metal rollers under pressure.

Super-calender

Superfund. See *Comprehensive Environmental Response, Compensation, and Liability Act of 1980 (CERCLA).*

superimpose. To position negatives or positives on a new film flat that is prepared directly over another flat to obtain exact registration between them. This is frequently done when stripping up complementary color flats.

superior character. A letter and/or number positioned above the x-height of a related word or character positioned on the baseline. Like inferior characters, superior characters are also set in a smaller typeface. Alternative term: *superscript.* See also: *inferior character.*

supershift. A higher level or condition than the shift mode on many typesetting keyboards. Supershift is used to access additional characters or functions not readily attainable on the common two-level keyboard.

surprint. A print from a second negative superposed upon a previously printed image of the first negative. See also: *composite.*

sweep speed. The pace at which a squeegee travels across a screen printing screen. Thicker ink deposits are left when the sweep speed is increased below over-pressure range. When the overpressure range is exceeded, less ink is deposited.

switched 56. A communications link operating over a traditional telephone line conditioned for digital data transfer at a base rate of 56 Kbps. Switched connections, like regular modem and telephone connections, are established, maintained, and ter-minated on demand.

switched multimegabit data service (SMDS). A packet-switched com-munications link that can achieve speeds from 56 Kbps to 34 Mbps.

SWOP. See *Specifications for Web Offset Publications.*

sword. See *bayonet.*

synchronous optical network (SONET). A form of high-speed digital transmission based on the Synchronous Digital Hierarchy (SDH) interface standard for intelligent networking support to T1 and T3 lines. Its transmission speeds range from 51.84 Mbps to 9953.28 Mbps.

synchronous transmission. High-speed data transfer with timing set by the circuit signals in electronic clocks.

system. The combination or configuration of software and hardware components, consoles, peripherals, and connections necessary to perform specific processing oper-ations electronically.

system architecture. The particular configuration in which computer hardware is connected to various other components so that it fulfills its primary purpose.

T

T1/T3. AT&T specifications for high-bandwidth, leased digital transmission. Unlike switched lines in which the printer pays just for the time required to complete a transmission, T1 and T3 lines are dedicated to continuous data transfer and thus more costly. Data rates are 1.544 Mbps for T1 and 44.21 Mbps for T3. A fractional T1 line has its bandwidth partitioned into smaller channels for point-to-point communications.

tab. See *tabular material; quad left; quad right.*

table. The arrangement of text in more than one column.

tabloid. The newspaper page size, approximately 11¾ in. wide and from 15 to 17 in. long, or about half of the standard newspaper page size.

tabular material. Numeric and alphanumeric data set in parallel columns separated by blank spaces or divided by rules.

tack. The cohesion between ink particles, which is measured by determining the force required to split an ink film between two surfaces. See also: *ink tack.*

tagged image file format (TIFF). A file format for exchanging bitmapped images (usually scans) between applications.

tail. The back end of a sheet or printed image opposite the gripper edge.

tail pin. On a pin-register system, the pin at the back edge of the flat or plate.

tail-end hook. Paper curl that develops at the back edge of the sheet away from the printed side.

tape drive. A mechanism capable of reading information from magnetic tapes and writing information onto them.

Targa. A file format for exchanging 24-bit color files on personal computers.

tear sheet. A job sample torn from a book or newspaper, sometimes with corrections or changes marked on it.

telecommunications. (1) The transmission of data and/or voice over the network of telephone lines. (2) Any data transmission from one independent device to another, regardless of distance or method.

telephony. The marriage of digital computers and telephone service.

telnet. The Internet tool that enables users to connect to a computer at a remote location and search its databases for information. Unlike the files accessed during an FTP session, the information gleaned during a Telnet session cannot be downloaded to the user's computer for future reference.

tempera. A water-reducible, opaque, matte-finish paint in which an albuminous or colloidal medium (as egg yolk) is employed as a vehicle instead of oil or varnish.

tensile strength. The amount of stress needed to break paper.

tensile strength, z-direction. A measure of the force required to break a paper in a direction vertical to its surface.

terabyte. One thousand gigabytes or one million megabytes.

Terminal

terminal. A peripheral computer system device, consisting of a monitor and keyboard. It is usually connected to the mainframe through some sort of network.

terminal emulation. The process by which an individual computer behaves as if it were actually part of a remote computer network, such as when a user establishes dial-up connectivity to a public-access Internet service provider.

tertiary. Those colors obtained by mixing two secondary colors.

text. The body matter of a page composed in column or paragraph form. Display matter, headings, and illustrations do not fall into this category.

text processing. Computer systems, stand-alone devices, and application software products that are used to enter, modify, rearrange, format, display, and print out text.

text string. A term used to distinguish a sequence of characters to be typeset, as opposed to the format and command code strings that contain typesetting instructions.

thermal ink jet. See *bubble jet; hot-melt ink jet.*

thermal printer. A nonimpact printer that uses heat-sensitive paper to form the image. The paper passes over a matrix of heating elements that act to change its color.

thermal printing, direct. (1) That form of thermal printing in which the printhead comes in direct contact with the heat-sensitive paper. (2) Printing in which the image is created by using selectively heated nibs in a printhead to thermally trigger the reaction of components coated on a paper or film.

thermal transfer, resistive ribbon. (1) A method of thermal transfer printing in which the ribbon itself contains the heated element. (2) An imaging process in which ink is selectively melted from a resistive donor ribbon by passing an electric current generated by an array of electrodes in the printhead through the ribbon.

thermal transfer printing. A printing method in which heat emitted from a printhead softens a ribbon coated with wax-based inks and transfers the ink to the substrate.

thermographic paper. (1) A substrate in which an image is formed as a result of irreversible chemical changes that occur when heat is applied. (2) A substrate in which the image is formed as a result of physical changes that occur in a thin coating over the sheet.

thermography. Raised printing created by heating freshly printed ink that has been coated with a special powder.

thermoplastic. Any resin that can be melted by heat and then cooled to form a solid.

thermoplastic toner. Resin particles that melt when heated, fusing the image to the substrate.

thin space. A relative space of known value, usually one-fifth or one-quarter of an em space. See also: *em space.*

thixotropy. The property that causes lithographic inks to become fluid when worked and to return to a semi-solid state later. This can cause some inks to back away from the ink fountain rollers.

three-color process printing. A method of printing in which it is theoretically possible to reproduce all of the hues found in an original by using three separate printing plates, each recording one of the primary colors found in the original. These plates usually are made from three halftone color separation negatives or positives.

three-knife trimmer. See *trimmer, three-knife.*

Threshold Limit Value (TLV). The concentration of an airborne substance that an average person can be repeatedly exposed to without adverse effects.

through drier. A slow-acting drier that solidifies the ink film throughout and does not form a hard surface.

throughput. The capacity of a printing system to deliver printed products, usually expressed in sheets per hour, impressions per hour, feet per minute, pages per minute, or square feet per hour.

thumb edge. The outside edge of a book, directly opposite the binding edge.

thumbnail sketch. Crude, small layouts sketched in pencil to develop the initial concept for a design.

Thumbnails

TIFF. See *tagged image file format.*

time division multiple access (TDMA). A method of concurrently transmitting several communications signals over a single transmission media.

tinctorial strength. The relative ability of a pigment or dye to impart a color value to a printing ink.

tint. An image element with an even shading produced by either a halftone dot screen of various shapes and sizes or fine parallel lines. Tints produced with halftone dot screens are often used to measure dot area, dot gain, and print contrast while tints produced with parallel lines are used to measure slur. See *screen tint; halftone tint.*

tint block. A panel of low-intensity color over which illustration type may be printed.

tint sheet. A transparent overlay containing a pattern or texture of dots or other small designs. Rated by density of area coverage or by a pattern design number, tint sheets are used to provide flat tints of color values and to "fake" simple process color reproductions.

tinting. Ink pigment particles that bleed into the dampening solution causing an overall tint to quickly appear on the unprinted areas of the sheet. This tint may appear on the nonimage areas of the plates but can be washed off with water and a sponge; however, it reoccurs when printing is resumed.

tinting strength. The color intensity of an ink as determined by the amount of white ink that can be added to it and still produce a particular light shade of the original ink color.

tip-in. Using an adhesive to attach a leaf, illustration, or foldout to a book.

tissue overlay. A thin transparent sheet of paper placed over artwork or the pasteup to protect it. Instructions, corrections, and color breaks are usually indicated on the overlay.

T-marks. A configuration of thin, accurately ruled lines used in printing to identify folds, trims, and bleeds.

T-marks

toggle. The act of switching back and forth from one file or display to another to compare two images. The two images usually represent the "before" and "after" stages of image processing or manipulation.

token ring. A broadcast network standard that transmits all signals across the system, using a special configuration of bits called a token to determine access. Only the computer next in line for the token can transmit or receive data.

token-passing bus. A physical network standard in which signals are regenerated as the ring moves from one workstation to another.

tone. The degree of lightness or darkness in any given area of a print. Alternative term: *tone value.*

tone, three-quarter. A tonal value that is approximately 75% of the total dot area.

tone compression. The reduction in density (or tonal range) that occurs naturally in the printed reproduction of an original. It is possible to compensate for it, to improve the quality of the reproduction.

tone reproduction. A comparison of the density of every tone in a reproduction to the corresponding densities on the original.

tone reproduction curve. A graph depicting the relationship between the densities of the original and the corresponding densities on the printed reproduction.

tone-line technique. A process used to convert continuous-tone originals into line reproductions that resemble pen-and-ink sketches or other fine-line drawings.

toner. (1) The electrostatically charged carbon particles suspended in a liquid solvent that fuse to the substrate with heat during photocopying and laser printing, forming the printed image. (2) The powder or liquid used to form images in some color proofing systems. (3) The pigment or dye used to darken the value of an ink color.

toner, monocomponent. A toner that does not need a carrier. It is used in magnetic printing.

toning. Intensifying or changing the degree of lightness or darkness in any area of a photographic print after processing. Toners are used to produce various shades of brown and blue.

tool marks. Improper hand corrections that show up as printed results in gravure.

tooling. (1) Impressing book covers with a blind or gold leaf or color design formed by a heated stamp or die. (2) Hand-engraving to correct or repair blemishes or add detail and tone to the copper surface of gravure plates or cylinders.

topology. The physical layout of a computer network.

topping. Coating an engraved gravure cylinder with an ink resist to enhance coverage during printing.

total quality management (TQM). A management approach to long-term success through customer satisfaction. TQM is based on the participation of all members of an organization to continuously improve processes, products, services, and the company culture. See also: *continuous improvement.*

tracks. The parallel recording channels on a memory device (such as magnetic tape); the concentric recording channels on disk drives and high-performance optical drives; or the spiral recording patterns on devices such as a CD-ROM.

trade customs. The business terms, policies, and industry guidelines codified by trade associations for printers and service bureaus. This information provides the starting point for developing contracts and estimates.

transfer cylinders. The press cylinders that convey paper from one printing unit to another. Paper grippers mounted on the transfer cylinders hold the paper as it travels on the cylinder.

transfer lettering. See *alphabet sheets.*

transfer station. In electrostatic printing, the area where toner is removed from the drum and applied to the substrate.

transforms. The algorithms applied to image data to optimize the conversion from one color space to another.

translucent. Transmitting and diffusing light so that objects beyond cannot be seen clearly.

Transmission Control Protocol/Internet Protocol (TCP/IP). The system that monitors and performs data transfer over the Internet. TCP sends data and IP receives it. On individual computers TCP/IP is the software component that enables users to access the graphical aspect of the World Wide Web and utilize other features of a SLIP or PPP account.

transmission copy. A slide or transparency used as original art for reproduction. Such copy is viewed by the light transmitted through its surface and can only be photoreproduced with back illumination. See also: *reflection copy*.

transmission densitometer. See *densitometer*.

transmittance. The fraction of transmitted incident light that passes through any tone area without being absorbed or scattered.

transparency. A positive photographic record of an image, frequently a color slide, on film.

transparent. A material that permits the relatively free passage of light through it. Objects beyond or under the material are distinct.

transposition. The incorrect reverse-order positioning of two adjacent characters or words.

trap, apparent. A relative indication of how well (or how poorly) an overprint ink sticks or "traps" over the first-down ink as compared to how well the overprinted ink traps on bare paper. Apparent trap is usually measured only when printing a wet ink on top of another wet ink.

trap, apparent, Preucil. See *Preucil apparent trap*.

trapping. (1) Printing a wet ink over a previously printed dry or wet ink film. See also: *lifting.* (2) How well one color overlaps another without leaving a white space between the two or generating a third color. See also: *choke; spread.*

trapping, dry. Printing overprints, or one color on top of another, when the first color is already dry. Printing multicolor work on a single-color press.

trapping, wet. Overprinting one wet ink film over an other wet ink film. Wet trapping occurs in multicolor printing on presses with multiple printing units. A wet trap can be measured with a densitometer that has a trap-reading function or mode. Process solid ink patches and overprint ink patches are read with a densitometer. The densitometer then uses a formula to create a trap value expressed in percent. A 100% trap would be a perfect ink trap. This never happens in normal wet ink overprinting; the values are less than 100%.

trend chart. A simple graph on which measures of a particular variable are plotted over time, such as hours of machine downtime or the amount of paper waste generated each week. Alternative terms: *r chart; run chart.* See also: *control chart.*

trichromatic. Consisting of or using three colors.

trim. The excess area of a printed form or page in which instructions, register marks, and quality control devices are printed. The trim is cut off before binding.

trim margin. The white space on the open side of a signature.

trim marks. Guide marks on the original copy and the printed sheet to indicate where the sheet will be cut.

trim size. The final dimensions of a page.

trimask film. A film that combines the three color-correcting masks into a single color film for transparency- and camera-back masking.

trimmer, collecting. A machine that gathers two books, one on top of the other, and trims them. See also: *two-on binding.*

trimmer, three-knife. A cutting machine with three knives, two parallel and one at a right angle, used to trim books or booklets. It operates automatically, usually at the end of a saddle stitcher, perfect binder, or casebound book binding system.

trimout. The area between two books that is removed when a job bound two-up is cut apart by the fourth and fifth knife of a trimmer.

tristimulus values. Sets of three numbers used to designate the amounts of red, green, and blue light in an image.

tritone. A halftone printed with three colors.

truck. Two pages of a book, tabloid, or newspaper, set up and processed together. Alternative term: *double truck.*

tucker blade. A reciprocating knife used to force signatures into jaws to produce a jaw fold, or between rollers to produce a chopper fold.

tungsten halogen lamp. See *quartz-iodine lamp.*

turnkey system. All of the hardware and software components needed to perform a computer application as already contained in a single computer when it is purchased.

tusche. Special crayons or a liquid mixture of waxes and resins with lampblack used to write or draw on a lithographic plate. Today, only fine artists use this process.

tusche-glue printing screen. Using special crayons or a mixture of waxes and resins to draw a design directly on a mounted, stretched screen printing fabric. A coating of water-soluble glue is applied on one side and then the tusche is dissolved with mineral spirits. When the tusche is washed out, it leaves an open stencil design.

two-on binding. Term used to describe two books trimmed one on top of the other. See also: *trimmer, collecting.*

two-sheet detector. See *double-sheet detector.* Alternative term: *two-sheet caliper.*

two-up. Printing two identical pages on the same press sheet, usually by exposing the plate twice to the same negative. See also: *one-up.*

two-up binding. Binding two units at a time, then cutting them apart and trimming them.

type. The letters, numerals, and special figures produced in different faces and sizes by various composition methods.

type family. A set of typefaces derived from one basic design, e.g., the bold, italic, and condensed variations of the original face.

type gauge. (1) A rule that is graduated in various point units and used to measure the body of type matter or the spacing between lines of type. (2) A fixed caliper used to determine whether type is exactly type-high.

type high. (1) The height of a piece of type from its feet to its face. In the U.S. and Great Britain this measurement is standardized at 0.918 in. (2) Any printing form or material that is the same height as the type.

type size. See *point size*.

type "speccing." Marking up a manuscript with the information required for typesetting. See also: *specifications*.

type styles. A system of general classifications for type, as distinguished by four divisions: Roman, Italic, Script, and Gothic.

typeface. A distinctive type design, usually produced in a range of sizes (fonts) and variations, including bold and italic.

typefont. See *font*.

typefonts, "tuned." Digital type images that are hand-edited to optimize the visual quality of the characters in relation to the resolution (lines per inch) of a given imaging technology, the actual resolution, the image spot energy profile, and the interaction between adjacent image spots.

typeform. See *form*.

typescript. A manuscript ready to be typeset.

typeset. To compose type in a standardized form.

typesetter. (1) A machine that composes type according to certain standardized specifications. (2) The person who sets type. See also: *phototypesetter*.

typesetter, fourth-generation. See *imagesetter*.

typesetting. Composing type into words and lines in accordance with the manuscript and typographic specifications. See also: *composition; phototypesetting.*

typesetting, digital. Imagesetters and third-generation phototypesetting machines that eliminate the need for film fonts by storing digital codes in the computer unit and producing type characters as microscopic dots. See also: *imagesetter.*

typo. An unintentional error made during keyboarding or by the typesetting machine itself. The latter is often referred to as a *machine error.*

typography. The art and craft of creating and/or setting type professionally.

U

ultraviolet (UV) curing. Using ultraviolet radiation to convert a wet coating or printing ink film to a solid film.

ultraviolet (UV) curing units. An in-line conveyor that carries the printed substrate under a focused beam of ultraviolet light to dry it.

ultraviolet (UV) inks. Printing inks containing an activator that causes the polymerization of binders and solvents after exposure to a source of ultraviolet radiation.

ultraviolet radiation. The range of electromagnetic radiation (light wavelengths of 200 to 400 nanometers) that lies outside the visible spectrum. In the graphic arts, UV rays are used to induce photochemical reactions.

unbleached. A term used to describe papers with a light brown coloring that have been manufactured with unbleached pulp.

uncoated. A paper stock that has received no mineral applications.

undercolor. In process printing, the yellow, magenta, and cyan present in dark, neutral tones.

undercolor addition (UCA). The inverse function of undercolor removal (UCR). Undercolor addition is applied in conjunction with gray component replacement (GCR) because 100% GCR does not produce a good saturated black in a print. This makes it necessary to add a controlled amount of "undercolor" to the GCR in the black areas. Electronic scanners compute UCA. See also: *gray component replacement.*

undercolor removal (UCR). A technique used to reduce the yellow, magenta, and cyan dot percentages in neutral tones by replacing them with increased amounts of black ink. See also: *gray component replacement (GCR).*

undercut. (1) In lithography, the difference between the radius of the cylinder body and the radius of the cylinder bearers. (2) Engravings on which side-wall areas have been etched under the printing surface as in gravure. (3) The spread of light beyond the transparent design areas of a negative or positive during exposure. This problem results frequently if the film and plate are not in proper contact.

Undercut (1)

underexposure. A condition in which too little actinic light reaches a photo-sensitive paper, plate, or film, producing a thin negative, a dark slide, or a muddy-looking print that lacks detail.

underpacking. (1) In lithography, the sheets of paper placed under the plate and blanket to bring low surface areas up to printing height. (2) An adjustment to printing diameters that compensates for paper caliper variations while maintaining printing pressure. Alternative term: *underlay.*

underrun. Producing fewer printed sheets than specified or ordered. Trade customs permit a standard tolerance for overruns or underruns.

underscore. To set a rule under a word or sentence in type composition.

underset. (1) A loosely typeset line with excessive word space values. See also: *river.* (2) A line of type not filling a desired measure.

undertone. The color of a thin film of ink. It is actually the color of light reflected by the paper and transmitted through the ink film.

undertrapping. Overprinting an insufficient amount of ink on top of a previously printed ink film.

uniform resource locator (URL). The World Wide Web address of a company, service, or other information resource.

uniformity. The consistency of color reproduction and printing quality from unit to unit as one sheet passes through a press.

unit set. (1) A multipart business form with a carbon tissue interleaf or an individual NCR (carbonless) business form. (2) A term used to describe type characters in terms of unit dimensions instead of points.

unitack. A series of printing inks that have the same tack rating.

universal asynchronous receiver/transmitter (UART). The computer chips that facilitate synchronous and asynchronous serial communications.

UNIX. The computer environment in which the Internet has been and continues to be developed. It is used to run powerful workstations and networks where multitasking and multiuser access is essential. UNIX is also the parent operating system of DOS, which, in turn, spawned the Windows/95/NT operating systems prevalent on PCs today.

unjustified text. See *flush left; justification; quad left.*

unsharp masking (USM). The increase of tonal contrast where light and dark tones come together at the edges of the images. USM is accomplished electronically on a color scanner by comparing readings taken through two different-size apertures and then adding the signal difference in the two readings to the signal from the larger aperture; this signal reduces density in the lighter areas, and increases density in the darker areas of the original, creating the illustration of a sharper picture. USM is accomplished photographically by combining a low-density, unsharp photographic mask with the sharp image from which the mask was made. See also: *peaking.*

unwanted colors. The three color patches on the GATF Color Reproduction Guide that should record the same as the white patch when the guide is color-separated. For example, on the yellow separation, the blue, cyan, and magenta patches should record the same as the white patch. See also: *wanted colors.*

upload. To transmit a file from a local computer's hard drive to the hard drive of a remote computer. See also: *download.*

uppercase. The capitalized letters of the alphabet and other symbols produced when the "shift" key on a typewriter-style keyboard is depressed. Originally called uppercase because the lead type version was located in the upper portion of the California Job Case. See also: *lowercase.*

UseNet News The information forum subset of the Internet. It is organized first by broad categories (e.g., miscellaneous), then by topical groups (e.g., industry); and finally by special interest group (e.g., quality). The UseNet Newsgroup defined by the previous examples would be *misc.industry.quality,* an actual group dealing with total quality management. Forums on commercial online services and BBSs mimic the UseNet concept.

utilities. A set of computer routines, used primarily for system maintenance or to facilitate applications, such as copying to disks, creating directories, or searching for information.

uudecode. A UNIX utility program also used on personal computers to reconstruct, or decode, binary program or graphics files encoded as ASCII for transfer over the Internet. The complementary uuencode program transforms binary graphics and program files into ASCII-encoded text. The letters "uu" stand for "UNIX to UNIX."

V

V.32 bis. The CCITT standard that specifies modem transmission at 14.4 Kbps.

V.34. The CCITT standard that specifies modem transmission at 28.8 Kbps.

V.42 bis. The CCITT standard for data compression.

vacuum frame. A device that holds film or plates in place by withdrawing air through small holes in a rubber supporting surface. Alternative terms: *contact printing frame; vacuum back.*

Vacuum frame

value. Term used in the Munsell system of color notation to describe color lightness or brightness.

valve jet. A drop-on-demand ink jet printer in which a nozzle opens and closes to distribute ink to the substrate. Alternative term: *asynchronous ink jet.* See also: *bubble jet; drop-on-demand ink jet.*

Van dyke. (1) In lithography, a print made on an inexpensive photographic paper from a negative or an assembled flat prior to platemaking. Used for proofreading, to check lay, color registration, and for customer or agency approval. See also: *blueline; brownprint; silverprint.* (2) An early reversal or deep-etch process of lithographic platemaking using positives and a bichromated glue sensitizer.

variable printing. A function of ink jet printers and some typewriters and computer software programs in which specific, changeable information such as names, addresses, and other personalized messages can be inserted or merged into a standardized printed document, such as an advertisement or sweepstakes entry form.

variation. The inevitable difference among individual outputs of a process. Variation can be classified in terms of natural causes (common, normal) or assignable (special, abnormal). For example, some dot gain occurs naturally during prepress and presswork, but dot gain caused by improper plate-to-blanket squeeze or an excessive ink film thickness is abnormal.

varnish. (1) A thin protective coating applied to a printed sheet to protect the image and improve appearance. (2) The major component of an ink vehicle, consisting of solvent plus a resin or drying oil. See also: *vehicle.*

vector file. An electronic file that describes geometric shapes and dimensions in terms of coordinates or other symbols. It also contains page design commands. See also: *spline.*

vectors. Mathematical descriptions of images and their placement. In electronic publishing, vector graphics information is transferred from a design workstation to a raster image processor (RIP) that interprets all of the page layout information for the marking engine of the imagesetter. PostScript, or another page description language, serves as an interface between the page layout workstation and the RIP. See also: *bitmap; imagesetter; line art; object-oriented; page description language; Post-Script™; raster; raster image processor.*

vegetable parchment. A greaseproof paper with high wet strength. It is produced by passing a paper web through a sulfuric acid bath that fuses its fibers into a homogeneous mass.

vehicle. The liquid component of a printing ink. See also: *varnish.*

vellum. A fine cream-colored writing or printing material originally made from unsplit calfskin. It has a fine-grained finish, smoother than antique.

Velox. A photographic print prepared from a halftone negative. It is placed on pasteups and photographed with line copy, eliminating the need for further screening or stripping operations. Velox is a trade name for an Eastman Kodak photographic contact printing paper.

verso. The reverse, back, or left-hand side of a page, folded sheet, book, or cover. See also: *recto.*

vibrator rollers. See *oscillator.*

video display terminal (VDT). See *cathode-ray tube.*

view file. A low-resolution electronic file containing the actual data used to form the final output page. Its primary use is to drive (display an image) on the workstation's color monitor. The view file can be output to continuous-tone material to provide a low-resolution proof of a quality slightly better than that displayed on the workstation monitor.

viewing conditions. A set of American National Standards Institute (ANSI) specifications that dictate the conditions under which originals (transparencies and reflection prints), proofs, and reproductions are viewed. For the graphic arts, the standard specifies a color temperature of 5000 K (a light level of approximately 200 foot-candles), a color-rendering index of ninety, and, for viewing transparencies, a neutral gray surround. Large-format transparencies must be viewed with 2–4 in. of white surround and should never be viewed with a dark surround. It is also necessary to view the original or reproduction at an angle to reduce glare.

vignette. (1) A halftone, drawing, or engraved illustration in which the background gradually fades away from the principal subject until it finally blends into the nonimage areas of the print. (2) An image segment with densities varying from highlight to white. See also: *degradee.* (3) Any small decorative illustration or design used to ornament a book, periodical, or other printed matter, especially before the title page and at the ends of sections or chapters.

vignetted dots. Dots that gradually vary in density from center to edges.

virgin fiber. A substance derived directly from its original source and used for the first time in papermaking.

virtual elimination. Removing pollutants within a targeted cleanup area to the extent that they no longer pose a health or safety threat to humans or the environment.

virtual memory. Program that enables a computer to allocate information to a portion of the hard drive when RAM is exceeded.

virus. A computer program specifically designed to harm a computer's hard drive or certain applications stored therein. Viruses are transported across networks or through shared disks or via Internet downloads to computers lacking virus protection.

viscoelastic. A material, such as an offset printing ink, that behaves as both a fluid and an elastic solid.

viscometer. An instrument used to measure how well an ink, glue, or other fluid resists flow.

viscosity. A measure of how well a printing ink, glue, or other fluid resists flowing. Viscosity is the opposite of fluidity.

viscosity, absolute. A characteristic of one-component liquids that have a constant ratio of shear stress over shear rate (constant viscosity).

visible spectrum. See *prism; spectrum, visible; white light.*

volatile organic compound (VOC). Any organic compound that significantly participates in photochemical reactions. Presence in emissions (pounds/day) by which clean air standards are measured (e.g., 15 pounds VOC emissions per day). The cleaning solvents used in the printing industry are among those chemical substances that are subject to governmental regulations regarding safety hazards because of VOC emissions.

W

waffling. See *embossing*.

walk. The erosion and gradual disappearance of the printed image from the plate during the run. Fogged negatives or insufficient density in positives, particularly in the highlights or in fine printing detail, may cause this problem. Alternative terms: *walk-off*; *walk-away*.

wall. The side of the bridge or division between cells on a gravure cylinder or the thickness of material on a base cylinder shell.

wanted colors. The three color patches on the GATF Color Reproduction Guide that should record the same as the black patch when the guide is separated. For example, on the yellow separation, the yellow, red, and green patches should record the same as the black patch. See also: *unwanted colors*.

wanted density. A measure of the extent to which an ink absorbs the colors it should absorb.

warm color. A color that is reddish or yellowish. Red, yellow, and orange are regarded as warm colors.

warp. The direction of maximum strength on an offset blanket. The warp is indicated by lines across the back of the blanket. To minimize stretching, the blanket is mounted on the press with the warp running around the cylinder.

wash. In photography, removing fixer and unexposed silver salts from photographic film and papers.

wash bath. The circulating water system that removes chemical residues from photographic materials during processing.

wash drawing. A monochrome watercolor drawing usually prepared with sweeping applications of black and gray pigments that are soluble in water. Intended for reproduction as a halftone, the principal detail in a wash drawing is often emphasized with inked lines.

wash marks. Light or uneven densities at the lead edge of the printed image, increasing in density away from the leading edge. Wash marks are caused by excessive water on the plate. Alternative term: *water streaks*.

washing out. Using solvents to remove the image coating from the plate.

washup. The process of cleaning the rollers, form or plate, and fountain of a press with solvents to remove all ink as required after a day's run, or during a run for ink color changes.

waste. Unwanted materials left over from a manufacturing process. See *chemicals, hazardous; waste, hazardous; waste, industrial.*

waste, commercial. All solid waste emanating from business establishments, including printers.

waste, converting. The trimmings generated when paper is cut into various shapes and sizes.

waste, hazardous. By-products of society that can pose a substantial or potential hazard to human health or the environment when improperly managed. Such waste possesses at least one of four characteristics (ignitability, corrosivity, reactivity, or toxicity), or appears on special EPA lists. See also: *chemicals, hazardous; waste; waste, industrial.*

waste, industrial. Unwanted materials from an industrial operation; may be liquid, sludge, solid, or hazardous waste. See also: *chemicals, hazardous; waste; waste, hazardous.*

waste, post-consumer. Finished material that is recycled or deposed of as solid waste after its product life span is completed.

waste, post-mill. Any waste generated after the paper has left the mill, including pulp substitutes and preconsumer and post-consumer waste.

waste, preconsumer. See *mill broke, dry; mill broke, wet.*

waste, secondary. Fragments of finished products from a manufacturing process. Secondary waste includes printers' trimmings, but not the virgin materials such as mill broke.

waste, solid. Waste materials that are disposed of in their original form by burial in a landfill or incineration.

waste management facility, commercial. A treatment, storage, disposal, or transfer facility that accepts waste from a variety of sources.

waste management facility, private. A treatment facility that manages a limited waste stream generated by its own operations.

waste stream. The movement of waste from generation to disposal.

wastepaper. A paper or paper product that has lost its original value and has been discarded. Printing plant waste, waste generated during paper converting, and discarded boxes and newspapers fall into this category.

wastepaper, recoverability. The imprecise measure or estimate of the quantity or percentage of a wastepaper grade that could be recovered by intensive collection practices.

wastewater. Used water from residential or industrial facilities that contains dissolved or suspended matter.

water finish. A glossy coat obtained by moistening the paper web as its passes through the calender or by applying water to the calender rolls during papermaking.

water pan. See *fountain.*

water stop. One of a series of devices that are set against the surface of a dampening roller on an offset press. Water stops are commonly used in conventional dampening systems to reduce or meter the amount of dampening solution reaching lightly inked areas of a printing plate.

Water stop

water streaks. See *wash marks.*

water-based ink. An ink containing a water-soluble or water-dispersible resin instead of petroleum derivatives.

watercolor. An artistic medium made from transparent dyes dissolved in water.

water-in-ink emulsion. An emulsion of ink and water in which the water is broken up into fine droplets in the ink.

Water-in-ink emulsion

waterleaf. A paper that absorbs water instantly.

waterless printing. See *lithography, waterless.*

watermark. Translucent design impressed in the paper while it is still wet for purposes of identification.

wavelength. The distance between corresponding points on two successive waves of light or sound, etc.

wavy-edged paper. A paper with exposed edges that have absorbed excessive moisture.

Wavy-edged paper

wax. An ink additive that improves slip and resistance, prevents setoff, and reduces tack.

waxer. A machine used to apply a thin, uniform coating of hot, melted wax to photographic paper and reproduction proofs. The wax is used to adhere these materials to pasteup boards and mattes.

web. A roll of any substrate that passes continuously through a printing press or converting or finishing equipment.

web break detector. A sensing device that mechanically, electronically, or pneumatically determines whether the web is passing beneath the device and automatically stops the press when the web is absent to prevent damage to the equipment.

web browser. A graphical or text-based utility that enables users to navigate the World Wide Web. Netscape Navigator and Microsoft Internet Explorer are the two most popular graphical browsers while Lynx is a popular text-based browser.

web lead. The continuous strip of paper passing from supply roll, over various rollers, through press units, to the folder.

web lead rollers. Any of the rollers used to support the paper web as it is fed through a web press.

web offset. A lithographic printing process in which a press prints on a continuous roll of paper instead of individual sheets.

web press. A rotary press that prints on a continuous web, or ribbon, of paper fed from a roll and threaded through the press. See also: *sheetfed press.*

webfed. A printing press that prints on a continuous roll of paper instead of individual sheets.

wedding paper. A fancy paper with a very uniform, closed formation and a refined surface lacking glare.

weft. The direction of minimum strength on a web offset blanket.

weight. See *basis weight.*

weight, character. A typographic term is used to specify the variation of a letterform. Weight designations include light, medium, bold, extra bold, and ultra bold.

well. A single cell on a gravure cylinder.

wet collodion process. A method of photography in which glass plates are coated with salted (iodized) negative collodion, then sensitized by immersion in an acidified silver nitrate solution and exposed in a moist condition.

wet end. The forming section of the paper machine, that area between the headbox and the dryer section.

wet method. A process of preparing carbon tissue for screen printing. The carbon tissue is exposed while it is damp.

wet printing. In multicolor work, printing the second and any additional colors over a previously printed wet ink film. See *trapping.*

wet rub. A wet paper's resistance to scuffing.

wet strength. The firmness of a paper after it has been saturated with water for a specified time, as determined by its wet tensile or wet bursting strength.

wet trapping. See *trapping.*

wet-on-wet. See *trapping.*

wetplate. A photographic plate produced by the wet collodion process.

wet-strength paper. (1) A paper that maintains at least 15% of its dry tensile strength when wet with water. See also: *tensile strength.* (2) A substrate designed for the production of outdoor posters. It is weather- and tear-resistant and contains special longer fibers.

wettability. In printing, the ease with which a pigment can be completely wet by the ink vehicle.

wetting. Surrounding the ink pigment particles with varnish during the ink manufacturing process. Pigments that "wet out" easily will, in general, grind more easily, form better ink bodies, and result in a finer dispersion.

wetting agents. Any of various chemical substances that reduce the surface tension of a liquid, thereby promoting smoother and more uniform results. Alternative term: *dispersing agents.*

wetting up. In screen printing, placing ink in the printing screen and making one or more strokes with the squeegee to distribute the ink evenly before beginning the actual production run.

what-you-see-is-what-you-get. See *WYSIWYG.*

white. (1) The presence of all colors. (2) The visual perception produced by light in which each wavelength has the same relative intensity in the visible range as sunlight.

white component. The portion of wavelengths of other colors that dilutes, or desaturates, a saturated color.

white light. The visual sensation that results when the wavelengths between 400 and 700 nm are combined in nearly equal proportions. See also: *prism; spectrum; spectrum, visible.*

white space. The area in printed matter that is not covered by type and illustrations.

whiteboard. A software tool that promotes collaboration among colleagues in many different locations linked by a computer network and often a video conferencing program. See also: *groupware.*

wide-angle lens. A photographic lens with a shorter focal length and a wider field of view (includes more subject area) than a normal lens.

wide-area network (WAN). Two or more related LANs that are linked across a great distance, such as one state to another.

wideband. A communications channel characterized by data transmission speeds of 10,000 to 500,000 bits per second and a greater band-width than a voice-grade channel. Densitometers are also said to be wideband or narrowband devices.

widow. (1) Any objectionably short line at the end of a paragraph or headline. It may be expressed as anything less than four characters, less than a full word, less than a certain percentage of the line measure, or any other subjective definition. (2) Any single line on the top of a page. See also: *orphan.*

widow band. The blank strip surrounding the area of a press blanket that offsets the image and nonimage areas of the plate to the press sheet or web.

window method. A procedure in which a sized adhesive-backed red masking material is placed on the pasteup board wherever a halftone or separate artwork will print. When photographed, the mask produces a clear area on the negative into which the halftone or artwork is stripped during image assembly. See also: *Rubylith.*

Windows™. A graphical user interface (GUI) from Microsoft that runs "on top of" the DOS operating system. Data is displayed on the monitor in rectangular areas (windows). The user interacts with the software by selecting icons and menu items from a screen. See also: *graphical user interface.*

WinSock. The standards embodied by the Windows Socket Application Programming Interface. This API controls the link between Windows software and a TCP/IP and SLIP/PPP program. See also: *serial-line interface program; transmission control protocol/Internet protocol.*

wipe-on plate. In offset lithography, a plate on which a light-sensitive coating is wiped on or applied manually or by a machine.

wire side. The side of a sheet of paper that was formed in contact with the wire of the paper machine during manufacturing. See also: *felt side.*

wire stitch. See *saddle stitch.*

wireless data transmission. Using microwave and satellite communications or systems based on the exchange of infrared, laser, or radio frequency signals to enable the long-distance exchange of information even where cabling is not present.

wood base. The wooden block used as a mount for letterpress printing plates.

wood cut. A printing form in which the image area has been carved in relief in wood. Alternative term: *wood engraving.*

wood free. A paper not containing groundwood or mechanical pulp. Alternative term: *groundwood free.*

wood type. Blocks of wood into which type characters have been carved in relief. The sizes of wood type were specified in multiples of the pica, and were thus named 8-line, 10-line, etc. Use of wood type predates use of hot-metal composition.

word processor. A personal computer and special software program or dedicated electronic equipment used to create, store, retrieve, and edit text.

Word processor

word spacing. In phototypesetting, the variable space that the computer inserts between words used to justify lines of type. See also: *kerning; justification; spacing.*

word wrap. In word processing and phototypesetting, the ability of a computer to emulate a carriage return or end a line automatically (with a soft return) and then move the cursor immediately to the next line.

work-and-tumble. An imposition (layout) in which the front and back of a form is printed from a single plate. After the first run through the press, the stock pile is inverted so that the back edge becomes the gripper edge for the second printing. Work-and-tumble differs from work-and-turn in that the gripper edge changes, often leading to misregister unless the stock has been accurately squared. Alternative terms: *work-and-flop; work-and-roll.*

work-and-turn. A common printing imposition or layout in which all the images on both sides of a press sheet are placed in such a way that when the sheet is turned over and the same gripper edge is used, one half of the sheet automatically backs up the previously printed half. When the sheet is cut in half parallel to the guide edge, two identical sheets are produced. Work-and-turn impositions are preferred over work-and-tumble impositions for accuracy because the same gripper edge and the same side of the press sheet are used to guide the sheet twice through the press.

work-and-twist. A method of imposition in which a film flat produces two different images on a plate. After the first exposure, the flat is rotated 180° to produce the second exposure.

workstation. A full-featured computer typically dedicated to one person's use.

World Wide Web (WWW). A hypertext program that allows users to access related documents across global networks by navigating a series of electronic links. Developed by scientists at CERN, the European Particle Physics Laboratory in Geneva, Switzerland, in 1989, the WWW was originally text-based. Introduction of the graphical browser NCSA Mosaic in 1993 made it possible to access the color imagery, sound, and video that we commonly associate with the WWW today.

WORM (write-once, read-many). An optical digital storage medium useful for archiving purposes. It receives and stores information permanently on the disk. While, it cannot be erased or altered it can be "read back" many times.

wraparound. (1) A folio or insert placed around a signature prior to stitching and binding. (2) An increased gutter allowance for the outside pages of larger (32-, 48-, and 64-page) signatures to compensate for creep. See also: *creep; shingling.* (3) Method of printing from thin copper plates fastened around a plate cylinder in sheetfed gravure.

wrinkle. (1) A defective crease produced in paper during manufacturing or converting operations. It is classified as wet or dry depending on the moisture content of the sheet when the wrinkle is formed. (2) Marks formed on an ink surface during drying that make it appear uneven. (3) In web printing, a crease produced because of excess water or uneven tension.

write-once, read-many. See *WORM.*

writing black. The electrophotographic method in which the image elements are exposed by light, usually laser light, while the nonimage, or background, areas remain unexposed.

writing white. The electrophotographic method in which the image elements remain unexposed while the nonimage, or background, areas are exposed to light, usually laser light.

wrong font (WF). WF is a proofreading symbol denoting use of the incorrect typeface or size.

wrong-reading image. In Western countries, printed type that reads from right to left, or an image printed backwards from its normal orientation. Wrong-reading film images are read from right to left when the film is viewed from the base side.

WYSIWYG (what-you-see-is-what-you-get). Computer screen displays that approximate the true size and true shape of typographic characters, rules, tints, and graphics.

X

X.25. The oldest packet-switching option and most widely used data transfer protocol. It offers standard speeds between 56 Kbps and 64 Kbps and is still used on many internal corporate LANs.

X-Acto knife. Trademark for a sharp-edged tool used to cut galleys, film, etc.

x-coordinate. (1) The horizontal location of data on a graph, computer monitor, or page layout. (2) The horizontal distance from a selected reference point. Alternative term: *x-axis.* See also: *y-coordinate.*

xenon. A relatively inert gaseous chemical used in various gas-discharge lamps largely because it produces a white light. Pulsed-xenon lamps are commonly used in graphic arts camera work.

xerography. An electrostatic, nonimpact printing process in which heat fuses dry ink toner particles to electrically charged areas of the substrate, forming a permanent image. The charged areas of the substrate appear dark on the reproduction, while the uncharged areas remain white.

x-height. A term used to describe the body height of a type character. It is expressed as the total character height without ascenders or descenders. The letters "x" and "z" from each typeface are selected to serve as examples of the face body height because they rest on the baseline and vary less in height than curved letters. Alternative term: *z-height.*

X-height

x-line. The line that marks the tops of lowercase letters without ascenders. Alternative term: *mean line.*

XMODEM. A widely supported but slow communications protocol that transfers files in 128K blocks. See also: *modem transfer protocols; XMODEM-CRC; YMODEM; YMODEM-G; ZMODEM.*

XMODEM-CRC. The XMODEM communications protocol with error checking (cyclic redundancy check) included. See also: *cyclic redundancy check; modem transfer protocols; XMODEM; YMODEM; YMODEM-G; ZMODEM.*

X Windows. A network windowing environment for UNIX workstations. This device-independent application program interface (API) can create graphical user interfaces under a variety of operating systems, including mainframe, independent of the hardware on a minicomputer-based network. See also: *application program interface.*

Y

yankee dryer. A single, large steam-heated drying cylinder that produces a glazed finish on the side of a paper that dries against it during manufacturing.

y-coordinate. (1) The vertical location of data on a graph, display monitor, or page layout. (2) The vertical distance from a selected reference point. Alternative term: *y-axis*. See also: *x-coordinate*.

yellow. The subtractive transparent primary color that should reflect red and green, and absorb blue light. One of the process-color inks.

yellow printer. In process color printing, the plate used to print the yellow ink image, or the film used to produce the plate that prints the yellow image.

yield value. A term describing the flow properties of a printing ink. The minimum force required to produce flow.

YMODEM. A communications protocol that permits batch file transfer with error checking. See also: *modem transfer protocols; XMODEM; XMODEM-CRC; YMODEM-G; ZMODEM.*

YMODEM-G. A faster variety of the YMODEM protocol. It lacks error checking because it was designed for modems with built-in error checking hardware. See also: *modem transfer protocols; XMODEM; XMODEM-CRC; YMODEM; ZMODEM.*

Young-Helmholtz theory. A theory about color vision that was proposed in the early nineteenth century. It suggests that humans perceive color based on the messages received from three receptors in the eye, one of which is particularly sensitive to red, and the others to the green and blue areas of the visible spectrum respectively.

Yule-Nielsen equation. A modification of the Murray-Davies equation to compensate for light scatter within a substrate when measuring the apparent printed dot area. This equation calculates the physical dot area. See also: *Murray-Davies equation.*

Z

Zahn cup. A device used to measure the viscosity of flexographic or gravure inks.

Zahn cup

zero discharge. Discharge from a point source that has been determined to contain minimal or no pollutants.

zero lead. In phototypesetting, a line ending with no vertical advancement, similar to a carriage return with no line feed on word processing equipment.

zero-speed splicer. An automatic device that attaches a new roll of paper to an expiring roll without a press stop. The device is used in conjunction with a festoon to permit the expiring roll to come to a complete stop just before the splice is made and then to accelerate the new roll up to press speed. See also: *flying paster; festoon.*

z-height. See *x-height.*

zinc oxide. An opaque inorganic white pigment used in inks.

zinc yellow. A yellow pigment consisting essentially of zinc chromate.

zip sorting. The process by which mail is separated according to destination and grouped into bundles. This is often completed during postpress.

ZMODEM. A fast and reliable communications protocol that can resume file transfer after interruption without reactivating the entire process manually. See also: *modem transfer protocols; XMODEM; XMODEM-CRC; YMODEM; YMODEM-G.*

zomag. A special lightweight alloy used for relief etching in photoengraving.

zonal error. A defect in photographic lenses that causes the size of the image to change with the use of apertures or stops of different sizes.

zoom lens. A photographic lens in which the focal length can be adjusted over a wide range, giving the photographer, in effect, lenses of many focal lengths.

zooming. The process of electronically enlarging an image on a computer monitor to facilitate electronic retouching.

Abbreviations and Acronyms Used in Graphic Communications

1D-MH	one-dimensional modified Huffman
2D-MR	two-dimensional modified read (computer file)
3DMF	three-dimensional metafile
3GL	third-generation (computer) language
4GL	fourth-generation (computer) language
A	ampere
Å	angstroms (10 nanometers)
AA	author's alterations
AAL	ATM adaption layer
AAUI	Apple auxiliary unit interface
ABI	application binary interface
AC	author's corrections, alternating current
ACA	asynchronous communications adapter
ACE	(1) access control entry; (2) asynchronous communications element
ACH	automated clearing house
ACK	positive acknowledgement (of data transfer)
ACL	access control list
ACR	(1) achromatic color removal or reproduction; (2) automatic carriage return
ACS	asynchronous communications server
ACTS	advanced communications technologies and services
A/D	analog-to-digital (conversion)
ADB	Apple desktop bus
ADC	analog-digital converter
ADE	automatic directory exchange

ADP	automatic data processing
ADPCM	adaptive differential pulse code modulation
ADSI	analog display services interface
ADSL	asymmetric digital subscriber line
AF	auxiliary carry flag
AGE	asphaltum-gum emulsion
AGU	address-generation unit
AGV	automatic guided vehicle
AI	artificial intelligence
AIS	automated imaging systems
ALGOL	algorithmic-oriented language
ALU	arithmetic logic unit
AM	amplitude modulation
a.m.	ante meridiem
AMD	advanced micro devices incorporated
AMEL	active matrix electroluminescent display
AMLCD	active matrix liquid-crystal display
AMPS	advanced mobile phone standard
ANDF	architecture neutral distribution format
ANN	artificial neural network
ANPAT	American Newspaper Publishers Abstracting Technique, a computerized news editing system
ANS	American National Standard
AP	author's proof
APA	all-points addressable
API	application program interface
APIC	advanced programmable interrupt controller
APM	advanced power management
APPN	advanced peer-to-peer network

APR	automatic picture replacement
APS	advanced printing services
Ar	argon
ARA	Appletalk remote access
ARC	advanced reduced instruction set computing
ArCS	argon laser contact screen
ArEDG	argon laser electronic dot generation
ARLL	advanced run length limited
ARM	advanced RISC machines
AS	advanced server
ASCI	accelerated strategic computing initiative
ASCII	American Standard Code for Information Interchange
ASLM	Apple shared library manager
ASPI	advanced SCSI programming interface
ASR	automatic send-receive
AS/U	advanced server for UNIX
AT	(1) attention (command set); (2) advanced technology
ATAPI	(1) AT advanced protocol interface; (2) AT attachment packet interface
ATF	active thermal feedback
ATM	(1) asynchronous transfer mode; (2) Adobe Type Manager ™
ATT	advanced transport telematics
AV	audiovisual
AVD	alternating voice and data
AVI	audio video interleaved
B	(1) bytes; (2) billion (1,000,000,000); (3)blue or blue filter; (4) base
b	bits
B&W	black and white

BACP	bandwidth allocation control protocol
BACT	best achievable control technology
BAPI	business application programming interface
BASIC	beginner's all-purpose symbolic instruction code
BBSs	bulletin board systems
BCD	binary-coded decimal
BDA	BIOS data area
BDC	backup domain controller
BDE	Borland database engine
BDR	basic density range
BEDO	burst extended data out
BEDORAM	burst extended data out random-access memory
BEL	bell character (typesetting)
BER	bit error rate
BF	boldface
BFT	binary file transfer
BG	blue-green
BGA	ball grid array
BHR	budgeted hourly rate
BIOS	basic input/output system
BISDN	broadband integrated services digital network
BIST	built-in self-test
bit	*bi*nary digi*t*
BitBlt	bit aligned block transfer
BLOB	binary large object
BOND	bandwidth on-demand
BOPS	billion operations per second
BP	base pointer
BPB	BIOS parameter block

bpi	bits per inch
Bps; B/s	bytes per second
bps; b/s	bits per second
BRD	baud rate divisor
BRI	basic rate interface
BSP	bootstrap processor register
BTB	branch target buffer
Btu	British thermal unit
BUS	broadcast unknown server
BW	black and white
C	cyan
C, C++	computer programming languages
C1S	paper coated on one side
C2S	paper coated on both sides
CAA	Clean Air Act
CAAD	computer-aided architectural design
CAB	cellulose acetate butyrate
CAB-EDI	cyber-assisted business electronic data interchange
CAC	computer-aided creativity
CAD	(1) computer-aided design; (2) computer-aided drafting
CAE	computer-assisted estimating
CAFE	conditional access for Europe
CAI	computer-aided instruction
CALS	(1) computer-aided acquisition and logistic support; (2) continuous acquisition and lifecycle support
CAM	computer-aided manufacturing; computer-aided makeup
CAMIS	computer-aided makeup and imaging system
CAN	cancel character
CAP	carrierless amplitude/phase

cap(s)	capital, or uppercase, letter(s)
CAPI	common application programmers interface
carbros	carbon-bromide photographic prints
CAS	(1) column address strobe; (2) computing application specification
CASE	computer-aided software engineering
CATV	cable television
CBDS	connectionless broadband data service
CBR	constant bit rate
CBT	computer-based training
CC	(1) color compensating; (2) color correcting
cc	cubic centimeters
CCA	(1) character content architectures; (2) call control agent
CCCC	color calibration, communication, and control
CCD	charge-coupled device
CC filter	color compensating filter
CCNUMA	cache-coherent nonuniform memory access
CCSD	cellular circuit-switched data
CD	(1) compact disc; (2) carrier detect
CDE	common desktop environment
CD-E	compact disc—erasable
CDFS	CD-ROM file system
CD-I	compact disk—interactive
CDK	control development kit
CDM	conceptual data model
CDMA	code division multiple access
CDP	corporate document production
CDPD	cellular digital packet data
CD-R	compact disc—recordable
CDRAM	cached dynamic random-access memory

CD-ROM	compact disc—read-only memory
CDTP	color diffusion transfer paper
CD-XA	compact disc—extended architecture
CEPS	color electronic prepress system
CERCLA	Comprehensive Environmental Response, Compensation, and Liability Act
CF	carry flag
CFA	compact flash association
CFM	(1) cubic feet per minute; (2) code fragment manager
CFR	computerize facial recognition
CFS	caching file system
CGA	computer graphics adapter
CGI	(1) computer graphics interface; (2) common gateway interface; (3) computer-generated imaging
CGM	computer graphics metafile
CHAP	challenge handshake authentication protocol
CHRP	common hardware reference platform
CID	configuration, installation, and distribution
CIDR	classless interdomain routing
CIF	common interchange format
CIR	committed information rate
CIRC	cross-interleaved Reed-Solomon code
CISC	complex instruction set chip
CITED	copyright in transmitted electronic documents
CLI	(1) command-line interface; (2) call-level interface
CLIP	calling line identification presentation
CLIR	calling line identification restriction
CLOS	common LISP object system
CLV	constant linear velocity
cm	centimeters

CMM	capability maturity model
CMOS	complementary metal oxide semiconductor
CMSA	consolidated metropolitan statistical area
CMYK	cyan, magenta, yellow, and black
coax	coaxial cable
COBOL	*co*mmon *b*usiness *o*riented *l*anguage
COM	(1) computer-output microfilm; (2) component object model
comp	comprehensive design
contone	continuous tone
COP	control and optimization package
CORBA	common object request broker architecture
COSE	common operating system environment
CP	chemically pure
CPF	cold pressure fusing
CPI	characters per inch
CPL	characters per line
CPM	(1) copies per minute; (2) characters per minute
CPP	(1) characters per pica; (2) color photo paper
CPS	characters per second
CPU	central processing unit
CR	carriage return
CRC	cyclic redundancy check
CREF	(Scitex) computer-ready electronic file
CRI	cure rate index
CRT	cathode-ray tube
CRTC	cathode-ray tube controller
CS	(1) color scanner; (2) code segment
CSCS	conventional source contact screen
CSLIP	compressed serial-line Internet protocol

CSMA/CA	carrier sense multiple access with collision avoidance
CSMA/CD	carrier sense multiple access with collision detection
CSR	(1) customer service representative; (2) character shape recorder
CSRG	computer systems research group
CSU	channel service unit
CSU/DSU	channel service unit/data service unit
CSV	comma-separated value
CT	(1) continuous tone; (2) computerized tomography
CTCS	continuous-tone color scanner
CTG	control techniques guideline
CTI	(1) coherent toroidal interconnect; (2) computer telephony integration
CTP	computer-to-plate
CTS	clear to send
cu.	cubic (with length unit)
CUA	common user access
CUG	closed user group
CUI	common user interface
CVF	compressed volume file
CVRAM	cached video random access memory
CVT	configuration variable table
CW	(1) continuous wave; (2) cool white
CWA	(U.S.) Clean Water Act
CWT	hundred weight
DAA	data access arrangement
DAC	digital-to-analog converter
DAD	desktop application director
DAO	data access objects
DASD	direct access storage device

DAT	digital audio tape
DAV	digital audio video
DAVIC	digital audio-visual council
dB, db	decibel
DBCS	double-byte character set
DBML	database markup language
DBMS	database management system
DC	(1) direct current; (2) device context
DCD	data carrier detect
DCE	data communications equipment
DCI	display control interface
DCS	(1) desktop color separation; (2) digital cellular system; (3) distributed control system
DCT	discrete cosine transform
DD	double density
DDA	digital differential analyzer
DDAP	digital distribution of advertising for publications
DDC	data display channel
DDCMP	digital data communications message protocol
DDCP	direct-digital color proofing
DDCS	distributed data connection services
DDE	dynamic data exchange
DDES	digital data exchange standards
DDI	device driver interface
DDK	device driver kit
DDL	(1) data definition language; (2) dynamic data library; (3) document description language
DDNS	dynamic domain naming system/services
DDPP	direct-digital printing plate
DDS	digital data storage

DDVT	dynamic dispatch virtual table
DE	discard eligible
DEBI	DMA extended bus interface
DECT	digital European cordless telecommunications
DEF	device exchange formats
DEN	document enabled networking
DES	data encryption standard
DF	direction flag
DH	discretionary hyphen
DHCP	dynamic host configuration protocol
DHL	dynamic head loading
DI	destination index
DIB	device-independent bitmap
DICOM	digital imaging and communications in medicine
DIL	dual inline
DIMM	dual inline memory module
DIN	Deutsche Industrie-Norm
DIP	(1) dual inline package; (2) dual inline pin
DIS	draft international standard
DISADV	dispatch advice
DIT	directory information tree
DKS	digital keyline system
DLC	data-link control
DLL	dynamic link library
DLP	digital light processing
DLPI	data link provider interface
DLT	digital linear tape
DM	data mining
DMA	direct memory access

DMC	dynamic Markov coding
DMD	digital micromirror display
DMI	desktop management interface
DML	data manipulation language
DMS	document management systems
DMT	discrete multitone
DNS	domain name serve/service
DOD	drop-on-demand ink jet
DOE	distributed objects everywhere
DOLE	distributed object linking and embedding
DOS	disk operating system
DP	(1) draft proposal; (2) data processing; (3) dual processing
DPC	digital page composing
DPE	distributed processing environment
DPI	dots per inch
DPM	dynamic power management
DPMI	DOS protected mode interface
DPMS	display power management signaling
DPS	display PostScript
DPSK	differential phase change shift keying
DPSPAR	digital processing systems personal animation recorder
DQL	data query language
DR	dynamic recompilation
DRAM	dynamic random access memory
DS	data segment
DSA	directory system agent
DSOM	distributed system object model
DSP	(1) directory synchronization protocol; (2) digital signal processor
DSR	data set ready

DSS   digital signature standard

DSU   data service unit

DSVD   digital simultaneous voice and data

DT   diffusion transfer

DTA   disk transfer address

DTC   desktop color

DTD   document type definition

DTE   data terminal equipment

DTMF   dual-tone modulated frequency

DTP   (1) desktop publishing; (2) direct to plate; (3) direct to press

DTR   data terminal ready

DUA   directory user agent

DVC   desktop videoconferencing

DVD   (1) digital video disk; (2) digital versatile disk

DWMT   discrete wavelet multitone

DXI   data exchange interface

E   emulsion

EB   electron beam

EBCDIC   extended binary coded decimal interchange code

EBDA   extended BIOS data area

ECC   error correction circuits/ code

ECF   elemental chlorine-free (paper)

ECM   error correction mode

ED   extra density

EDG   electronic dot generation

EDI   electronic data interchange

EDIFACT   electronic data interchange for administration, commerce and transport

EDO   extended data out

EDORAM   extended data out random-access memory

EDOSRAM   extended data out static random-access memory

EDOVRAM   extended data out video random-access memory

EDP   (1) electronic design in print; (2) electronic data processing

EDR   early developer release

EDRAM   enhanced dynamic random access memory

EDSS1   European digital subscriber signaling system 1

EEL   Epsilon extension language

EEMS   enhanced expanded memory specification

EEPROM   electrically erasable programmable read-only memory

e.g.   for example

EGA   extended graphics adapter

EIDE   enhanced integrated disk electronics

EIP   electronically integrated processes for print

EISA   expanded/extended industry standard architecture

EL   extra lightfast

ELAN   emulated local-area network

EMB   expanded memory block

EMC   enhanced memory chip

EMF   enhanced metafile format

EMI/RFI   electromagnetic interference/radio frequency interference

EMM   expanded memory manager

EMMS   empty multimedia extensions state

EMS   expanded memory specification

EMSI   electronical mail standard identification

EMX   enterprise messaging exchange

END   equivalent neutral density

ENS   enterprise network services

EOF   end of file

EOL	end of line
EOM	end of message
EOT	(1) end of transmission; (2) end of take
EPBX	electronic private branch exchange
EPCRA	Emergency Planning and Community Right-to-Know Act
EPDF	embedded portable document format
EPP	enhanced parallel port
EPPF	encapsulated prepress format
EPROM	erasable programmable read-only memory
EPS	(1) encapsulated PostScript; (2) electronic printing systems
EPSS	electronic performance support system
ER	entity relationship
ES	extra segment
ESC	escape character
ESD	electronic software distribution
ESDI	enhanced small device interface
ETB	end of transmission block
etc.	and so forth
E-to-B	emulsion-to-base
E-to-E	emulsion-to-emulsion
ETX	end of text
FAQs	frequently asked questions
FAT	file allocation table
fax	facsimile
FCAL	fibre channel arbitrated loop
FCB	file control block
FCS	frame check sequence
FDDI	fiber distributed digital interface

FDM	frequency division multiplex
FDMA	frequency division multiple access
FED	field emission display
FF	form feed character
FIFO	first in, first out
FIR	fast infrared
flexo	flexographic or flexography
FLOPS	floating point operations per second
fl. oz.	fluid ounce
FOD	fax on demand
FORTRAN	formula translator
FP	floating point
FPI	family programming interface
FPM	(1) fast page mode; (2) feet per minute
FPM-DRAM	fast page mode dynamic random-access method
FPNW	file and print services for NetWare
FPO	for position only
FPU	floating-point unit
FRAD	frame-relay assembler/disassembler
FRAM	ferroelectric random-access memory
FRC	functional redundancy check
FSI	free-standing insert
FSR	free system resource
ft.	foot
FTP	file transfer protocol
G	(1) giga, or one billion (1,000,000,000); (2) green
g	gram
gal.	gallon

GAN	global-area network
GB	gigabyte
Gb	gigabit
Gbps	gigabits per second
GCR	gray component replacement
GDE	generic decryption engine
GDI	graphical device interface
GDT	global descriptor table
GERDIEN	general European road data information exchange network
GGCA	geometric graphics content architecture
GIBR	graphics industry bar code
GIF	graphics interchange format
GIGO	garbage in, garbage out
GIS	geographic information system
GKS	graphical kernel system
GL	graphics language
GMR	giant magneto-resistive
GNP	gross national product
GPE	general protection error
GPF	general protection fault
GPIO	general-purpose input output
GPR	general-purpose register
GPRS	general packet radio service
GPS	global positioning system
gr.	grain
gsm	(1) grams per square meter; (2) global system for mobile communications
GSS-API	generic security services application programming interface
GUI	graphical user interface
GUID	global universal identification

H	hue
HA	host adapter
H&J	hyphenation and justification
HAL	hardware abstraction layer
HBA	host bus adapter
HCS	hazard communication standard
HDLC	high-level data link control
HDSL	high-bit-rate digital subscriber line
HDSS	holographic data storage system
HDTV	high-definition television
HDVD	high-definition volumetric display
HeCd	helium cadmium (laser)
HEL	hardware emulation layer
HeNe	helium neon (laser)
HeNeCs	helium neon laser contact screen
HFC	hybrid fiber coax
HIF	hyper-G interchange format
HiPPI	high-performance parallel interface
HLS	hue, lightness (or luminance), and saturation
HMD	head-mounted display
HMIS	Hazardous Materials Identification System
HMM	hidden Markov model
HPC	high-performance computing
HPCN	high-performance computing and networking
HPFS	high-performance file system
hr.	hour
HRI	horizontal retrace interval
HSM	(1) hardware specific module; (2) hierarchical storage management
HSP	high-speed printer

HST	high-speed technology
HSV	hue, saturation, and value
HT	halftone
HTF	hyper-G text format
HTML	hypertext markup language
HTTP	hypertext transfer protocol
HVHA	high-velocity hot-air (dryer)
Hz	hertz
IAC	interapplication communication
IAF	intelligent arc furnace
IAL	Intel architecture lab
IANA	Internet assigned numbers authority
I-BASIC	Internet beginners all-purpose symbolic instruction code
IBC	integrated broadband communications
IC	integrated circuit
ICA	intelligent console architecture
ICF	interconnect fabric
ICM	independent color matching
ICO	Internet connectivity option
ICR	intelligent character recognition
ICU	instruction control unit
IDC	Internet database connection
IDDE	integrated development and debugging environment
IDE	(1) integrated development environment; (2) integrated disk electronics
IDEA	(1) interactive digital electronic appliance; (2) international data encryption algorithm
IDL	interface definition language
IDMS	integrated data management system

IDO	interface definition object
IE	(1) information engineering; (2) Internet Explorer (Microsoft)
i.e.	that is
IEMSI	interactive electronic mail standard identification
IER	interrupt enable register
IF	interrupt flag
IFS	installable file system
IFT	ink film thickness
IGES	initial graphics exchange specification
IIOP	Internet interoperable ORB protocol
IIR	interrupt identification register
IIS	Internet information server
IKP	Internet keyed payments
IMAP	Internet mail access protocol
IMC	image color matching
IMM	interactive multimedia
IMR	interrupt mask register
in.	inch
in.^{2}	square inches
INN	Internet news server
I/O	input/output
IOC	ISDN ordering code
IP	(1) Internet protocol; (2) instruction pointer
IPA	isopropyl alcohol (isopropanol)
IPC	inter-process communication
IPH	impressions per hour
IPI	interprocessor interrupt
IPM	intelligent power management
IPng	Internet protocol next generation

IPP	in-plant printing
IPS	inches per second
IPv6	Internet protocol version 6
IPX	Internet packet exchange
IR	(1) infrared; (2) information retrieval
IRB	instruction reorder buffer
IRC	Internet relay chat
IRDA	infrared device association
IRLAP	infrared link access protocol
IRQ	interrupt request
IRR	internal rate of return
ISA	industry standard architecture
ISAM	indexed sequential access method
ISAPI	Internet server application programming interface
ISBN	International Standard Book Number
ISDN	integrated services digital network
ISM	Internet service manager
ISP	Internet service provider
ISR	Interrupt service routine
ISSN	International Standard Serial Number
IT	(1) information technology; (2) image technology
ITV	interactive television
IU	integer unit
IVR	interactive voice-response
JDK	Java development kit
JIT	just in time
JND	just-noticeable difference
JOE	Java objects everywhere
JPEG	Joint Photographic Experts Group (image file format)

K   (1) kilo (or 1,000); (2) black; (3) Kelvin

KB   (1) kilobyte; (2) kauri-butanol

Kb   kilobit

Kbps   kilobits per second

kg   kilogram

km   kilometer

KPH   keystrokes per hour

kW   kilowatt

L   liter

l. or **ll.**   line or lines

LAER   lowest achievable emission rate

LAN   local-area network

LANE   local-area network emulation

LAPM   link access procedure for modems

laser   light amplification by stimulated emission of radiation

LATA   local access and transport area

lb.   pound(s)

LC   (1) lowercase; (2) Library of Congress

LCA   lowercase alphabet

LCD   (1) liquid-crystal display; (2) lowest common denominator

LCS   liquid-crystal shutter

LD   laser diode

LD-CELP   low delay codebook excited linear prediction

LDN   long-distance network

LE   LAN emulation

LE-ARP   LAN emulation—address resolution protocol

LECS   LAN emulation configuration server

LED   light-emitting diode

LES	LAN emulation server
LF	line feed character; lightface
LIF	low insertion force
LIFO	last in, first out
LIG	lasers in graphics
LIM	Lotus Intel Microsoft
LIMDO	light intensity modulation—direct overwrite
LIMM	light-intensive modulation method
litho	lithographic or lithography
LLC	logical-link control
LMB	line mode browser
LMDS	local multipoint distribution service
LMU	LAN manager for UNIX
LOD	level of detail
LPC	lines per centimeter
LPD	line printer daemon
LPH	lines per hour
LPI	lines per inch
LPM	lines per minute
LPR	line printer remote
LPR/LPD	line printer remote/line printer daemon
LR	link register
LRPC	lightweight remote procedure call
LSB	least-significant bit
LSI	large-scale integration
LSL	link support layer
LSR	line status register
LTT	liquid toner transfer
LU	logical unit

LUID	locally unique identifier
LUT	look-up table
LVM	logical volume manager
LWK	lightweight kernel
LWP	lightweight process
LZW	Lempel-Ziv-Welch (compression scheme)
M	(1) mega (or 1,000,000); (2) magenta
m	(1) meter; (2) milli
MAC	(1) medium-access control; (2) media access control; (3) metropolitan area exchange; (4) multiply accumulate
MADD	multiply-add
MAE	Macintosh application environment
MAN	metropolitan-area network
MAPI	messaging application programming interface
MAU	multi-station access unit
MB	megabyte
Mb	megabit
MBps	megabytes per second
Mbps	megabits per second
MBR	master boot record
MC	microchannel
MCA	microchannel architecture
MCGA	memory control gate array
MCI	media control interface
MCM	multichip module
MCR	modem control register
MDA	(1) monochrome display adapter; (2) multidimensional analysis
MDDBMS	multidimensional database management system
MDI	multiple document interface

MDRAM	multibank dynamic random access memory
MEK	methyl ethyl ketone
MEPS	monotone electronic prepress systems
MES	manufacturing execution system
MESI	modified, exclusive, shared, invalid
MFC	Microsoft foundation classes
MFLOPS	million floating point instructions per second
MFM	modified frequency modulation
MFP	multifunction peripheral
mg	milligram
MGS	media gateway server
MHS	message handling system
MHz	megahertz
mi.	mile
MIB	management information base
MICR	magnetic ink character recognition
MIDI	musical instrument digital interface
MIF	management interface file
MIMD	multiple instruction multiple data
MIME	multipurpose Internet mail extensions
min.	minute
MIPS	million instructions per second
MIS	management information systems
M-JPEG	Motion Joint Photographers Experts Group
mL	milliliter
MLID	media layer interface device
mm	millimeter
MMCD	multimedia compact disc
MMCX	multimedia communications exchange server

MMU	memory management unit
MMX	multimedia extensions
MNP	microcom networking protocol
MNP10EC	microcom networking protocol 10 enhanced cellular
MO	magnetical-optical
MOB	memory order buffer
modem	modulator-demodulator
MOM	message-oriented middleware
MOO	multi-user object-oriented dungeon
MOS	multimedia operating system
MOSS	MIME object security services
MMX	multimedia extensions
MP	multilink point-to-point protocol
MPC	multimedia personal computer
MPC2	multimedia personal computer 2
MPEG	Moving Picture Experts Group (video file format)
mph	mile(s) per hour
MPI	message passing interface
MPMD	multiple processor multiple data
MPOA	multi-protocol over asynchronous transfer mode
MPP	massive parallel processing
MPR	multiprotocol router
MPS	multi processing specifications
MPTS	multi-protocol transport services
MPU	multiprocessor unit
MR	magneto-resistive
MRA	Macintosh RISC architecture
MRC	message routing component
MRI	magnetic resonance imaging

MRP	material-resource planning
MRP-2	manufacturing-resource planning
MS	manuscript
MSA	metropolitan statistical area
MSB	most-significant bit
MSC	mobile switching center
MSDS	material safety data sheet
MSF	Microsoft solution framework
MSL	mirrored server link
MSM	media support module
MSN	Microsoft Network
MSO	multiple system operator
MSP	military services protocol
MSR	modem status register
MT	(1) machine translation; (2) multithreading
MTBF	mean time between failures
MTD	memory technology driver
MTE	mutation engine
MTT	multi-transaction timer
MTU	maximum transmission unit
MUD	multiuser domain
MVIP	multi-vendor integration protocol
MVP	multimedia video processor
MXS	Microsoft Exchange server
n	nano (10^{-9} or 0.000000001)
NAAQS	National Ambient Air Quality Standard
NAD	name and address
NAK	negative acknowledge

NAP	network access point
NAPLPS	North American presentation-level protocol syntax
NAS	numerical aerodynamic simulation
NASIRC	NASA automated systems Internet response capability
NAUN	nearest active upstream neighbor
NC	network computer
NCP	network control protocol
NCR	no-carbon-required paper
NCS	(1) natural color system; (2) NetWare connect services
NDIS	network device interface specification
NDPS	NetWare distributed print services
NDS	NetWare directory service
NEO	networked object
NEST	Novell embedded systems technology
NetBIOS	network basic input/output system
NFS	Network file system
NIC	network interface controller/card/component
NiMH	nickel metal hydride
NIP	nonimpact printer
NIS	network information services
NIS+	network information services plus
NLC	new-line character
NLM	NetWare loadable module
NLP	natural language processing
NLQ	near-letter quality
NLSP	NetWare link services protocol
nm	nanometer (0.1 angstroms)
NMI	non-maskable interrupt
NMS	NetWare management system

NNTP   network news transfer protocol

NOMS   network operations management system

NOS   network operating system

NPCS   narrowband personal communications services

NPV   net present value

NSAPI   Netscape server application programming interface

NSM   Netscape server manager

NSP   native signal processing

NT   new technology

NT-1   network terminator type 1

NTFS   new technology file system

NTSC   National Television Standard Code

NUMA   nonuniform memory access

NUMA-Q   nonuniform memory access with quads

NURBS   nonuniform rational B-splines

NWPA   NetWare peripheral architecture

NWS   NetWare web server

OA   office automation

OBR   (1) optical bar reader; (2) optical bar recognition

OCF   objects components framework

OCR   (1) optical character reader; (2) optical character recognition

OCX   object linking and embedding control

ODA   office document architecture

ODBC   open database connectivity

ODBMS   object-oriented database management system

ODF   Opendoc development framework

ODG   optical dot gain

ODI   open datalink interface

ODL	object description language
ODM	original design manufacturer
ODMA	open document management API
ODP	open distributed processing
ODSI	open directory service interface
OEM	original equipment manufacturer
OF	overflow flag
OFS	object file system
OGIS	open geodata interoperability specification
OID	object identifier
OK	okay
OLAP	online analytical processing
OLE	object linking and embedding
OLTP	online transaction processing
OLVWM	open look virtual Windows manager
OMA	object management architecture
OMG	object management group
OMR	(1) optical mark reader; (2) optical mark recognition
OMT	object modeling technique
ONC+	open network connectivity plus
OO	object oriented
OOA	object-oriented analysis
OOAD	object-oriented analysis and design
OODB	object-oriented database
OOP	object-oriented programming
OOPS	object-oriented programming system
OOW	object-oriented workflow
OPI	open prepress interface
OPX	off-premises extension

OQL	object-oriented query language
ORB	object request broker
ortho	orthochromatic
OS	(1) operating system; (2) optical storage
OSA	open scripting architecture
OSHA	Occupational Safety and Health Act
OSI	open system interconnection
OSM	off-screen model
OSPF	open shortest path first
OTA	operation-triggered architecture
OTJ	on-the-job
OWL	object Windows library
oz.	ounce
p., pp., pg.	page or pages
p	pica
P5	Pentium computer
P6	Pentium Pro computer
PACE	priority access control enabled
PACS	picture archiving and communications systems
PAD	packet assembler/disassembler
PALCD	plasma-addressed liquid-crystal display
PAP	password authentication protocol
par.	paragraph
PBX	public branch exchange
PC	(1) personal computer; (2) print contrast
PCI	peripheral component interconnect
PCL	printer control language
PCM	pulse code modulation

PCMCIA	personal computer memory interface adapter
PCR	(1) print contrast ratio; (2) phase change recordable
PCS	password connection security
PDA	personal digital assistant
PDC	(1) page description communications; (2) primary domain controller
PDES	product data exchange standard
PDF	portable document format
PDG	physical dot gain
PDH	plesiochronous digital hierarchy
PDL	(1) page description language; (2) program design language
PDM	physical data model
PDO	portable distributed objects
PDT	performance diagnostic tool
PE	printer's error
PEL	(1) picture element; (2) permissible exposure limit
PEM	privacy enhanced mail
PEP	professional electronic publishing
Perl	practical extraction and report language
PF	parity flag
PGA	pin-grid array
PGP	Pretty Good Privacy (encryption software)
pH	potential of hydrogen
PHIGS	programmer's hierarchal interactive graphics
pi.	pint
PIC	programmable interrupt controller
PICS	platform for Internet content selection
PID	proportional, integral, derivative
PIF	program instruction file
PIG	process ink gamut

PIM   (1) page imaging mode; (2) personal information manager

PIN   processor-independent NetWare

PIO   programmable input output

pixel   picture element

PKCS-7   public key cryptography standard 7

PL/1   programming language/1

PLA   programmable logic array

PLAR   private-line auto ringdown

PLB   pipelined burst

PLC   programmable logic controller

PLIP   parallel line Internet protocol

PLL   phase-locked loop

PM   photomultiplier

p.m.   post meridiem

PML   page modeling language

PMMU   paged memory management unit

PMS   Pantone Matching System

PMT   (1) photomechanical transfer; (2) photomultiplier tube

PNG   portable network graphics

PNNI   private network-to-network interface

PnP   plug and play

PO   position only

POP   (1) post office protocol; (2) point of presence; (3) point of purchase

POS   programmable option select

POSIX   portable operating system interface for UNIX

POST   power-on self-test

POTS   plain old telephone service

POTW   publicly owned treatment works

POWER   performance optimization with enhanced RISC

PPGA	plastic pin grid array
PPM	(1) pages per minute; (2) parts per million
PPP	point-to-point protocol
PPTP	point-to-point tunneling protocol
PReP	PowerPC reference platform
PRI	primary rate interface
PRISM	photorefractive information storage materials
PRML	partial-response maximum likelihood
PRO	precision RISC organization
progs	progressive proofs
PROLOG	programming in logic
PROM	programmable read-only memory
PS	(1) PostScript; (2) point size
PSE	paper surface efficiency
PSK	phase shift keying
PSP	program segment prefix
PSTN	public switched telephone network
pt., pt	(1) point; (2) pint
PTE	page-table entry
PUS	performance upgrade socket
PV	(1) present value; (2) physical volume
PVA	polyvinyl alcohol
PVC	(1) polyvinyl chloride; (2) permanent virtual circuit
QBASIC	quick beginners all-purpose symbolic instruction code
QC	quality control
QCIF	quarter common interchange format
QD3D	QuickDraw 3D
QIC	quarter-inch cartridge

QOS	quality of service
QPSK	quadrature phase shift-keying
qt.	quart
QTM	quadratic texture map
QWERTY	standard keyboard layout
R	red
r	radians
RA	rapid access (films)
R&D	research and development
RACT	reasonably available control technology
RAD	rapid application development
RADSL	rate adaptive digital subscriber line
RAM	random-access memory
RAMDAC	random-access memory digital/analog converter
RAS	(1) remote access service; (2) row address strobe
RAT	register alias table
RAVE	rendering acceleration virtual engine
RC	resin-coated (paper)
R-CGI	remote common gateway interface
RCRA	Resource Conservation and Recovery Act
RCS	reference color space
RDBMS	relational database management system
RDR	receiver data register
RDRAM	rambus dynamic random-access memory
ReTINA	real-time telecom. information networking architecture
RFC	request for comment
RFQ	request for quote
RGB	red, green, blue

RGCA	raster graphics content architectures
RH	relative humidity
RIP	(1) raster image processor; (2) routing information protocol
RISC	reduced instruction set computer
RLL	run length limited
RLP	radio link protocol
RMI	resource manager interface
RMP	refiner mechanical pulp
ROB	reorder buffer
ROD	rewritable optical disc
ROLAP	relational online analytical processing
ROM	read-only memory
ROOM	real-time object oriented modeling
ROP	(1) run of press; (2) raster operation; (3) RISC operation
RPC	remote procedure call
rpm	revolutions per minute
RRF	retirement register file
RSI	repetitive strain injury
RSVP	resource reservation protocol
RTC	(1) real-time clock; (2) return to control
RTF	rich text format
RTG	retargetable graphics
RTOS	real-time operating system
RTP	real-time protocol
RTS	request to send
SAFHAZ	safety and hazard data sheet
SAP	service advertising protocol
SAPI	speech application programming interface

SARA	Superfund Amendment and Reauthorization Act of 1986
SATAN	security administrator tool for analyzing networks
SB	standards board
SC	(1) small caps; (2) subcommittee
SCADA	supervisory control and data acquisition
SCAM	SCSI configured automatically
SCI	scalable coherent interconnect
SCSA	signal computing system architecture
SCSI	small computer systems interface
SD	(1) single density; (2) super density
SDH	synchronous digital hierarchy
SDI	single document interface
SDK	software development kit
SDL	system description language
SDLC	synchronous data link control
SD-R	super density recordable
SDRAM	synchronous dynamic random-access memory
SDSL	symmetrical digital subscriber line
sec.	second
SEH	structured exception handling
SEM	SQL enterprise manager
SEPP	secure electronic payment protocol
SET	secure electronic transactions
SF	sign flag
SFT	system fault tolerance
SFX	self-extracting archive
SG	study group
SGML	standard generalized markup language
S-HTTP	secure hypertext transport protocol

SI	source index
SIC	standard industrial classification
SID	security identification
SIG	special interest group
SIMD	single instruction multiple data
SIP	single inline package
SIPP	single inline pinned package
SLIP	serial-line Internet protocol
SLM	spatial light modulator
SLU	spoken language understanding
SMART	self-monitoring analysis and reporting technology
SMB	server message block
SMD	surface-mounted device
SMDS	switched multimegabit data service
S/MIME	secure multipurpose Internet mail extensions
SMIT	system management interface tool
SMP	symmetric multiprocessing
SMPT	simple mail transfer protocol
SMS	(1) short message service; (2) storage management services
SMT	surface-mounted technology
SNA	systems network architecture
SNAP	Specifications for Nonheatset Advertising Printing
SNMP	simple network management protocol
SO-DIMM	small outline dual inline memory module
SOH	start of heading
SOHO	small office home office
SOM	system object model
SONET	synchronous optical network
SOP	service object pair

SP	(1) space character; (2) stack pointer
SPARC	scalar processor architecture
SPC	statistical process control
SPDL	standard page description language
SPI	service provider interface
SPID	service profile identifier
spool	simultaneous peripheral operation on line
SPP	(1) scalable parallel processing; (2) standard parallel port
SPR	special-purpose register
SPX	sequenced packet exchange
sq.	square
SQC	statistical quality control
SQG	small-quantity generators
SQL	structured query language
SRAM	static random-access memory
SRAPI	speech recognition application programming interface
SRE	standard for robot exclusion
SRM	server request manager
S.S. or **S/S**	(1) same size; (2) stack segment
SSD	solid-state disk
SSFDC	solid-state floppy disk card
SSL	secure sockets layer
SSP	system service processor
STEP	standard for exchanging product definition data
STL	standard template library
STP	shielded twisted pair
STT	secure transactions technology
SUR	shell update release
SVC	switched virtual circuit

SVGA	super video graphics adapter
SVRAM	synchronous video random-access memory
SWOP	Specifications for Web Offset Publications
SYSOP	system operator
T	tera, or one trillion (1,000,000,000)
TA	terminal adapter
TAB	tape automated bonding
TAO	telephony application object
TAPI	telephony applications programmers interface
TB	terabyte
Tb	terabit
TC	technical committee
TCF	totally chlorine free (paper)
TCL	tool command language
TCP/IP	transmission control protocol/Internet protocol
TDM	time division multiplex
TDMA	time division multiple access
TDS	tabular data system
TERI	trailing edge ring indicator
TF	trap flag
TFT	thin film transistor
TG	task group
THR	transmitter holding register
TI	tone index
TIB	technical information bulletin
TIFF	tagged image file format
TLI	transport level interface
TLV	threshold limit value

TMP	thermomechanical paper pulp
TMR	triple modular redundancy
TOC	table of contents
TOP	technical and office protocols
TP	transaction processing
TPA	transient program area
TPI	tracks per inch
TPM	(1) total preventive maintenance; (2) total production maintenance; (3) transactions per minute
TPS	transactions per second
TQM	total quality management
TR	technical report
TSA	target service agent
TSAPI	telephony services API
TSOP	thin small outline package
TSR	terminate and stay resident (computer program)
TT	TrueType
TTA	transport-triggered architecture
TTCN	tree and tabular combined notation
TTS	teletypesetting
typo	typographical error
U&LC	uppercase and lowercase
UAE	unrecoverable application error
UART	universal asynchronous receiver transmitter
UC	uppercase
UCA	undercolor addition
UCR	undercolor removal
UCS	Uniform Color Space
UDF	user-defined field

UDP	used datagram protocol
UDT	uniform data transfer
UEF	user exchange format
UI	user interface
UIMS	user interface management system
ULSI	ultra-large-scale integration
UMA	unified memory architecture
UMB	upper memory block
UNC	universal naming convention
UPA	Ultrasparc port architecture
UPS	(1) uninterruptible power supply; (2) upgrade performance socket
URI	universal resource identifier
URIF	use-right interchange format
URL	uniform resource locator
USB	universal serial bus
USM	unsharp masking
UST	underground storage tank
UTP	unshielded twisted pair
UUCP	UNIX-to-UNIX copy
UV	ultraviolet
V	volt
VAFC	video electronics standard (association) advanced feature connector
VAN	value-added network
VAR	value-added reseller
VBA	Visual Basic for applications
VBI	virtual binary interface
vBNS	very-high-speed backbone network service
VCC	virtual channel connection

VCPI	virtual control program interface
VCSEL	vertical cavity surface emitting laser
VDA	visual data analysis
VDD	virtual device driver
VDI	virtual device interface; virtual data interchange
VDM	virtual device machine
VDS	virtual device services
VDT	video display terminal
VDU	video display unit
VFAT	virtual file allocation table
VGA	video graphics adapter
VIM	vendor-independent messaging
VIP	(1) vertically integrated printer; (2) VSLI ISDN processor
VIS	visual instruction set
VKD	virtual keyboard device
VLB	VESA local bus
VLD	variable-length decoder
VLIW	very long instruction word
VLM	virtual loadable module
VLSI	very-large-scale integration (computer chip technology)
VM	virtual machine
VMC	Vesa media channel
VMM	virtual memory manager
VOC	volatile organic compound
VOD	video on demand
VON	voice on/over the Net
vol.; vols.	volume; volumes
VPN	virtual private network
VPT	virtual printer technology

VR	virtual reality
VRAM	video random-access memory
VRI	vertical retrace interval
VRM	voltage-regulator module
VRML	virtual reality modeling/markup language
VRT	voltage reduction technology
VRU	voice-response unit
VSAM	virtual storage access method
VSM	visual system manager
VTD	virtual timer device
VxD	virtual device driver
W	watt
WABI	Windows application binary interface
WAIS	wide-area information server
WAN	wide-area network
WAP	wired access point
WATS	wide-area telecommunications service
WDM	Win32 driver model
WF	wrong font
WG	working group
WINS	Windows Internet naming service
WORM	write once, read many
WOSA	Windows open services architecture
WP	word processing
WPM	words per minute
WPS	word processing system
WPVM	Windows parallel virtual machine
WRAM	Window random access memory

WRB	web request broker
WSAPI	web site application programming interface
WWW	World Wide Web
WYSIWYG	what-you-see-is-what-you-get
WYSIWYP	what-you-see-is-what-you-print
XA	extended architecture
XDF	extended density format
XDR	external data representation
XGA	extended graphics adapter
XMM	extended memory manager
XMS	extended memory specification
XT	extended technology
XTI	X/open transport interface
Y	yellow
YAG	yttrium-aluminum-garnet (laser)
YMC	yellow, magenta, and cyan
YMCK	yellow, magenta, cyan, black
ZF	zero flag
ZIF	zero insertion force
ZM	zoomed video
ZPV	zoomed port video

Association and Business Acronyms

AAAA	American Association of Advertising Agencies (also called the 4A's)
AAP	Association of American Publishers
ABP	American Business Press
ACM	Association for Computing Machinery
AFNOR	Association Francaise de Normalisation (France)
AGA	Association of the Graphic Arts
AGAT	Association of Graphic Arts Trainers
AIGA	American Institute of Graphic Arts
ANPA	American Newspaper Publishers Association, now Newspaper Association of America (NAA)
ANSC	American National Standards Committee
ANSI	American National Standards Institute
AP	Associated Press
APDF	Association of Professional Design Firms
API	American Paper Institute
ARPA	Advanced Research Projects Agency (U.S. Defense Department)
ASA	American Standards Association
ASQC	American Society of Quality Control
ASTM	American Society for Testing and Materials
ATypl	Association Typographique Internationale
AWMA	American Waste Management Association
BIA	Binding Association of America
BMI	Book Manufacturers Institute, Inc.
BPI	British Printing Institute
BSI	British Standards Institution
BSR	Board of Standards Review

CBEMA   Computer and Business Equipment Manufacturers Association

CCITT   International Telegraph and Telephone Consultative Committee

CEN   European Committee for Standarization

CENELEC   European Committee for Electrotechnical Standardization

CERN   Conseil European Pour le Recherche Nucleaire (The European Particle Physics Laboratory)

CGATS   Committee for Graphic Arts Technologies Standards

CIE   Commission Internationale de l'Éclairage (International Commission on Illumination)

CPPA   Canadian Pulp and Paper Association

CS   Central Secretariat (ISO)

DEC   Digital Equipment Corporation

DIN   Deutsch Institute for Normalization

ECB   Environmental Conservation Board of the Graphic Communications Industries

ECMA   European Computer Manufacturers Association

EFTA   European Free Trade Association

EIA   Electronic Industries Association

EPA   See *USEPA (United States Environmental Protection Agency)*

FCC   Federal Communications Commission

FDA   Food and Drug Administration

FIEJ   Federation Internationale des Editeurs de Journaux et Publications (International Federation of Newspaper Publishers)

FPA   Flexible Packaging Association

FTA   Flexographic Technical Association

GAA   (1) Gravure Association of America; (2) Graphic Arts Association

GAERF   Graphic Arts Education and Research Foundation

GASC	Graphic Arts Show Company
GASF	Graphic Arts Sales Foundation
GATF	Graphic Arts Technical Foundation
GCA	Graphic Communications Association
GCI	Graphic Communications International
GPI	General Printing Ink
GPO	See *USGPO (United States Government Printing Office)*
GTA	Gravure Technical Association, now Gravure Association of America (GAA)
IAC	International Advisory Committee
IARIGAI	International Association of Research Institutes for the Graphic Arts Industry
IBN	Institut Belge de Normalisation (Belgium)
ICA	International Communications Association
ICI	Imperial Chemical Industries
IEC	International Electrotechnical Commission
IEEE	Institute of Electrical and Electronic Engineers
IFIP	International Federation for Information Processing
IGAEA	International Graphic Arts Education Association
IOP	Institute of Printing
IPA	International Prepress Association
IPMA	In-Plant Management Association
IPTC	International Press Telecommunications Council
ISCC	Inter-Society Color Council
ISO	International Standards Organization
ISSB	Information Systems Standards Board (ANSI)
IT8	Image Technology Committee number eight (ANSI)
ITSB	Image Technology Standards Board (ANSI)
ITU	(1) International Telecommunications Union, (2) International Typographic Union

JBMA	Japan Business Machine Makers Association
JISC	Japan Industrial Standards Committee
JPEG	Joint Photographic Experts Group
JSA	Japanese Standards Association
LC	Library of Congress
MPA	Magazine Publishers Association
MPEG	Moving Pictures Experts Group
NAA	Newspaper Association of America
NADD	National Association of Diemakers and Diecutters
NALC	National Association of Litho Clubs
NAPIM	National Association of Printing Ink Manufacturers
NAPL	National Association of Printers and Lithographers
NAQP	National Association of Quick Printers
NASTA	National Association of State Textbook Administrators
NBS	National Bureau of Standards, now NIST (National Institute of Science and Technology)
NCA	National Composition Association
NCGA	National Computer Graphics Association
NEMA	National Electrical Manufacturers Association
NIST	National Institute of Science and Technology
NPES	The Association for Suppliers of Printing and Publishing Technologies
NPIRI	National Printing Ink Research Institute
NSTF	National Scholarship Trust Fund
NTSC	National Television Standards Committee
OMB	Office of Management and Budget
OSA	Optical Society of America

OSHA   Occupational Safety and Health Administration

PIA   Printing Industries of America
Pira   Printing Industry Research Association (of the UK)
PDI   Printing Developments, Inc.

RIT   Rochester Institute of Technology

SCC   Standards Council of Canada
SET   Standard D'Exchange et De Transfer
SGAUA   Scitex Graphic Arts Users Association
SOF   Society of Fellows (GATF)
SPAI   Screen Printing Association International
SPSE   Society of Photographic Scientists and Engineers

TAGA   Technical Association of the Graphic Arts
TAPPI   Technical Association of the Pulp and Paper Industry
TIA   Typographers International Association

USEPA   United States Environmental Protection Agency
USGPO   United States Government Printing Office

Common File Extensions

While Macintosh computers have always supported longer file names, this convention is relatively new in the PC world. Many PC systems in use today still rely on three-character extensions. Four-character extensions often indicate a file created on a Mac. Of course, many Mac files do not include extensions. Nevertheless, the PC/UNIX nature of the Internet requires familiarity with the extensions that appear after many files received via electronic communications regardless of the internal computer system used.

.$$$	temporary work file
.$DB	dBase temporary file
.$VM	Windows 3.x virtual memory temporary file
.??_	compressed file
.??~	compressed file
.000	doublespace compressed volume file
.1ST	instruction file for running software
.386	Windows 3.x protected mode driver
.3DS	3D Studio graphics file
.3FX	Corel Chart effect file
.4SW	4Dos swapfile
.A	ADA source code
.ABK	Corel Draw automatic backup file
.ACB	associative coder data file
.AD	After Dark screen saver
.ADL	adapter description library
.AFM	Adobe PostScript font support file
.AI	Adobe Illustrator file
.ALL	WordPerfect printer and font definition files
.ANN	Windows help annotation file
.ANS	ANSI graphics file
.ARC	compressed file archive

.ARJ	compressed file archive
.ART	First Publisher graphics file; CorelXara file
.ASC	ASCII text file
.ASI	Borland C Assembler include file
.ASM	assembly language source code
.ASP	Procomm communications program script file
.ATM	Adobe Type Manager data file
.AU	audio data file
.AVI	audio video interleaved file
.BAK	backup file
.BAS	BASIC program file
.BAT	batch file
.BCP	Borland C++ makefile
.BDR	Microsoft Publisher border
.BGI	Borland graphical interface device driver
.BIB	bibliography file
.BIN	binary file
.BIT	LOTUS Manuscript graphics file
.BLD	saved BASIC binary file
.BMK	Windows 3.x Help bookmarks file
.BMP	bitmap graphics file
.BPT	Corel Draw bitmap fills file
.C	source code for the C programming language
.CAL	calendar file
.CAT	master catalog file for MSBACKUP in DOS 6
.CBL	COBOL source file
.CCH	Corel chart file
.CDR	Corel Draw graphics file

.CFG	configuration file
.CFL	Corel flow file
.CFN	configuration file
.CGM	computer graphics metafile
.CHK	DOS CHECKDISK command file
.CLASS	Java class file
.CLP	Windows clipboard file
.CMD	OS/2 batch file
.CMF	(1) Corel metafile; (2) creative music file
.CMV	Corel move animation file
.CMX	Corel presentation exchange
.COB	source code for the COBOL programming language
.COD	object code file used by compilers
.COM	command file
CONFIG.SYS	ASCII file containing the system configuration commands used to boot, or start, an MS-DOS/Windows computer
.COR	Corel Draw installation backup file
.CPI	code page information file (for a foreign character set)
.CPL	Windows control panel file
.CPP	C++ file
.CPT	Corel Photopaint file
.CRD	Windows card file
.CRF	cross reference file
.CST	terminate cost file
.CSV	comma-separated value ASCII text file
.CUR	cursor file
.CUT	Halo I, II, III graphics file
.DAT	data file
.DB	(1) database file; (2) Netscape cache index file

.DB2	dBASE II file
.DB3	dBASE III file
.DB4	dBASE IV file
.DBF	dBASE or compatible database file
.DCT	dictionary file
.DEF	C definition file
.DEV	device driver file
.DHP	Dr. Halo PIC graphics format file
.DIB	device-independent bitmap graphics file
.DIC	dictionary file
.DIF	data interchange format ASCII spreadsheet file
.DIZ	shareware text file describing software; description in ZIP file
.DJP	Hewlett-Packard Deskjet printer softfont file
.DLL	(Windows) dynamic link library file
.DOC	(1) Microsoft Word file; (2) documentation text file
.DOT	(1) Corel Draw line-type definition file; (2) Microsoft Word template file
.DRV	hardware driver file
.DRW	Corel Draw or Micrographx graphics file
.DSW	Turbo C context file
.DVP	DESQview configuration file
.DVR	device driver file
.DWG	Autocad drawing file
.DXF	Autocad graphics file
.EMF	enhanced Windows metafile
.END	Corel Draw arrow file
.EPS	encapsulated PostScript file
.EVY	WordPerfect Envoy document
.EXE	executable file
.EXT	extension file

.FAQ	frequently asked questions file
.FIF	Fractal image format file
.FLT	Microsoft filter file
.FMT	dBASE III formatting file
.FNT	font file
.FON	font file
.FOR	FORTRAN language source code file
.FOT	TrueType scalable outline font for Windows
.FOX	FoxBASE database file
.FRM	form file
.FUL	full backup catalog file for DOS 6
.GEM	vector graphics file
.GDI	GEM metafile
.GIF	graphics interchange format file
.GRP	Windows program manager group data file
.GX1	partner graphics file
.H	C language header file
.HDX	help index file
.HLP	help file
.HPF	Hewlett-Packard printer control language Bitstream SoftFont file
.HPG	Hewlett-Packard graphics language file
.HPJ	Windows help project file
.HST	program history file
.HTM	hypertext markup (language) file
.HTML	hypertext markup language file
.HYC	hyphenation list file (WordPerfect)
.ICO	icon graphics file (Windows Program Manager)
.ID	disk identification file

.IDE	Borland C project file
.IDX	FoxBASE database index file
.IFF	Deluxe Paint II graphics file
.IMG	GEM Paint graphics file
.INC	incremental backup file (DOS 6)
.INF	information file
.INI	Windows initialization (configuration) file
.ISF	IBM image support facility file
.JPEG	Joint Photographic Experts Group compressed graphics image file
.JPG	JPEG (Joint Photographic Experts Group) compressed graphics image file
.KEY	keyboard macro definition file
.LBM	Deluxe Paint graphics file
.LEX	lexicon dictionary file
.LIB	computer language compiler library file
.LNK	Windows 95 Shortcut
.LRF	Microsoft C linker response file
.LST	list of files
.LTR	letter file
.LZH	compressed archived file
.MAC	(1) MacPaint graphics file; (2) macro file
.MAK	Turbo C makefile
.MAN	software program manual
.MAX	3D Studio scene file
.MDB	Microsoft Access database file
.MEU	DOS Shell menu group
.MGF	Micrografx font file

.MID	musical instrument digital interface audio file
.MIDI	musical instrument digital interface audio file
.MNU	(1) menu file; (2) mouse control file
.MOD	file to support data exchange between DOS and Windows
.MPEG	Moving Pictures Expert Group video file
.MPG	Moving Pictures Expert Group video file
.MRB	multiple-resolution bitmap (MS C)
.MSC	Microsoft C makefile
.MSG	message file
.MSP	Microsoft Windows graphics file
.MTH	derive math file
.MUS	music file
.NAM	Print Shop name file
.NCD	Norton change directory data file
.NDX	dBASE index file
.NFO	information file
.NG	Norton Guides database file
.NTX	dBASE index file
.OBD	Microsoft binder file
.OBJ	object code file
.OBT	Microsoft binder file
.OCX	object linking and embedding custom control
.OLD	backup file renamed "old"
.OVL	overlay file
.OVR	overlay file
.OPT	Quarterdeck Enhanced Memory Maker optimize support file
.P	Pascal language source code
.PAK	compressed archived file

.PAL	palette file
.PAS	PASCAL programming or source code file
.PAT	Corel Draw vector fill file
.PCC	Z-Soft graphics file
.PCD	Kodak Photo-CD graphics file
.PCH	Microsoft C precompiled header file
.PCX	PC Paintbrush graphics file
.PDF	(1) printer definition file; (2) portable document format file
.PDV	Microsoft Paintbrush device driver file
.PDX	Paradox file
.PFB	Type 1 font file
.PFM	Type 1 font metric file
.PGM	binary program file
.PGP	Pretty Good Privacy encrypted file
.PIC	graphics file
.PICT	Mac graphics file
.PIF	Windows program information file
.PIM	permanent image file
.PKG	installer script file
.PKT	Fidonet packet (Internet) file
.PLT	plotter file
.PMR	PageMaker file
.PNM	Print Shop name file
.POG	Print Shop graphics file
.PPT	Microsoft Powerpoint file
.PRD	printer definition file
.PRG	programming source file
.PRJ	project file
.PRN	print text file
.PRS	WordPerfect printer definition file

.PRT	print file
.PS	PostScript interpreted file
.PSO	PostScript page description language printer file for Bitstream Soft-Fonts
.PUB	Microsoft Publisher file
.PWL	password list file (Windows 95)
.QDK	Quarterdeck Extended Memory Manager installation backup files
.QLB	Microsoft C quick library file
.QTM	QuickTime Movie file
.QTW	Apple QuickTime for Windows file
.QWK	quick reader message file
.QXP	QuarkXPress file
.RAM	teal audio file
.RAR	compressed file
.REC	Windows macro recorder file
.REG	registry file
.RES	C compiled resource file
.RLE	run-length-encoded graphics file
.RPT	report file
.RSP	response file
.RTF	rich text format file
.SAM	AmiPro word processing file
.SAV	backup file
.SCR	(1) telecommunications script file; (2) screen (capture) file; (3) DOS debug script file; (4) screen saver file
.SCT	(1) LOTUS Manuscript screen capture text file; (2) Scitex CT bitmap file
.SCX	RIX/EGA and ColoRix graphics file

.SDN	compressed archived file
.SDR	Printmaster name file
.SEA	self-extracting archive file
.SET	(1) MSBACKUP set; (2) setup options file
.SFL	Hewlett-Packard printer control language [4] bitmapped SoftFont file (landscape orientation)
.SFP	Hewlett-Packard printer control language [4] bitmapped SoftFont file (portrait orientation)
.SFS	SoftFont screen font file
.SHB	Corel Show background file
.SHP	Printmaster graphics file
.SHW	(1) Corel Show presentation file; (2) Harvard Graphics presentation file; (3)Word Perfect presentation file
.SIG	signature file (for Internet email)
.SIT	compressed archive file
.SK	SideKick Plus utility file
.SND	sound file
.SQL	structured query language database file
.STY	WordPerfect Style file
.SYM	symbol file
.SYS	operating system device driver file
.TC	Turbo C configuration file
.TCH	Turbo C help file
.TD	Turbo debugger configuration file
.TF	Turbo profiler configuration file
.TGA	Targa 16
.THS	WordPerfect thesaurus file
.TIF	tagged image file format (raster graphics)
.TIFF	tagged image file format (raster graphics)
.TMP	temporary file

.TPU	Turbo Pascal unit
.TST	test file
.TTF	Windows header file for a TrueType scalable outline font
.TUT	tutorial file
.TXT	text file
.UC2	(1) compressed file archive; (2) Ultracompressor II datafile
.UPD	updated history file
.UUE	UNIX-to-UNIX encoded compressed binary file; often a graphic
.VBX	Visual Basic control file
.VOC	Soundblaster audio file
.VXD	Windows virtual device driver
.WAV	Windows audio file
.WIZ	Microsoft Publisher page wizard
.WK1	LOTUS spreadsheet version 2.0 file
.WK?	LOTUS spreadsheet temporary work file
.WKE	LOTUS educational worksheet file
.WKQ	QUATTRO spreadsheet file
.WKS	LOTUS spreadsheet version 1A file
.WMF	Windows metafile graphics format file
.WPG	WordPerfect graphics file version 5.0 and later
.WPK	WordPerfect keyboard macro file
.WPM	WordPerfect macro file
.WQ1	QUATTRO spreadsheet version 1.0 file
.WRI	Windows Write text file
.WRK	Symphony spreadsheet file
.WSD	WordStar file
.WVL	wavelet compressed bitmap

.XLS   Microsoft Excel spreadsheet file

.XLT   translation table file

.XTP   Xtree overlay file

.ZIP   compressed file archive

.ZOO   compressed file archive

Bibliography

What follows is a select bibliography of sources that the reader may wish to consult to learn more about the terms defined in the *Glossary of Graphic Communications.*

Banta Resource Handbook. Menasha, Wis.: Banta Corporation, 1995.

Binding and Finishing. Lyman, Ralph. Pittsburgh: Graphic Arts Technical Foundation, 1993.

Color and Its Reproduction. Field, Gary G. Pittsburgh: Graphic Arts Technical Foundation, 1988, revised in 1992.

Color for the Electronic Age. White, Jan V. New York: Watson-Guptill, 1990.

Color Scanning and Imaging Systems. Field, Gary G. Pittsburgh: Graphic Arts Technical Foundation, 1990.

Computer and Internet Dictionary, 6th ed. Pfaffenberger, Bryan, Ed. Indianapolis: Que Books, 1995.

Computing Dictionary Illustrated. Lincoln, Nebr.: PCNOVICE Publishing, 1996.

Dunn's Acronyms, Terminology, and Abbreviations for the Graphic Arts Industry (DATA). Dunn, Dr. S. Thomas and Dunn, Patrice. Vista, Calif.: Dunn Technology Incorporated, 1990.

Editing for Print. Rogers, Geoffrey. Cincinnati: Writers Digest Books, 1985.

Electronic Prepress Essentials, Vols. 1–4. Stone, Vicki. Pittsburgh: Graphic Arts Technical Foundation, 1995, 1996.

EPA Terms of the Environment: Glossary, Abbreviations, and Acronyms. Washington, D.C.: USEPA, 1993.

Flexography Primer. Mulvihill, Donna C. Pittsburgh: Graphic Arts Technical Foundation, 1985.

Glossary of Color Terms. Philadelphia: Federation of Societies for Coatings Technology, Inter-Society Color Council, 1981.

Glossary of Lithographic Terms. Erlanger, Ky.: Metroweb Company, 1987.

Glossary of Paper Terms for Web and Sheetfed Offset Printing. Atlanta: Technical Association of the Pulp and Paper Industry, 1971.

Glossary of Reprographic and Nonimpact Printing Terms for the Paper and Printing Industries. Atlanta: Technical Association of the Pulp and Paper Industry, 1990.

Glossary of Screen Printing Terms. Fairfax, Va.: Screen Printing Association International, 1987.

Glossary of Typographic & Computer Terminology, 2nd edition. Washington, D.C.: Typographers International Association, 1989.

Graphic Arts Glossary. Ann Arbor: Edwards Brothers, 1987.

Graphic Arts Photography: Black and White. Cogoli, John E. Pittsburgh: Graphic Arts Technical Foundation, 1988.

Graphic Arts Photography: Color. Wentzel, Fred, et. al., Pittsburgh: Graphic Arts Technical Foundation, 1988.

Graphic Design for the Electronic Age. White, Jan V. New York: Watson-Guptill, 1988.

Graphically Speaking: An Illustrated Guide to the Working Language of Design and Printing. Beach, Mark. Manzanita, Oreg.: Elk Ridge Publishing, 1992.

Guide to Desktop Publishing, 2nd edition. Cavuoto, James and Beale, Stephen. Pittsburgh: Graphic Arts Technical Foundation, 1995.

IBM Dictionary of Computing, 10th edition. Research Triangle Park, N.C.: International Business Machines, 1994.

Imaging Glossary: Electronic Document & Image Processing Terms, Acronyms, and Concepts. Moore, Andy. New York: Telecom Publishing, 1991.

Implementing Quality Management in the Graphic Arts. Apfelberg, H. and Apfelberg, M. Pittsburgh: Graphic Arts Technical Foundation, 1995.

Inside Photo CD. McIlroy, Thad and Pease, David, Eds. San Francisco: The Color Resource, 1993.

Introduction to Digital Color Prepress. Wilmington, Mass.: Agfa Corporation, 1990.

ISDN for Dummies. Angell, David. Foster City, Calif.: IDG Books, 1995.

LAN Glossary. San Francisco: Miller Freeman Publications, 1990.

The Lithographers Manual, 9th edition. Pittsburgh: Graphic Arts Technical Foundation, 1994.

Lithographic Press Operator's Handbook. Groff, Pamela, et. al. Pittsburgh: Graphic Arts Technical Foundation, 1988.

Maclopedia. Alpasch, T., et. al. Indianapolis: Hayden Books, 1996.

Nonimpact Printing. Nothmann, Gerhard A. Pittsburgh: Graphic Arts Technical Foundation, 1989.

Prepress Glossary. South Holland, Ill.: International Prepress Association, 1987, rev. 1991.

Printing Ink Handbook. Harrison, N.Y.: National Association of Printing Ink Manufacturers, 1976.

Quick Printing: The Printshop in Transition. Newtonville, Mass.: BIS CAP International, 1990.

Screen Printing Primer. Magee, Babette. Pittsburgh: Graphic Arts Technical Foundation, 1985.

Sheetfed Offset Press Operating, 2nd edition. DeJidas, Lloyd P. and Destree, Thomas M. Pittsburgh: Graphic Arts Technical Foundation, 1994.

SNAP Glossary. Arlington, Va.: Committee on Specifications for Nonheatset Advertising Printing, 1989.

Solving Offset Ink Problems. Eldred, Nelson R. Pittsburgh: Graphic Arts Technical Foundation, 1987.

Solving Sheetfed Offset Press Problems. DeJidas, Lloyd P., et. al. Pittsburgh: Graphic Arts Technical Foundation, 1987.

Spectrum Glossary. Arlington, Va.: Graphic Communications Association, 1988.

Stripping: The Assembly of Film Images. Peck, Harold L. Pittsburgh: Graphic Arts Technical Foundation, 1989.

Technical Guide to the Gravure Industry. New York: Gravure Technical Association, 1975.

Understanding Digital Color. Green, Phil. Pittsburgh: Graphic Arts Technical Foundation, 1995.

Understanding Electronic Communications. Ajayi, A'isha and Groff, Pamela. Pittsburgh: Graphic Arts Technical Foundation, 1996.

Warren Standard, Vol. 2, No. 5. Boston: S.D. Warren Company, 1995.

Web Offset Press Operating, 4th edition. GATF staff. Pittsburgh: Graphic Arts Technical Foundation, 1996.

Webster's New World Dictionary of Media and Communications. New York: Simon and Schuster, 1990.

What the Printer Should Know about Ink. Eldred, Nelson R. and Scarlett, Terry. Pittsburgh: Graphic Arts Technical Foundation, 1990.

What the Printer Should Know about Paper. Bureau, William H. Pittsburgh: Graphic Arts Technical Foundation, 1989.

Wired Style: Principles of English Usage in the Digital Age. Hale, Constance, Ed. San Francisco: HardWired Books, 1996.

About the Author

Pamela Groff is a senior technical writer at the Graphic Arts Technical Foundation in Pittsburgh. In addition to editing all three editions of this book, she is coauthor of *Understanding Electronic Communications: Printing in the Information Age,* coauthor of *Careers in Graphic Communications: A Resource Book,* coauthor of *Understanding Digital Media,* and the author of the *GATF-World* magazine series "The Internet for Printers." Since receiving her bachelor's degree in English and business administration from La Roche College, she has studied digital media at the University of Pittsburgh's Graduate School of Library and Information Science and book publishing in the twenty-first century through the New School for Social Research's computer-based distance-learning program. Groff is also a beta tester of new media products for several major publishers.

About GATF

The Graphic Arts Technical Foundation is a nonprofit, scientific, technical, and educational organization dedicated to the advancement of the graphic communications industries worldwide. Its mission is to serve the field as the leading resource for technical information and services through research and education.

For 74 years the Foundation has developed leading edge technologies and practices for printing. GATF's staff of researchers, educators, and technical specialists partner with nearly 2,000 corporate members in over 65 countries to help them maintain their competitive edge by increasing productivity, print quality, process control, and environmental compliance, and by implementing new techniques and technologies. Through conferences, satellite symposia, workshops, consulting, technical support, laboratory services, and publications, GATF strives to advance a global graphic communications community.

The GATF*Press* publishes books on nearly every aspect of the field; learning modules (step-by-step instruction booklets); audiovisuals (CD-ROMs, videocassettes, slides, and audiocassettes); and research and technology reports. It also publishes *GATFWorld*, a bimonthly magazine of technical articles, industry news, and reviews of specific products.

For more detailed information on GATF products and services, please visit our website *http://www.gatf.org* or write to us at 200 Deer Run Road, Sewickley, PA 15143-2600 (phone: 412/741-6860).

Other Books of Interest from GATF*Press*

- *Understanding Digital Color* by Phil Green

- *Guide to Desktop Publishing* by James Cavuoto and Steven Beale

- *On-Demand Printing: The Revolution in Digital and Customized Printing* by Howard Fenton and Frank Romano

- *Understanding Electronic Communications: Printing in the Information Age* by A'isha Ajayi and Pamela Groff

- *Professional Print Buying* edited by Phil Green

- *Handbook of Printing Processes* by Deborah Stevenson

- *Screen Printing Primer* by Sam Ingram

- *Flexography Primer* by J. Page Crouch

- *Lithography Primer* by Dan Wilson

- *The Magazine* by Leonard Mogel

- *Digital Photography: A Primer for Printers* by David Milburn and John Carroll

- *The GATF Encyclopedia of Graphic Communication* by Frank Romano and Richard Romano

- *Creating Your Career in Communications and Entertainment* by Leonard Mogel

- *Careers in Graphic Communications: A Resource Book* by Sally Ann Flecker and Pam Groff

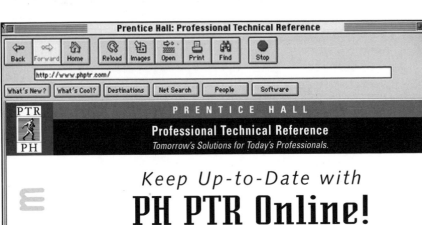